FAIR GAME?

FAIR GAME?

POLITICS
TACKLING
SPORT!

JOHN LEONARD

First published by Pitch Publishing, 2016

Pitch Publishing
A2 Yeoman Gate
Yeoman Way
Worthing
Sussex
BN13 3QZ
www.pitchpublishing.co.uk

ISBN 978-1-78531-141-3

Typesetting and origination by Pitch Publishing

Printed by TJ International, Padstow, Cornwall

Contents

ABOUT THE AUTHOR

John Leonard is a journalist with more than three decades experience. He began his career on local newspapers in Staffordshire as a reporter for the *Stafford Newsletter* and then the *Leek Post and Times* before working for BBC News in London. He moved to ITN, employed there as a Sports Producer before becoming a Programme Editor for Five News and ITV News. A life-long Stoke City fan; he enjoyed an ill-starred brief sporting career as an athlete running for Staffordshire Moorlands AC.

Introduction: Strutting the World Stage

AS Vladimir Putin stood for the Russian national anthem at the opening ceremony of the Sochi Winter Olympics, diplomatic storm clouds were gathering over the capital cities of athletes from the Western nations gathered before him. Ukraine was in turmoil. Russia was preparing to make a land grab. World leaders were contemplating how to deal with a rapidly unfolding political, diplomatic and military nightmare. Surely nothing would happen during an Olympics dubbed cynically by his critics as 'Putin's Games'? These were the Games in which the Russian president was anxious to promote his nation as one with its self-confidence restored. No longer would it be overshadowed by the United States and its Western allies after the collapse of the Soviet Union.

The 2014 Sochi Winter Olympics gave the Kremlin the chance to demonstrate to the world Russia was once again a global power, a force to be respected and feared. For Putin's Western critics, it appeared as a chilling reminder of the 1930s and Hitler's Games; the Berlin Olympics. Few of them realised at the time the extent to which the Russian state was going in its aim to achieve international sporting supremacy with allegations emerging of a sinister and corrupt doping programme.

Backed with the promise of European Union money, Ukrainian nationalists, in the months prior to the Sochi Olympics, deposed their president, a man backed by Putin. Perhaps they felt the Russian ruler would not exact revenge during a forthcoming sporting jamboree with the eyes of the world upon him. He would just bask in the glory of staging the Olympics Games. If so, they were wrong. Within weeks of Ukraine's president Viktor Yanukovich fleeing to Moscow, Crimea had been annexed; Ukraine forced to give up its Black Sea naval bases. Russian tanks were being gathered on the eastern borders of Ukraine. It was eerily similar to the Anschluss of Hitler's Germany some 80 years earlier; a ruthless land grab. Hitler's Games and international sporting contact with Nazi Germany went on regardless. The Olympic torch was lit for Putin's Games as his tanks lined up to open fire on Ukrainian nationalists. Putin's Olympics meant global sport was tied to global politics, a political leader exploiting the platform given to him by strutting on the ultimate world sporting stage.

Almost two years after Winter Olympians had left Sochi, the sinister nature of Russia's elite sporting programme was laid bare. An independent investigation for the World Anti-Doping Agency (WADA) supported claims from the German television channel ARD of state-sponsored doping of athletes. It was so extensive agents from Russia's Federal Security service (FSB), the successor to the KGB, were working in the country's anti-doping labs during the Sochi Winter Olympics. Their job was simple. It was to cover up any positive tests of Russian athletes tacking performance-enhancing drugs (PEDs); to ensure Russian cheats enjoyed global sporting glory. In assessing the Moscow Laboratory of the Russian Anti-Doping agency, an independent commission set up by WADA found 'its impartiality, judgment and integrity were compromised by the surveillance of the FSB within the laboratory during the Sochi Winter Olympic Games'.

Such was the extent of the state-sponsored Russian doping programme, the world athletics governing body, the IAAF, an organisation under heavy criticism for its almost laissez-faire attitude to the illicit use of performance-enhancing drugs (PEDs) and blood doping, had no choice but to provisionally suspend Russia's track and field team from the Olympic Games. What was the Russian reaction to these disturbing revelations? Well predictably it was to denounce it all as a Western plot. Without a hint of irony, Maria Zakharova from the Russian Foreign Ministry accused WADA's investigators of being 'biased and politicised'. One Russian MP, Valery Shestakov, a member of the State Duma's sports committee, even went as far as suggesting the drugs allegations from the German TV station ARD came in revenge for Russia being awarded the hosting of football's World Cup.

Putin himself played a cleverer game on this occasion, offering conciliatory promises to clean up Russian sport. After all, he would never admit as much but he was shamelessly using sport as a diplomatic tool; the Sochi Games, now sullied by the drugs revelations, a brazen propaganda opportunity to promote a 'Greater Russia'. On Russia winning the right to stage football's World Cup in 2018, Putin planned to do much the same. It mattered little to him the sport's governing body, FIFA, became mired in allegations of 'rampant, systemic and deep-rooted' corruption over the awarding of the most popular sport's prestigious competition. The fact Russia's nemesis, the United States, was leading investigations into malpractice at FIFA, only emboldened Putin; sport reflecting geo-political rivalries.

Briefly Ukrainian athletes did consider boycotting those 2014 Sochi Olympics; Putin's Games. Eventually they decided to compete, despite their fellow countrymen and women's anger over the annexation of Crimea by Putin's armed forces, believing as so many do sport and politics don't mix. Sadly too many others think otherwise; these include the likes of Putin and Hitler. Now, any Western democratic leader opposed to Putin and Hitler would resent of course being put in the same category as those autocrats. Yet even with these advocates of democracy and freedom there is an unsavoury record of exploiting sport. They revel in the feelgood factor from their compatriots winning gold medals, World Cups, and European Championships. Athletes are summoned to the White House and Downing Street with gleeful politicians vicariously celebrating sporting success; doing so in some countries as playing fields are bulldozed over to become building sites and gymnasiums closed down. Even more cynically, athletes are ordered by political leaders to boycott sporting events held in countries run by governments deemed as rogue regimes; yet little or nothing is done to stop business and trade with those self-same regimes. Sport and politics are not supposed to mix. Sadly, inevitably they do mix. They mix with chilling results. Occasionally, though seldom intentionally, they mix with comical results.

All of this occurs when governing bodies of sports claim to be above politics; apolitical organisations with solely a sporting and cultural agenda. Yet those same organisations often dabble in politics. FIFA, the world governing body of association football or to use the nickname soccer, and the International Olympic Committee both expelled South Africa from international competition even long before those running world cricket were forced to act over the apartheid regime's treatment of England cricketer Basil D'Oliveira. The IOC, rightly, had decided a country with an apartheid regime discriminating on the basis of the colour of a person's skin could not send athletes to compete in the planet's greatest multi-sport competition. Those men at Lord's running world cricket took a while to come to the same conclusion.

It took decades for the international rugby community to respond with one voice to oppose apartheid. Yet, when the International Rugby Board (IRB) decided to stage its first World Cup in 1987, it made one crucial decision. The IRB, for all its previous protestations of being an organisation operating outside the grubby sphere of politics, excluded South Africa from the competition. It was a blow to the Afrikaans' pride. Rugby was their sport. They had been snubbed by even those who had supported them for decades by controversially sending international touring teams. Even to the IRB, though, allowing South Africa to compete in the inaugural World Cup seemed a step too far. The South African Springboks rugby side was banned. Can it be a coincidence the apartheid regime was dismantled in less than a decade after its chief opponent, Nelson Mandela, was released from prison?

In fairness, the opposition to apartheid from the IOC and FIFA is a rare example of sports' rulers dabbling in global politics. Many exist in their own strange little bubble, oblivious of human rights abuses, so there's bizarrely some merit in their claims of being apolitical as a result. Some, though, are also inextricably linked with the sporting and cultural history of their country; the national aspirations of their country, tragically at times the divided politics of their country. It is perhaps no coincidence the National Football League, despite being an organisation desperate to give its code of football an international profile, has the American flag proudly incorporated into its logo. The NFL, though, barely compares with Ireland's Gaelic Athletic Association in being almost part of the DNA of a country. The GAA claims to be non-political. Yet this was an organisation promoting a nationalist vision of an Irish-Ireland. It once did so to the extent of banning anyone from its organisation from going along to watch a 'foreign sport' (i.e. an English sport such as rugby, association football or cricket); let alone playing a foreign sport.

The zealous enforcement of the GAA's infamous rule 27 led to one of the most embarrassing incidents in modern Irish history. Remarkably, the GAA decided to boot out its patron, president Douglas Hyde, for attending an international soccer match in his role as head of state. It mattered little to the GAA that Hyde was a true patriot, recognised by many as father of the Irish-Ireland movement, promoter of the Gaelic language and a leading advocate of GAA sport. Hyde was dumped. By indulging in a brand of politics its critics warned bordered on fascism, the GAA's protests of being non-political rang hollow.

The GAA apologised decades later; most of its infamous bans dismantled and abolished. Relations were repaired with organisations promoting sports with rules drawn up by English public schoolboys; most notably rugby union. Relations too were repaired with the established Irish political classes. They even invited the Queen of England to their Croke Park headquarters; scene of a massacre by crown forces loyal to her grandfather during Ireland's war of independence. For the GAA to impose its own form of boycotts in the guise of bans on the support of 'foreign' sports, ostracising even the president of Ireland in the process, was perhaps in a bizarre sense somewhat appropriate. After all, the term 'boycott' was coined in Ireland. It came about thanks to a Mayo landlord, Captain Thomas Boycott. His tenants and the rest of the community refused to co-operate with him as part of the land agitation protests in 19th-century Ireland. The GAA's bans imposed in the late 19th and early 20th centuries were the original sporting boycotts. More were to controversially follow worldwide.

It simply was not enough for sporting organisations to impose their own boycotts such as the apartheid bans from cricket and the IOC. Government leaders saw the propaganda value of sport. They sought to impose boycotts, flexing their political muscles. A few countries boycotted the Melbourne Olympics of 1956, either in protest at the crushing of the Hungarian uprising or the invasion of Suez. Different countries took their pick.

Many African nations boycotted the 1976 Montreal Olympics in protest at New Zealand maintaining links with South Africa in the sport of rugby union. Four years later, Jimmy Carter, president of the United States, and Margaret Thatcher, prime minister of the United Kingdom, took their chance. Carter succeeded in imposing a boycott, preventing his athletes from attending the Moscow Olympics in protest at the Soviet Union's invasion of Afghanistan. Thatcher's pleas for a British boycott of the Moscow Games fell on deaf ears. The British team went. It did not help Thatcher that the British and Irish Lions rugby team were touring South Africa in the summer of 1980; a controversial decision supported by her own backbenchers. Sport and politics had formed a toxic mix.

Of course revenge from the Soviets for the Americans' failure to turn up in Moscow was inevitable. They boycotted the Los Angeles Olympic Games four years later, ordering Eastern Bloc countries do to the same. In between came an opportunity at a Winter Olympics to play out the Cold War on ice and indulge in some classic nationalistic tub-thumping for an American president and his electoral rival. The 'miracle on ice', an Olympic ice hockey semi-final between the Soviet Union and the United States, served as a remarkable propaganda coup for Jimmy Carter and Ronald Reagan, a triumph for the 'land of the free' over the dark forces of communism. The Americans won, eventually securing gold in the final. The players, all-American heroes, were given a White House reception. Their sporting achievement as amateurs and students pitted against to all intents and purposes full-time professionals was acknowledged. Their value, though, as propaganda tools at the height of the Cold War as the USA tried to strangle the life out of the Soviet Union, was of more importance.

At least in the cases of these sporting boycotts no athletes or coaches died at the hands of the politically motivated. Sadly though many sporting tragedies have been born out of politics; chief among them the massacre at the Munich Olympics of 1972. It seems inconceivable the Games carried on despite the deaths of Israeli athletes; murdered by the Palestinian terrorist group Black September. Yet the event continued regardless.

Too often commentators refer to sporting failure as a tragedy. This glib, lazy and ignorant use of the word is put in context by the murder of Israeli athletes and coaches at Munich in the autumn of 1972 and the massacre of spectators at Croke Park in Dublin half a century earlier. Politics has also played a part in the tragic history of the world's most popular team sport, association football. Two countries, El Salvador and Honduras, went to war ostensibly on face value over the result of a World Cup match. It may have served as an excuse for countries with strained relations, yet remarkably a sport, football, gave them no better excuse for committing young men into battle. Arguably, soccer also played a role in the Arab spring; football matches between club sides serving as a focal point for protest with tragic, fatal results. Even if organised rallies were banned or prevented by the authorities, there was always the opportunity to go along to a football match, mass spectator sport the ideal cover for political protest.

Occasionally the sporting world appears to embrace rather than merely mix with the political world, despite administrators and athletes claiming to the contrary. One such controversial example is as whether an athlete is a drugs cheat; just who carried out and sanctioned the pharmaceutical doping? Often it was done at government level during the Cold War era, especially in the Soviet bloc; also there were growing suspicions that some Western capitalist nations such as West Germany indulged in the dubious practice too. Now, in a throwback to the Cold War era, Russia is accused of indulging in state-sponsored doping, though whether it is the only country to engage in such a dubious practice is perhaps open to question.

Dick Pound, the chairman of WADA's independent commission investigating the doping allegations declared with a degree of exasperation, 'It's pretty disturbing. It's disappointing to see the nature and the extent of what was going on and to reach the conclusions that it could not possibly have happened without everybody knowing about it and consenting to it. It's worse than we thought. It has the effect unlike other forms of corruption of affecting the results on the field of play.'

Russia had, in playing its own geo-political games, choreographed what the chastened president of the IAAF, Sebastian Coe, described as a 'horror show'; one his own organisation appeared unable or reluctant to pull the curtain down on. In recognising his own organisations' failings, one far too susceptible to being manipulated by malevolent political influences, Lord Coe commented, 'The whole system has failed the athletes, not just in Russia, but around the world. This has been a shameful wake-up call and we are clear that cheating at any level will not be tolerated.'

It is not just the scourge of drugs. Financial doping causes heated argument in sport. Did a football club effectively buy a league title or a European Cup with its rivals unable to compete with the owners' financial firepower? Those owners are occasionally foreign governments seemingly on a diplomatic and public relations mission to boost their status in the international community; Qatar investing in Paris St Germain, Abu Dhabi's ruling family injecting money into Manchester City. Forget the abilities of the players on the pitch. It's the size of the wallet of the owner sitting in the boardroom which matters. At the Olympics, did a nation win a clutch of gold medals by pumping millions of dollars of public money into nurturing athletes and coaching programmes? Most times the answer is yes; Great Britain's improved performance, for example, at successive Olympic Games from the mid-1990s onwards being largely down to extra public money in the form of lottery funding.

Worse still, the spectre of corruption hangs over many sports; especially the influence of money on key policy decisions, such as the award of a World Cup or an Olympic Games. Again politics becomes entangled. How much a nation state can influence an individual's vote in a key policy decision of a sporting governing body is always open to question. Allegations of bribery are common, though more than often never proven. Dark rumours abound of delegates being persuaded by their own national governments to vote one way or another for reasons of trade and commerce. Sport, in the guise of the bureaucrats running its governing bodies, does little to dispel lingering suspicions. It is almost as though those in charge thrive on controversy.

This is a select sample of controversial episodes; the potent mix of sport and politics. The aim is to give a simple guide to those events, some tragic, others plain sinister, a few bizarre; all the subject of hot dispute. Here are just a few examples of how sports and politics do not only mix but collide, how sporting governing bodies can by cynically manipulated at times by the most unsavoury of characters. Ultimately, it is the athletes, the coaches and the fans being manipulated. Worse still, lives have been lost thanks to the potently toxic mix of politics and sport.

1

Hitler's Olympics: Berlin 1936

JUST who was responsible for the modern Olympics; this multi-billion pound orgy of sport and largesse? Forget the history books, forget Athens 1896 with Baron Pierre de Coubertin's Games. These were the innocent Games in the Corinthian spirit, a sporting festival promoted as the modern industrial nations of the time began to embrace organised professional sport. De Coubertin insisted his Olympics was to be amateur, strictly a festival for 'gentlemen'. The French aristocrat was inspired by Shropshire farmers trying to bring ancient Greece to the English Midlands. It was a quaint vision; a remarkable legacy to leave to future generations. Yet strictly in many respects, Pierre de Coubertin is not the answer. The true solution, the sinister and depressing outcome, might well be Adolf Hitler. He instituted the ritual of the torch relay; a curious tribute to ancient Greek and Nordic mysticism. He is to blame for everything from the largesse to the mind-numbing jingoistic and nationalistic tub-thumping; using a sporting jamboree to showcase a country. Berlin 1936 served as a blueprint for the organisation of the modern Olympic Games.

One other man could and should be credited for creating the modern Olympics – Hitler's propaganda minister Joseph

Goebbels. Hitler was no fan of sport. He saw little value in it apart from the need for physical exercise to build up fitness in soldiers for war. As for the Olympics, Hitler condemned the movement in predictable racist rhetoric as a 'plot by Freemasons and Jews'. Goebbels thought otherwise. He spotted an opportunity; not for improving one's health, nor for friendly competition in the spirit advocated by de Coubertin, but for political exploitation. Goebbels recognised the award of the Olympic Games to Berlin gave Germany's Nazi regime the perfect platform for launching a global propaganda coup. He persuaded Hitler to embrace the Olympics, not to promote sport but to showcase Nazi Germany; to hoodwink the world into perhaps believing the Third Reich was governing a modern, benevolent state.

To do so, not a single Reichmark would be spared; the best stadia, the best training facilities, the perfect living quarters built for the world's athletes. Crucially, money would be poured into providing state-of-the-art media facilities. These were the first games to be televised. Letting the world know who had won gold, silver and bronze was of secondary importance to the arch propagandist Goebbels; promoting Nazi efficiency was the primary concern. He wanted to showcase a 'new Germany'. By 1935, the British ambassador to Berlin, Sir Eric Phipps, felt moved to comment on the 'tightening' of the Nazi regime's control of German sport. He also lamented the Nazi 'exploitation' of German sporting victories. In the months leading up to the Berlin games, the Nazis had published a manual of political education, which stressed the importance of sport. Deutschland über Volk, Staat, Leibesübungen or in English 'Germany, about people, state, physical exercises' asserted among other things, 'Gymnastics and sport are thus an institution for the education of the body and a school of the political will in the service of the State. Apolitical, so-called neutral gymnasts and sportsmen are unthinkable in Hitler's state.'

Bruno Malitz, the man in charge of the Nazi Brownshirts sports programme in Berlin, declared, 'For us National Social-ists, politics belongs in sport. First, because politics guides everything; and second, because politics is already inherent in sport.' Evil politicians had hijacked the world's biggest sporting spectacle for their own sinister ends.

The International Olympic Committee had unwittingly handed Hitler and Goebbels their propaganda coup, one even Hitler himself was slow to recognise. The games of the 11th Olympiad were awarded to Berlin in May 1931, before the Nazis came to power in Germany. Those games to be staged in 1936 would come 20 years after Berlin was originally due to stage the Olympics. Instead, those Games were cancelled because of the First World War.

Hitler was about to provoke the Second World War. In the early years of the Nazi regime he was recognised as a threat to world peace and the IOC was urged to reconsider a decision made before the rise of the Nazis, not least because of the sickening growth in anti-Semitism across Germany. The president of the German Olympic Committee, Theodor Lewald, was forced to stand down from his lead role in organising the Games because his paternal grandmother was Jewish. Instead, Lewald was forced to take up a liaison role between the Nazis and the International Olympic Committee, the acceptable face of German sport. His successor, the Nazi sports boss Hans von Tschammer und Osten, set about excluding Jewish athletes from German teams. Gypsies were also excluded. Sport and politics toxically mixed thanks to the Nazis' anti-Semitic and racist policies. Critics worldwide, including leading politicians in Great Britain and the United States, thought it inconceivable the Olympics could be staged in Nazi Germany. Yet the IOC pressed ahead with the staging of the Berlin Games in 1936. Not only would the summer Games go ahead in Germany but also the Winter Olympics in the Bavarian town of Garmisch-Partenkirchen in February 1936. Those Games were staged just a fortnight after German troops entered the de-militarised zone of the Rhineland, set up between Germany and France after the First World War.

Not even the prospect of staging both the winter and summer Olympics would stop the Nazis from flexing their military muscle, the International Olympic Committee appearing weak and manipulable. An inspection team from the IOC visited Germany in 1934 and found no problem with the treatment of Jewish or Gypsy athletes. It was a remarkable observation. The Nazis were so intent on pursuing their all-Aryan policies that world class athletes were prevented from participating in sport. Jewish and Gypsy athletes were deemed inferior, members of races the Nazis dismissed as sub-human. They were barred from sports clubs, training facilities or competing as individuals. In such a depressing context, sporting integrity counted for nothing.

Avery Brundage, president of the American Olympic Committee, posed as a zealot advocate of Corinthian values. He would emerge as president of the IOC, a controversial and divisive figure firmly believing in the amateur ethic and of sport being kept apart from politics. Curiously despite advocating this view, Brundage initially appeared hostile to the staging of the Games in Berlin and favoured any boycott by America and other nations if necessary. It was clear the unsavoury political creed of the Nazi regime threatened the Olympic ideal. He declared, 'The very foundation of the modern Olympic revival will be undermined if individual countries are allowed to restrict participation by reason of class, creed, or race.'

Nevertheless, once Brundage was feted by the Nazis; given full VIP treatment with lavish hospitality by Goebbels and his fellow henchmen; it led to him changing his mind. Brundage carried out his own inspection of Germany once US sports administrators indicated they were unhappy with the IOC giving the Nazis a clean bill of health. He remarkably concluded Nazi Germany was pursuing the 'true spirit of the Olympics' and pompously asserted, 'The Olympic Games belong to the athletes and not to the politicians.' This politically astute sports administrator ignored the potential propaganda value for a vile regime. He apparently appeared to believe Nazi pledges to include Jewish athletes on their Olympic team; pledges Hitler's regime had no intention of keeping.

Brundage backed the Berlin Games and worked towards persuading his American colleagues to ignore calls for a boycott; despite deep reservations especially from not just the Jewish community but Christian groups, including the Catholic Church. Its American journal *The Commonweal* declared that going to the Berlin Games would set the seal of approval on radically anti-Christian Nazi doctrines. It called the Nazis not only anti-Semitic but 'pagan to the core' and pleaded, 'In the interests of justice and fairness we suggest that no Catholic, and no friend of the sports activities of Catholic institutions, ought to make the trip to Berlin.'

The United States still appeared in the months before the Games the most vociferous opponent of a Nazi Olympics; boycott movements in other countries, including the European powers of Great Britain and France, gaining little traction. Brundage still had his work cut out to persuade the American Athletic Union to send a track and field team. Its president, Jeremiah Mahoney, clearly recognised the Olympics were being cynically manipulated by a racist and totalitarian regime; the Nazis. He dismissed German assurances given to Brundage, concluding, 'I am convinced, and I do not see how, you can deny that German Jews are being excluded from the possibility of competing in the Olympic Games merely because they are Jews.

'I believe that participation in the Games under the Swastika implies the tacit approval of all that the Swastika symbolises. Surely, it does not imply the disapproval and the abhorrence, which so many Americans feel. I believe that for Americans to participate in the Olympics in Germany means giving American moral and financial support to the Nazi regime, which is opposed to all that Americans hold dearest. Therefore, I hope that all Americans will join me in opposing American participation in the Olympic Games and aid me in having the Games transferred to another country.'

Support for this position came from Jesse Owens, the athlete destined to become the inspirational figure of the Berlin Games. Owens told a radio station in November 1935, 'If there is discrimination against minorities in Germany, then we must withdraw from the Olympics.'

Walter White, the secretary of the American civil rights group the National Association for the Advancement of Coloured People (NAACP), wrote to Owens congratulating him on his stance. Yet even White admitted he felt 'somewhat divided' over the issue of a boycott of the Berlin Games. White explained that he found Nazi policies 'a duplication of what we Negroes have suffered for three centuries in America'. He mused, 'There have been times when I have felt that there might be a certain psychological value in having blond Nazis run ragged by yourself and others.' As it turned out, Owens had already changed his mind. He wanted to go to Berlin and compete; so did most of his black colleagues.

A vote on whether or not to boycott the Berlin Games was held at a convention of the American Athletic Union at the Commodore Hotel in New York City in December 1935. Brundage, not his arch opponent Mahoney, narrowly won the day. Brundage had seen no irony or any contradiction in his statement the Olympics were meant for 'athletes not politicians', despite a despicable bunch of politicians clearly hijacking the games for their own sinister motives. Crucially, the US president Franklin D. Roosevelt had stayed out of the Olympic boycott debate, taking a neutral stance. If American opponents of going to the Nazi Olympics hoped for support from their president, it was not forthcoming. On hearing American participation in the Berlin Olympics had been guaranteed, Sigfrid Edstrom, the Swedish member of the IOC and an ally of Brundage, sent him a cable couched in racist terms to congratulate him on foiling what he described as a 'plot by the dirty Jews and politicians'. He further suggested Brundage's reward might be a seat on the IOC. Brundage's place was duly offered by the committee prior to the Berlin Games in July 1936.

The Berlin Games were going ahead and involving American, British and French participation. Of the major nations, only the Soviet Union was absent, not coming into the Olympic fold until the Helsinki Games of 1952. In all, 49 teams took part; more than in any previous Games. One of the American participants seeking a gold medal was a certain Avery Brundage. He took part in the strangest of sporting disciplines, the art competition.

Prior to the world's top athletes gathering for the Games, the Nazis had gone out of the way to lavish competitors, officials, travelling fans and journalists with hospitality. They made sure Berlin was a pristine city, shorn of incriminating anti-Semitic Nazi propaganda. Instead the city was adorned with Olympic flags; alongside the Nazi German flag. 'Jews not welcome' signs, seen all over Germany since Hitler came to power, were removed from hotels, restaurants, bars and other public places. Anyone deemed 'undesirable', people likely to embarrass the Nazis, were rounded up and locked up; out of sight from tourists and inquisitive foreign journalists. On just one infamous day, 16 July 1936, more than 800 Gypsies were detained by police and frogmarched to a camp on the outskirts of Berlin. The Nazis had not just built an Olympic village for athletes; they built a detention centre for Gypsies. As for Berlin's Jewish population, Hitler's notorious elite army corps, the SS, were apparently ordered to refrain from taking any action against them. For once, they were to be left alone. However, any foreign journalist, wanting to speak to Jewish leaders and gain an insight into life under the Nazis, had to go to the Gestapo for permission. From that point, those journalists would be closely monitored for the duration of the Games. Just as an added measure, another act of deceit, the anti-Semitic publication *Der Stürmer* was absent from newsstands. It would be back in circulation after the games. In pulling off a grand propaganda coup nothing was left to chance.

It helped the previous summer Games in Los Angeles four years earlier had been something of a flop, thanks largely to the depression. Only half the number of competitors present for the 1928 Games in Antwerp turned up in Los Angeles. President Edgar Hoover decided not to attend. Given a record number of countries and competitors were descending on Berlin, the Nazis were presented with a golden opportunity to showcase their country, to send a positive message to the rest of the world. Crucial in all this was the ability to exploit technological advances in 1930s media. These were the first televised Games, though the pictures were deemed poor with the medium only in its infancy. A viewing room was set up in the Olympic village. Berliners were able to watch the Games live on television at designated venues across the city; very few had a TV at home.

Radio was a different matter. It had grown into a reliable and popular medium worldwide. The Nazis ensured the world's broadcasters were able to operate the best equipment available. More than 20 outside-broadcast vans were made available to the foreign media with radio journalists given prominent commentary positions. Once Joseph Goebbels was congratulated by a producer from the American broadcaster NBC for the facilities on offer, the Nazi propaganda chief was able to reflect on a personal triumph. He had persuaded Hitler to embrace the Games; one to confirm Germany's status as a modern country recovering from economic depression and defeat in the Great War; one dishonestly able to portray itself to the world as culturally tolerant and inclusive. The world's media, while suspicious, appeared to conform, promoting a positive view of the Berlin Games.

Goebbels must have been delighted with the favourable press on offer from the international media for the Berlin Olympics of 1936. Athletes, officials and journalists were impressed with the impeccable organisational skills of their German hosts and in awe of the state-of-the-art sporting facilities. In justifying the 20m Marks spent on the 1936 Games, Hitler declared it as 'absolutely necessary in light of the impression this creation will make on the rest of the world'. Final estimates put the cost of the Berlin Games as more than 100m Marks. The Olympic village, spread over 130 acres, served as a model for future Games; better than anything built for the competitors at previous Olympiads. Yet for all the cold efficiency here there was a dark side to the Nazis, one to be spotted years later and not known at the time to the outside world. It was designed by Captain Wolfgang Fuerstner of the German army and built by the men under his command. There were more than 140 buildings, including a post office and a bank. The residential accommodation consisted of apartment blocks with 13 twin bedrooms and separate provision made for stewards able to act as interpreters for their foreign visitors. A 400-metre athletics track and an indoor Olympic-size pool on site made it easy for the competitors to access training facilities.

There was just one snag though as far as the Nazis were concerned; Feurstner was of Jewish descent. Therefore, despite the brilliant job he had done in designing the village, Feurstner was demoted. Here there appeared to be a dark pattern. It followed the decision to force the head of Germany's Olympic Committee, Theodor Lewald, to accept a lesser role because of his paternal Jewish grandmother. Instead of Feurstner, Lt Colonel Werner Gilsa was given the credit, and thanked and honoured by the Nazis at a lavish reception. Feurstner, devastated by the snub, went back to his barracks from the party in honour of Gilsa and shot himself. The Nazi propaganda machine responded by burying him with full military honours and falsely claiming he had died in a road accident. Hitler's

Games had claimed a life. Millions more were to follow in war and concentration camps.

In the summer of 1936, though, the Nazis were intent on holding out the hand of friendship to a sceptical world, attempting to showcase a modern and vibrant nation. In doing so they assured the best facilities were available, the competition venues just as impressive as the Olympic village. The main stadium housed 100,000 spectators and it still stands to this day, though it was refurbished and modernised to stage football's 2006 World Cup Final. Three other stadiums were built along with a polo field and an outdoor theatre. As the athletes lined up to enter the Olympic Stadium for the opening ceremony there were some notable absentees. Avery Brundage accepted Nazi assurances of fielding a German Olympic team selected on merit rather than race or creed. Yet just a fortnight before the Games, Jewish athlete Gretel Bergmann was dropped from the German team despite being the joint world record holder in the women's high jump. She was the favourite to win gold. Other world-class Jewish athletes were excluded from the German team in a brazen act of racial discrimination. Gypsies were also not allowed to compete, among them the boxer Johann Trollmann, who was the German middleweight champion. This evil political regime had ruined the sporting dreams of its country's own citizens. Later, of course, they were to do far, far worse, embarking on war and genocide.

Yet the exclusion of Jews and gypsies from the German Olympic team proved politics and sport mixed in a disturbing poisonous cocktail; the most ruthless of politicians able to exploit sport for their own dubious ends. It showed the world had been hoodwinked but frankly very few people noticed or cared. As the Games progressed the Nazis managed to build a favourable impression of the Games; thanks to their own organisational skills but also the infamous 'feelgood' factor from world-class sporting competition.

On Saturday 1 August 1936 Adolf Hitler greeted the world's athletes at the opening ceremony for the Games of the XI Olympiad. For the ceremony, the grey skies hovering overhead served as a reminder of the metaphorical dark clouds gathering over Europe in the build-up to the Second World War. Yet the Olympics were about triumph and joy, tempered only by sporting despair and disappointment. How competitors would greet Hitler was just one of the thorny issues at stake; specifically the offering of the Nazi salute to the German leader. Most teams chose not to do so as they paraded around the stadium. Controversially though, the French team did salute Hitler, causing fury back home in France. The French team insisted the salute offered was the 'Olympic salute', a gesture similar to the Nazi salute; one not seen at any Games since 1936. It was uncomfortably far too similar to the familiar gesture to greet Adolf Hitler. For all the protestations of innocence, the French team's decision to offer a form of salute to Hitler was greeted with despair and disappointment by their own supporters. The British and American teams, in contrast, merely marched past Hitler; not a smile on a face, not a wave to the crowd who were giving them polite applause.

Hitler had already completed the first stage of his propaganda triumph with tens of thousands of German citizens enthusiastically flocking to freshly-built stadia to welcome the world and greet its best young athletes. His own citizens were impressed with the show on offer; the world's media giddy with praise. Frederick T. Birchall of the *New York Times* filed copy describing the scene and asserting it was a triumph for sport over politics. He did note the mixed reaction given to the parading teams from the crowd; notably enthusiastic applause for the Nazi-saluting Hungarians and a muted greeting for the Americans and the British. Yet on Hitler he observed, 'Adolf Hitler was receiving the plaudits of a league far removed from politics, a league of peaceful sport to which he had become the proud host. There can be no doubt that he was proud at this moment of the climax of two years' patient preparation and endeavour. For once pride in an achievement showed in his bearing.'

Perhaps Birchall was trying to be balanced with just the faintest hint of criticism. Yet he gave a ringing endorsement of the Nazi Olympic Games in tones echoed by others from the international media contingent, 'For him [Hitler] it has been a day of triumph, exceeding perhaps any that have gone before. From soon after dawn, when a military parade down Unter den Linden and back revived the old imperial custom of "Great

Waiting", until he retired past midnight, he was the object of enthusiasm exceeding all bounds.'

Birchall concluded, 'These Olympic Games have had an opening notable even beyond expectations, high as these were. They seem likely to accomplish what the rulers of Germany have frankly desired from them, that is, to give the world a new viewpoint from which to regard the Third Reich: It is promising that this viewpoint will be taken from an Olympic hill of peace.' That peace yearned for by the *New York Times* correspondent was, of course, to be shattered only three years later.

For all the plaudits from those normally suspicious of Nazi intent, one man memorably ensured Hitler and the Nazis would be thwarted in their aims of promoting Aryan racial superiority; thwarted in making the Berlin Olympics a complete propaganda triumph. He was Jesse Owens, who would later be shamefully treated by Avery Brundage, the sporting plutocrat who asserted that the Olympics was above the murky world of international politics. Owens was one of ten African American athletes in the US track and field team and for all the Nazi boasts of Aryan superiority he was a clear favourite to strike gold in Berlin.

Just a year earlier, he had remarkably set three world records in the space of 45 minutes at the 'Big Ten' meeting in Michigan. Owens first equalled the world record for the 100-yard dash, clocking 9.4 seconds. He then broke the world record for the long jump before going back on the track to break the world record for the 220-yard dash with a time of 20.3 seconds; also in the process breaking a world record for the metric equivalent, the 200 metres. Just to round off his day Owens then broke the world record for the little-run 220 yards low hurdles in 22.6 seconds, again a world best in the metric equivalent. His achievement was all the more remarkable because he was complaining of a bad back and didn't bother to warm up because it would have been too agonising. Given Owens's record breaking feats it was odd of the Nazis, to put it mildly, to mock the Americans for relying on black athletes to bring the United States Olympics glory; people the Nazis considered to be an 'inferior race'. One Nazi officially shamefully dismissed them as 'Black Auxiliaries'.

In his quest for gold medal glory, Owens was only seriously challenged in the long jump; Germany's Lutz Lang offering the challenge before finally conceding defeat and warmly congratulating his American opponent. Hitler, so the narrative goes, was less than impressed and apparently stormed out of the Olympic Stadium, although there is little evidence he actually did so. In all, Owens won four gold medals: the 100 metres in 10.3 seconds, the 200 metres in 20.7 seconds, the long jump and the 4x100 metres sprint relay. It was in the latter more controversy emerged thanks to the intervention of Avery Brundage. Despite winning the individual sprint events, the US track and field management decided to leave Owens out of the relay team for the heats. He was rested and the US sprint relay team was doing quite nicely without him, comfortably making the final with gold seeming certain. Brundage then intervened. He insisted Owens, and Ralph Metcalfe, another black athlete, ran in the final instead of Marty Glickman and Sam Stoller; both Jewish athletes. They were the only Jewish members of the American track and field team at Berlin. They were also the only American Olympians not to take part in the Games. It was a clear snub to Glickman and Stoller; one based not on sporting integrity as it might have appeared at face value but it seems on the basis of their religion and race. Observers alleged Brundage deliberately blocked the selection of the Jewish athletes to appease the Nazis; remarkable if true.

At no point did Hitler present medals to black athletes, despite the men's 100 metres sprint being viewed widely in sport as one of the Olympics' 'Blue Riband' events. He was not to be seen shaking hands with any black athletes, least of all Owens, the greatest athlete of his generation and perhaps arguably of any generation; the man shattering Hitler's myth of Aryan supremacy. Yet years later it emerged Owens himself was unfazed by the so-called snub from the Nazi leader. Instead, he poured scorn on his own political leaders at home in the United States; a country openly at the time practising racial segregation in professional team sport. Owens remarked, 'It was all right with me, I didn't go to Berlin to shake hands with him, anyway. When I came back, after all those stories about Hitler and his snub, I came back to my native country, and I couldn't ride in the front of the bus. I had to go to the back door. I couldn't live where I wanted. Now what's the difference?'

Owens lived in 'Jim Crow America', individual states imposing segregation by passing laws branding African Americans as 'separate but equal'. It is no wonder Owens challenged the notion of the United States being a morally superior nation. Instead of criticising Adolf Hitler, he castigated his own president Franklin Roosevelt. 'Hitler didn't snub me. It was our president who snubbed me,' he told American journalists. Owens added, 'The president didn't even send me a telegram.' He even went further by claiming Hitler waved to him; a gesture none of the 110,000 people in the stadium seemed to notice. Owens's coach Larry Snyder reasoned he was trying 'to take the sting out of Hitler's apparently rude behaviour toward him and other American blacks'.

Owens was unquestionably the hero of the Berlin Olympics and yet his achievements were, as he bluntly pointed out, largely ignored by the American political establishment. Not for another 40 years would he receive an invitation to the White House, where he was honoured by president Gerald Ford with the Medal of Freedom, the highest civilian honour for an American citizen. Furthermore he was unable to capitalise on his new-found fame and was instantly stripped of his amateur status for daring to ignore a call to go on a post-Olympic European tour with the American team. Owens complained he was tired, missed his wife after three months away from home, and wanted to return to the United States. Brundage stripped him of his amateur status, a decision he defended years later as president of the International Olympic Committee. Brundage told *Sports Illustrated*, 'They said I declared Jesse Owens a professional. Jesse is a fine man. I have the utmost respect for him. His accomplishments in the '36 Games were remarkable. But Jesse had agreed to go with a group that was to visit Sweden. Well, some smart fellow in New York had a bright idea on how to make a quick bundle of money and he sent Jesse a telegram offering him $40,000 to turn professional. $40,000 is a great deal of money, and Jesse was just a young fellow, so he announced that he was going to accept the offer. And he didn't go to Sweden, as he had promised. All right; he was suspended. What did the headlines say? The headlines said "Brundage declares Jesse Owens a professional"! His face was truculent again and his voice rose slightly in intensity.

"Brundage had nothing to do with it"! Jesse Owens declared Jesse Owens a professional. I think it was a shame.'

Brundage was indignantly unrepentant. For him even the promise of money was enough to punish Owens; just weeks after his triumph at the Berlin Olympics. Brundage insisted sport and politics did not mix, despite being an arch-political manipulator. He certainly made sure sport and money would not mix as far as athletes were concerned, just for administrators to give people like himself a decent living. Brundage was right to view it as 'a shame'. The shame was on him. Owens's treatment was shameful.

Hitler's apparent reluctance to meet and greet Owens along with the other black athletes competing in Berlin oddly suited Goebbels and his propagandists. They possibly felt it was a good thing for Hitler to take a low profile during the duration of the Games. It also suited the IOC; Hitler's background role, once the opening events were over, ensuring prominence given to sport. Few members of the IOC recognised they were being cynically manipulated for political propaganda; a Nazi strategy ruined, though only in part, by the brilliance of Jesse Owens. The world went away by and large with a favourable but distorted view of German life and also of a Nazi regime already flexing its military muscle. Brundage was smugly satisfied with events in Berlin. In his assessment of the Games he said, 'The Games of the XI Olympiad at Berlin, Germany, was the greatest and most glorious athletic festival ever concluded – the most successful and colourful of all time.'

He praised the Nazis for throwing millions of marks into staging the Games and concluded without irony that the Games had been 'far more than an athletic spectacle'. He was right, but it appears not to have dawned on Brundage that he was endorsing Hitler's Nazi regime. At the outbreak of war, the American correspondent William L. Shirer expressed his despair at the naivety of Brundage and the Olympic movement. He wrote, 'Hitler and his Nazi thugs had succeeded in making the XI Olympiad the most colourful in history and, what was more important, had used the Olympics to fool the world into believing that Nazi Germany was a peaceful, civilised and contented nation.'

Post-Berlin, there was not to be another Olympics for a dozen years. At the closing ceremony on Sunday 16 August 1936 the call was made for 'the youth of every country to assemble in four years at Tokyo, there to celebrate with us the 12th Olympic Games'. Instead, Germany and Japan were allies as the youth of the world was at war; one engineered by Adolf Hitler, the man feted by the international Olympic movement in Berlin, August 1936.

2

England's Football Shame: The Nazi Salute

HOW do you address Adolf Hitler? How do you respond to the playing of Nazi Germany's national anthem? 'Don't bother' might be the glib answer for the 21st century. Yet in the 1930s this posed something of a diplomatic and political headache for the British Foreign Office and the governing bodies of UK sports teams, all anxious to avoid upsetting the Nazis. It was resolved comfortably at the opening ceremony of the Berlin Olympics – just eyes right and carry on walking was the tactic employed by the British contingent as they paraded before Adolf Hitler and his Nazi henchmen.

Perhaps in hindsight the England football team should have followed suit when they turned up in the very same stadium some two years later. Hitler was not even there, preferring to visit his fascist ally Mussolini rather than watch football. Yet England's players still gave the Nazi salute. It further compounded the Football Association's decision to unwisely organise a friendly against a country just weeks after it had 'annexed' another country, Austria. The 'Anschluss', which incidentally included scrapping the Austrian national football team and incorporating its best players into a 'Greater Germany' team, did not stop the FA offering the English handshake of friendship to their

German counterparts. It failed to stop the England team from making the Nazi salute in still the most infamous dark moment in English sporting history. Unlike the Berlin Olympics, it was a propaganda gift the Nazi propaganda chief, Goebbels, did little to work for. He probably could not believe his luck.

How this act of infamy came about subsequently became a matter of dispute; presumably out of sheer embarrassment on the part of the various parties involved, the players blaming the FA and the British Foreign Office, the authorities blaming the players. For the players to be deemed solely responsible seems odd. Ever since the Nazis rose to power their willingness to exploit sport for propaganda purposes had long exercised the minds of Britain's diplomatic corps and their political masters; not least the eventual decision to avoid persuading the British Olympic Association to boycott the Berlin Games of 1936. This football match on 14 May 1938 in Berlin's Olympic Stadium also came against the backdrop of a diplomatic strategy of 'conciliation' with Germany, or 'appeasement' as Winston Churchill preferred to call prime minister Neville Chamberlain's policy.

England went to Berlin just three years after hosting Germany in a politically controversial friendly at White Hart Lane, the home of Tottenham Hotspur – one traditionally with a Jewish following. The Football Association extended the invitation to its German counterparts. Hans von Tschammer und Osten, the Nazis' boss of German sport, gleefully accepted and his players would travel to London 'in homage to the inventors of football'. He further promised that 10,000 German supporters would go along as 'ambassadors of goodwill'. Any feelings of goodwill were certainly not reciprocated by horrified opponents of the Nazis. Labour politicians, trade union leaders and Jewish organisations called on the government to stop the FA from staging the game. British ministers resisted the pressure, preferring instead to utter the mantra of keeping sport out of politics. It did not dawn on them that the Nazis were already doing the exact opposite; preparing for the Berlin Olympics and manipulating this 'goodwill' game for propaganda purposes.

The home secretary, Sir John Simon, in justifying the British government's stance, told a group of TUC delegates, 'I think that we have to keep up in our country a tradition that a sporting fixture is carried through without any regard to politics at all.' As far as Sir John was concerned, this was a private matter of little government concern. Perhaps it was pure coincidence that it helped to maintain workmanlike diplomatic relations with a Nazi regime already happy to embrace sport as a political propaganda tool. The game went ahead with the Nazi flag of Germany flying above an English football ground for the first and only time. England comfortably won 3-0 in front of a capacity crowd, including those estimated 10,000 German fans. Despite the defeat one German newspaper told its readers, 'For Germany it was an unqualified political, psychological and sporting success.' As for the Brownshirt leader Tschammer, he opined dreamily at a post-match dinner of the 'blue sky of friendship between the two Nordic countries'. Thanks to the Nazi salute from England players in Berlin's Olympic Stadium two and a half years later, the Germans were to enjoy another dubious 'political and psychological' success despite losing the actual football match.

There appeared little or no debate over whether England would travel to Berlin to play Germany, despite the growing international tension brought about by the annexation of Austria. Czechoslovakia was also coming under threat from the Nazis yet the British government, unlike Hitler and Goebbels, expressed a determination to avoid using sport as a political and diplomatic tool. At least it ignored calls for bans and boycotts. Actually, doing little or nothing to stop England's footballers from travelling to Berlin and then allegedly encouraging them to offer a Nazi salute inside the Olympic Stadium suited Chamberlain's diplomatic policy; the appeasement much derided by Churchill. It was a rare foray for English soccer on foreign soil and it was also legendary winger Stanley Matthews's first game of football outside the British Isles. The Germans were also confident of victory with the English on a poor run of form since the game at White Hart Lane in December 1935. Germany, in contrast, had enjoyed an undefeated run of 14 matches after the 1936 Olympics. It also helped they were able, thanks to the Nazi 'Anschluss' to co-opt Austria's best players, with one notable exception.

A blip in Germany's impressive form had come in a defeat to Austria just before the Nazis decided to gobble it up. Matthias Sindelar was among the Austrian scorers and upon annexation refused to join the 'Greater Germany' squad to play England. Within a year he was dead. A Gestapo file labelled him as 'pro-Jewish' and a 'social democrat'. Sindelar died in his girlfriend's flat of carbon monoxide poisoning; a death officially recorded as an 'accident'. Rumours of suicide quickly abounded but friends thought it was suspicious, blaming the Nazis.

Even without Sindelar, the presence of other players from Austria, formerly a major force in 1930s world football, meant growing grounds for optimism among German fans. The Olympic Stadium in Berlin held 110,000 spectators yet it was four times oversubscribed. Such was the enthusiasm for watching German sides taking on British sides in a game of football, the Nazi authorities were able to sell out a game between a German XI and Aston Villa to be staged in the same stadium the day after the international match.

Preparation for those fixtures was thorough, the German and Austrian players going into a training camp in the Black Forest for a fortnight before the game. In contrast, the FA had to beg the English clubs to release their players for the game against Germany before making an arduous train journey to Berlin, arriving just a couple of days before the game. The Nazis were sensing victory for Germany; defeat for the country which gave the sport of association football to the world. Neville Henderson, the British ambassador to Berlin, dryly noted, 'The Nazis are looking for victories to boost their regime. It is their way of claiming a super-race.'

The man in charge of the English touring party was London solicitor Charles Wreford-Brown, an England football captain in the 1890s. In the 1930s England had no manager or coach and the team was selected by committee, then expected just to go out and beat the opposition heavily. Foreign teams were deemed inferior to England. Only Scotland, and on occasions the Welsh and the Irish were shown any respect. As a bizarre act of sporting snobbery, the English, Scots, Welsh and Irish all refused to have anything to do with FIFA's new-fangled competition, the World Cup. On arrival in Berlin on 12 May 1936, Wreford-Brown and the English footballers must have been more aware of the importance being place on this game by their Nazi hosts and the subsequent diplomatic pitfalls. Weeks earlier, no less a dignitary than the chief diplomatic officer at the Foreign Office, Sir Robert Vansitartt, had contacted FA secretary Stanley Rous to warn him that this international friendly of association football between Germany and England was more than just a game. Sir Robert stressed, 'It is really important for our prestige that the British team should put up a really first-class performance. I hope that every possible effort will be made to ensure this.'

In reply the Football Association assured the government that 'every member of the team will do his utmost to uphold the prestige of his country'. So much then for the pretence put up from the British government of the day of sport having nothing to with politics; it was pure nonsense. Given the frenzied preparations for the game it seems odd no protocol had been worked out on how to address the German crowd and the Nazi regime during the anthems being played before the game. Basically whether or not the Nazi salute would be offered by the English footballer, something not countenanced by the British Olympians at the Berlin Games of 1936.

On the eve of the match Wreford-Brown told English journalists that a decision would be made in the morning at a special meeting being held just hours before kick-off. They were left with the impression he had already made his mind up. The players, who indicated to their friends in the press that they were not happy with the prospect, would be told after this meeting to make the Nazi salute as the German anthem was being played before kick-off. For the FA committee men to leave such an important diplomatic decision that late seems distinctly odd. For there to be no British government input into the decision given the chief diplomatic officer's almost panic-stricken missive to the FA only weeks earlier was also curious. For all the concerted efforts from the FA and the British government to lay all the blame on the players for making a Nazi gesture, roundly criticised back home, it appears clear considerable pressure was put on the players by diplomats, government ministers and FA committee men. Indeed similar pressure was exerted on the Aston Villa team for their upcoming fixture.

At the meeting to decide on the appropriate 'etiquette', if that's the polite word, for the players to adopt, Stanley Rous alleged that the British ambassador to Berlin, Sir Neville Henderson, advised the FA to ask the players to make the Nazi salute. Rous claimed Sir Neville told him it was a 'matter of courtesy'. Rous insisted Sir Neville had offered this advice, 'When I go to see Herr Hitler I give the Nazi salute because that is the formal courtesy expected. It carries no hint of approval of anything Hitler or his regime may do. If I do it, why should you or your team not do it?'

As a result of this advice, England's footballers were told by FA officials to make the Nazi salute. They may not have been happy about it but they complied with the order, lining up to give the salute during the playing of the German national anthem 'Deutschland über alles'. Their hosts also made the Nazi salute during the playing of the British anthem, 'God Save the King'. Perhaps any anger at being forced to make this infamous gesture emboldened them during the game itself. They gave what even German football writers of the day declared as a 'masterclass'. *Fuseball Woche*, the in-house journal of the German Football Federation, even went as far as hailing England as world champions. The Germans had been thrashed 6-3 yet were magnanimous, and bizarrely also quite comfortable with how events unfolded. The Nazis' propaganda victory was no doubt of more importance than a humiliating defeat in a football match.

Once the English players had delivered the infamous salute and won the match convincingly the British ambassador seemed insufferably pleased with himself, ignoring the furore developing back home on the following day from a hostile press. He deemed not only England's performance in winning 6-3, but also the pre-match salute with its warm reception from the German crowd, a success. He boasted that the match 'undoubtedly revived in Germany British sporting prestige'. History would record it as one of the most infamous moments in British sport, yet the senior British diplomat to the Nazi regime was fulsome in his praise. It led to the Foreign Office to take the unprecedented step of writing to the FA to thank the organisation for its role in helping to cement Anglo-German relations.

Yet for the Foreign Office and officials of the FA, this dubious diplomatic initiative on a sporting weekend in Berlin did not go quite as smoothly as they hoped thanks to the recalcitrant and noble behaviour of Aston Villa players. Their game against a German XI, containing ten former Austrian internationals, turned out to be an ill-tempered affair. Villa won 3-2, much to the displeasure of the crowd, who booed the English side throughout. Those boos came to a deafening crescendo at the end of the game. The German XI made the Nazi salute. The Villa team, unlike England the previous day, refused. Most of them ran straight off the pitch at the end of the game, leaving their captain Allen in the middle with one or two others. He tried to call his team-mates back but they refused to return. Allen and the others gave up and also left the field to a chorus of catcalls from the hostile German crowd.

The Villa players, though, were adamant. They were not going to make the Nazi salute. Frank Broome was not going to repeat the same mistake he made when lining up for England the day before. Their manager, Jimmy Hogan, revealed that they had been asked by the FA to make the Nazi salute. Indeed, they assured the FA that they would do so. Their decision to refuse, he reasoned, was entirely 'spontaneous' and due to the bad-tempered nature of the game. Hogan did not say so but it was also entirely honourable.

Remarkably, FA officials took a dim view of the Aston Villa players' behaviour. They were of the belief the offering of the Nazi salute by the England football team served as a diplomatic triumph. It was a job well done but they considered all their 'good work' had been destroyed by the stubborn refusal of the Villa players to repeat the gesture. Publicly, they passed off the refusal to stay behind after the game and give the Nazi salute as a 'misunderstanding'. Aston Villa's club president Sir Patrick Hannon went as far as contradicting match reports from the English press. Sir Patrick, the Conservative and Unionist MP for Birmingham Moseley and a man with known pro-fascist sympathies, insisted the press gave an exaggerated impression of what occurred. He commented, 'The game was clean and undisturbed by any untoward incident from beginning to end. Such trouble as arose was due to the fact that the vast array of spectators – something like 110,000 – were not accustomed to decisions arising out of the offside rule.'

He went on, 'The incident at the end of the game when the Villa players did not stay behind to salute was due entirely to a misunderstanding, and I am satisfied that there was no want of courtesy on the part of the Aston Villa players.'

Indeed he insisted his players would make the Nazi salute at a subsequent tour match against Stuttgart. This time they went ahead with a salute. They collectively offered up a 'two fingers' gesture to the crowd, one the delighted spectators, oblivious of English customs, wrongly mistook for a Nazi salute. Sir Patrick, anxious as ever to maintain good diplomatic relations with the club's Nazi hosts, presumably did not bother to tell them the true meaning of a 'two fingers' gesture.

As for the FA boss Stanley Rous, he felt he was in no position to ignore the angry response to England's international players giving the Nazi salute. He made excuses, citing the dubious advice given by the British ambassador Sir Neville Henderson and for good measure blamed the players as willing participants. Rous claimed, 'All agreed that they had no objection, and no doubt saw it as a bit of fun rather than of any political significance.'

It was curious then that Stan Cullis, the one man who stubbornly refused to give in to pressure and go along with the plan, was dropped from the side to play Germany on the day of the game. The rest agreed, yet contrary to the version of events given by Rous felt coerced into making the Nazi salute. As far as the players were concerned, they were not willing participants. All in later years spoke of their subsequent shame. Eddie Hapgood of Arsenal, the team's captain, observed after the Second World War, 'I've been V-bombed in Brussels before the Rhine crossing, bombed and "rocketed" in London, I've been in a shipwreck, a train crash, and inches short of a plane accident. But the worst moment of my life, and one I would not willingly go through again, was giving the Nazi salute in Berlin.'

Stanley Matthews, the star player of the England team in Berlin and one of its scorers in the match, also commented in later years. In his autobiography published in 2001 entitled *The Way it Was*, Matthews described bedlam in the dressing room once Wreford-Brown had told them to give the Nazi salute. He wrote, 'All the players were livid and totally opposed to this, myself included. Everyone was shouting at once. Eddie Hapgood, normally a respectful and devoted captain, wagged his finger at the official and told him what he could do with the Nazi salute, which involved putting it where the sun doesn't shine.'

According to Matthews, Sir Neville Henderson had not only advised them to give the Nazi salute but had delivered a 'direct order' to do so; one endorsed by Rous. Again, this account directly contradicts Rous's version of events. By the time Matthews had given his side of the story at the turn of the 21st century, his former FA boss had long since died.

Beyond Matthews and Hapgood, all of the players felt they had been badly let down and hung out to dry. Matthews wrote, 'I sat there crestfallen thinking what on earth my family and the people back home would think if they saw me and the rest of the England team paying lip service, so to speak, to the Nazi regime and its leaders.'

Matthews believed the team had little choice given the pressure being asserted by Henderson on behalf of the British government. He said the players were told by the hapless Wreford-Brown the political situation between Great Britain and Germany was so volatile it only needed a 'spark to set Europe alight'. If it was the advice given by Henderson, a football match being the precursor or excuse for a world war, it was rather ludicrous. Hitler hardly needed to feel affronted by the behaviour of England's international footballers to order the invasion of Czechoslovakia just weeks after the Germany and England game; or to invade Poland just over a year later.

Matthews concluded, 'Faced with the knowledge of the direst consequences, we felt we had little choice in the matter and reluctantly agreed to the request.' He described the publication of the photograph of them giving the Nazi salute the next day was to the 'eternal shame of every player and Britain as a whole'. Matthews felt they had let their country down; something the Foreign Office clearly didn't consider in its congratulatory missives to the Football Association.

Quite who was responsible for this infamous act will remain a matter of dispute and conjecture with most or all of the participants no longer with us. Yes, the England players, including Matthews and Hapgood, could and should have followed the example of their team-mate Stan Cullis and refused point blank to give the Nazi salute. Yet it now seems clear they were young men under considerable pressure from individuals in power, men such as Henderson and Rous refusing to take responsibility for their own actions in ordering the salute. Young men, proudly wearing the three lions on their shirts, were being led by metaphorical donkeys.

England won 6-3; Matthews describing it as the finest England performance he had ever been involved in. For the record the goalscorers were Cliff Bastin, Frank Broome, Len Goulden, Matthews and a couple from Jackie Robinson. Although in football terms it was a great victory, sadly the real winners were the Nazi regime, Adolf Hitler, and his propaganda chief Joseph Goebbels. Sport itself was a loser, beaten by evil and manipulative Nazi politicians thanks to the weakness of their British counterparts.

3

The Black Power Salute

FOR the Olympic movement to deny that politics had no place in the sporting arena seemed just a little odd as the world's youth gathered in Mexico City in 1968. The International Olympic Committee had banned South Africa from competing years earlier because of its racist apartheid policies. South African athletes were not welcome at the Games in Tokyo in 1964; the same would apply for the Olympiad in Mexico, though only after prevarication on the part of some IOC members. Quite rightly the IOC eventually deemed it wrong for competing nations to select athletes on the basis of the colour of their skin, though only did so after considerable international pressure. South Africa was in purdah (the time between an announced election and the final results). By suspending the apartheid nation the IOC had made its own political statement; one heartily approved by the watching world; though perhaps not among racists in one part of the world, the United States of America.

Ever since a black woman, Rosa Parks, refused to obey a bus driver's order to give up her seat for a white man in 1955, the American civil rights movement had grown in strength. African Americans vigorously campaigned against racial discrimination in a country where slavery had only been abolished less than a century earlier, only to be followed by a succession of discriminatory laws declaring black people as 'equal but separate'. By 1968, the civil rights movement was at its height. In Martin Luther King Junior the movement had its martyr; the inspirational leader of the civil rights movement shot dead by an assassin. His movement had already successfully campaigned for the US Congress to legislate to abolish racial segregation in the American southern states; a Civil Rights Act in 1964; and a Voting Rights Act in 1965. Yet as the American nation mourned for King in April 1968 there remained a deep social and economic divide along racial lines in the United States. It was a problem two young American athletes were determined to highlight and address as they took to the world stage. Tommie Smith and John Carlos, favourites for sprint titles at the Mexico Olympics, decided to make their own unique quiet protest, giving us one of the most iconic images in sporting history – their black power salute.

Carlos cites his faith as the inspiration for his protest on the Olympic podium, the 200 metres bronze medallist raising his black-gloved left arm as gold medallist Smith raised his black-gloved right arm at the playing of the American national anthem. Carlos explained, 'I had a moral obligation to step up. Morality was a far greater force than the rules and regulations they had. God told the angels that day, take a step back – I'm gonna have to do this myself.'

Yet the protest, at least the chance to protest, was nearly abandoned. As African American athletes prepared for the Mexico games, many favoured a boycott. It was fine for the Olympic movement to banish the South Africans for their racist policies yet racism in American society remained endemic despite the passing of the Civil Rights Act and the restoration of voting rights. In the autumn of 1967, a group of black athletes formed the Olympic Project for Human Rights, Tommie Smith being one of its leading advocates. Smith and his colleagues felt they were being cynically exploited by the American establishment to give the impression to the world of American black people enjoying success in a racially harmonious nation.

Outside of the sporting world, especially the disciplines of track and field athletics, boxing and gridiron football, the truth was the opposite. The OPHR's founding statement summed up the athletes' frustration, 'We must no longer allow this country to use a few "Negroes" to point out to the world how much progress she has made in solving her racial problems when the oppression of Afro-Americans is greater than it ever was. We must no longer allow the sports world to pat itself on the back as a citadel of racial justice when the racial injustices of the sports industry are infamously legendary. Any black person who allows himself to be used in the above matter is a traitor to his country because he allows racist whites the luxury of resting assured that those black people in the ghettos are there because that is where they want to be. So we ask why should we run in Mexico only to crawl home?'

Given the strength of the statement, it seemed a boycott from black American athletes of the Mexico Olympic Games was inevitable. There were other demands from the OPHR: the restoration of Muhammad Ali's world heavyweight boxing championship (he had been stripped of his title because of his anti-Vietnam War stance); the sacking of Avery Brundage as president of the US Olympic Committee; the hiring of more black coaches; a boycott of the New York Athletic Club and also the banishment of South Africa and Rhodesia from the Olympic movement. In the case of South Africa the IOC had already done so, banning South African athletes from competing in the 1964 Tokyo Games. Given there was no change in South Africa's apartheid regime, it was a little odd for Brundage and his IOC colleagues to invite the country back. Brundage and his cohorts did so only to withdraw the invitation a couple of months later, fearing a boycott by African nations. The IOC also decided to withdraw the invitation for Rhodesia to send a team to Mexico; both decisions credited arguably more to pressure from African and British Commonwealth nations rather than perhaps the American civil rights campaigners.

In the months leading up to the Mexico Games, there was no sign of Brundage being sacked or resigning despite his botched attempt to allow apartheid South Africa to compete, nor any chance of Muhammad Ali's title being restored. These though were the least significant of the OPHR's aims. More importantly, there remained a strong appetite for a boycott of the Olympics from African American athletes in support of the US civil rights movement. It was a year of turmoil, campaigns for social justice, protests against the ongoing Vietnam War, springing up around the world, the oratory of assassinated civil rights leader Martin Luther King serving as an inspiration.

A metaphorical call to arms came from Tommie Smith. In a magazine article published in March 1968 Smith wrote, 'We learn through observation and education. I know more now than I did when I was a boy. I know now, for instance, that Negroes do not have equality in the United States and do not have all of the rights supposedly granted to them by the constitution of the United States. What is right is right. What is wrong is wrong. I recognise wrongs and I am willing to fight for right. I am not a militant. I am an extremist only where a fight for my rights as a human being are concerned. I recognise that Negroes have had greater opportunities in sports in general and the Olympics in particular than they have in any other field.'

Smith concluded he had no choice but to give up his chance of Olympic glory, 'To emphasise my point, I have said I would give up my right arm to win a gold medal in the Olympics, but I would not give up my personal dignity. I am not entirely sure of my actions. No one could be. But I have searched my conscience and I am acting as I believe I should act. I am concerned that I may have harmed my "image" and thus damaged the future I hope to make for my family. I would be a fool not to be concerned. But I would be less than a man if I did not act for what I believe.'

Smith and his colleagues from the Olympic Project for Human Rights rattled the American establishment. Future US president Ronald Reagan was among the most scathing critics. The then Californian governor reserved his ire for the organisation's founding father Dr Harry Edwards; a sociologist based at San Jose State College. He ranted, 'I disapprove greatly of what Edwards is trying to accomplish. Edwards is contributing nothing toward harmony between the races.' Edwards's response was hardly diplomatic, calling Reagan 'a petrified pig, unfit to govern'.

Such a response would hardly endear him to critics of his organisation from within the African American community. Doc Young, one of the leading black sports writers of the time, wrote in the *Chicago Tribune*, 'I have nothing but contempt for people who complain because we don't have enough heroes but who spend their time trying to destroy the showcases for which heroes are produced and displayed. The charge that "America is as racist as South Africa" is the most extravagant lie in our times.' Most of Young's criticism was reserved for Tommie Smith, a view apparently shared by boxing legend Joe Louis. The *Washington Afro-American* reported, 'Joe Louis says coloured athletes should consider themselves Americans first and coloured Americans second and disagrees with those pushing for a boycott.' It quoted Louis as saying, 'Whenever you are asked to do something for your country, you do it.'

Crucially, though, the dissenting athletes were being offered support by other leading figures in politics and sport. Jackie Robinson, the first African American to play Major League Baseball, praised the athletes, recognising the sporting sacrifice they were prepared to make. He commented, 'I do support the individuals who decided to make the sacrifice by giving up the chance to win an Olympic medal. I respect their courage. We need to understand the reason and frustration behind these protests... it was different in my day, perhaps we lacked courage.'

Shortly before he was murdered in April 1968, Martin Luther King also offered his crucial support, 'This is a protest and a struggle against racism and injustice and that is what we are working to eliminate in our organisation and in our total struggle. No one looking at these demands can ignore the truth of them. Freedom always demands sacrifice and they have the courage to say we're going to be men and the United States of America have deprived us of our manhood, of our dignity and our native worth, and consequently we're going to stand up and make the sacrifices.'

Dr King's murder hardened attitudes among those calling for a boycott, yet for all the hyperbole it curiously never materialised. Instead, the athletes decided to go to Mexico, to compete for medals, to make their own protests on the greatest world stage, with Smith and Carlos destined to make the greatest of all.

Pragmatism motivated the African Americans eschewing calls and thoughts of a boycott rather than the criticism of the white-American establishment led by Avery Brundage and the likes of Ronald Reagan. Being typically bombastic, Brundage offered this opinion, 'If these boys are serious, they're making a very bad mistake. If they're not serious and they're using the Olympic Games for publicity purposes, we don't like it.' He was hardly going to like what was about to follow with the podium protest from Smith and Carlos.

The United States fielded its strongest possible team simply because the athletes were not going to give up their chance of sporting glory. There were other ways to protest against the injustice being meted out to black Americans. Lee Evans, who won gold medals in the individual 400 metres and 4x400 metres relay in Mexico City, reflected on the clever role being played by Harry Edwards in drumming up publicity for the cause of the Olympic Project for Human Rights. He said, 'Harry was media savvy. He said all year that we were going to take a vote at the Olympic trials and all year there was commentary in all the newspapers. Some editors made fools of themselves. They would write, "Look at these narrow, stupid black guys. They don't know what they're doing." They just said things that exposed themselves to who they really were. The athletes of course voted down the boycott. I was hoping it was going to be voted down because I wanted to run in the Olympics. I knew that this would happen, that the proposal was a way for us to get leverage. Tom and I had talked about it and I said let's say we're going to boycott so we can get some things done but we all knew that we were going to run in Mexico. Push comes to shove we were going to be there.'

Despite months of agonising over a boycott, the American athletes decided to pack their bags and travel to Mexico City. The Olympics there would give them a global platform to promote the cause of American civil rights. Attempts by the US Olympic Committee to dissuade Smith and Carlos or any other American athlete from making their protests had failed. Once they were aware of the athletes' intentions, Avery Brundage and his colleagues had even roped in Jesse Owens to try to stop them from going ahead. Owens had met the Olympic team prior to the Games to make his case but the 1930s Olympic legend was sent packing, though many of the athletes felt sorry for him. Given he was treated appallingly by Brundage in the aftermath of the

1936 Olympic Games, Owens was an odd choice of emissary from the American establishment. Lee Evans summed up the athletes' feelings; insisting they felt nothing but admiration for Owens. Evans ruefully recalled, 'He was confused coming to talk to us like that because we knew that he was being victimised. He was a victim and we felt sorry for him actually.'

Among those listening to Jesse Owens was an apparently disgruntled John Carlos. He preferred a boycott strategy and was unhappy with the decision to participate in the Games. Yet he still went to Mexico to win his medal and make his protest. He recalled in an interview with US journalist David Zirin, 'A lot of the athletes thought that winning medals would supersede or protect them from racism. But even if you won the medal it ain't going to save your momma. It ain't going to save your sister or children. It might give you fifteen minutes of fame, but what about the rest of your life?' Instead of a boycott a different strategy was adopted; a series of high-profile protests, preferably on the victory podium.

First of all a race had to be won; at the very least a podium place secured. For Smith and Carlos, they were joint favourites to win the 200 metres, the medal ceremony for the race providing them with an ideal opportunity to make their civil rights protest. Carlos had won the American trials in an unratified world record time but his achievement was not recognised because he wore too many spikes in his shoes. As they lined up for the Olympic final in Mexico City, the odds had been tipped further in the favour of Carlos thanks to an injury suffered by Smith in the semi-finals. He had pulled an abductor muscle and went to the blocks for the final with his thigh heavily strapped.

Smith later explained he feared he had lost his chance of winning Olympic gold and thoughts of a civil rights protest on the podium were cast from his mind. He said, 'My psychology immediately changed to running the race with that pulled muscle. How could I get up to speed without that muscle? I was deeply worried about winning.' The injury made little difference to Smith. A false start did little for any nerves among the athletes lining up for the race and they were eventually up and sprinting at the second time of asking with Carlos quickest off the blocks. Carlos ran by far the better bend going into the finishing straight a couple of metres ahead of the rest of the field. With 80 metres to go he was still leading comfortably, then Smith applied what he called his 'Tommie burners'; a devastating turn of speed leaving Carlos and the rest of the field trailing in his wake. Smith even slowed down as he crossed the line in a new world record of 19.83 seconds. Carlos tightened up as he saw his great rival race away from him, with Peter Norman of Australia pipping Carlos on the line to claim the silver medal. For the planned protest on the podium, Norman, a white Aussie, would play his part.

Smith recalled the moment he crossed the line and won Olympic gold, 'About three strides after I hit the tape, you can see the genuine smile on my face, but you'll see that smile immediately diminished. All of a sudden, "Oh, oh, it's time." There was another chapter. If I won the race, the next chapter was how am I going to do this? This has to be done so that people will understand.'

On the evening of 16 October 1968, an hour after crossing the line in the Olympic 200 metres final, Smith, Carlos and Norman prepared to walk out for the medal ceremony. Smith had a pair of black gloves bought for him by his wife, though she was puzzled by his request for a pair of gloves to wear in the warmth and suffocating altitude of Mexico City. Carlos had forgotten his gloves so Norman, a willing collaborator, suggested they each wore a glove, one to raise his fist with his left hand and the other the right. Norman also wanted to make his own personal contribution to the protest about to be made by Smith and Carlos by wearing the badge of the Olympic Project for Human Rights. There was just one snag. He didn't have one. Fortunately members of the US Olympic rowing team were sitting in the stands as fans, all of them white and all of them from Harvard while being most sympathetic to the OPHR. The rowers issued a statement, 'We, as individuals, have been concerned about the place of the black man in American society in their struggle for equal rights. As members of the US Olympic team, each of us has come to feel a moral commitment to support our black teammates in their efforts to dramatise the injustices and inequities which permeate our society.'

Norman approached Paul Hoffman from the American rowing team and asked for his OPHR badge. Hoffman explained with some fondness, 'He came up to me and said, "Have you got one of those buttons, mate?" If a white Australian is going to ask me for an Olympic Project for Human Rights badge, then by God he would have one. I only had one, which was mine, so I took it off and gave it to him.'

Everything was set for the protest; Smith and Carlos both feeling conflicting emotions as, along with Norman, they were about to book their place in sporting history – not for winning an Olympic medal but bringing politics into the sporting arena.

Their sense of apprehension was understandable in hindsight given the furore about to unfold from those angered by their protest. Smith recalled the walk into the stadium, 'Peter Norman was in front. I was in the middle. John was behind. We had discussed that as soon as the American flag went up; we had to make a joint move. I said, "My head will be bowed and my hand will go to God and I will pray during the national anthem because this country needs a lot of prayer."'

Carlos, in his autobiography *The John Carlos Story*, described the moments before the band was about to strike up the American national anthem. His thoughts were both personal and political; remembering his father on the one hand, Martin Luther King and Malcolm X with their political mantras on the other. Among those mantras was 'be true to yourself even when it hurts'. He wrote, 'Damn, when this thing is done, it can't be taken back. I know that sounds like a lot of thoughts for just a few moments standing on a podium, but honestly this was all zigzagging through my brain like lightning bolts.'

Their medals were presented by Lord Burghley, a British Olympic gold medallist from the 1932 Los Angeles Games and president of the International Amateur Athletic Federation; African American athletes having already indicated they did not want to see their US compatriot Avery Brundage anywhere near the podium. True to their word, as soon as the American flag began to rise, as soon as the band struck the opening bars of the US national anthem, Smith defiantly raised his right arm towards the heavens with his black gloved fist clenched and his head bowed. Carlos followed suit, this time a left arm raised though slightly bent, black gloved fist clenched, head also bowed. Peter Norman stood impassively in front with hardly anyone noticing the OPHR badge pinned to his Australian tracksuit. The resulting image captured by photographers is one of the most iconic, if not the most iconic, in world sport.

Smith, who tucked his gold medal inside his tracksuit top at the end of the ceremony, explained at the time, 'We are black and we're proud to be black. White America will only give us a credit for an Olympic victory. They'll say I'm an American but if I did something bad, they'd say a Negro. Black America was with us all the way, though.' Carlos offered similar sentiments, 'We feel that white people think we're just animals to do a job. We saw white people in the stands putting thumbs down at us. We want them to know we're not roaches, ants or rats.'

Carlos later explained in his autobiography the reason for bending his arm rather than holding it straight up in the sky. It was so, if necessary, he was able to thump anybody trying to stop the protest. He wrote, 'I wanted to make sure, in case someone rushed us, I could throw down a hammer punch. We had just received so many threats leading up to that point, I refused to be defenceless at that moment of truth.'

Norman, before he died in 2006, recalled the atmosphere inside the Olympic Stadium, 'I couldn't see what was happening. I had known they had gone through with their plans when a voice in the crowd sang the American anthem but then faded to nothing. The stadium went quiet.' Carlos remembered the response from the crowd with colourful language, 'You could have heard a frog piss on cotton. There's something awful about hearing 50,000 people go silent, like being in the eye of a hurricane.'

Smith had no regrets, later explaining to the BBC, 'What I had to do was necessary, though it took a very, very devastating step towards me being vilified because of what had to be done. Did I want to do it? No. But I had to do it.

'There are many cases where people might ask did you regret doing it? The only regret was it had to be done; and I was the one that did it.' As for the bronze medallist Carlos, he was quizzed by the BBC just after the medal ceremony, the interviewer wondering whether it was a publicity stunt just to earn notoriety and perhaps money. Carlos retorted, 'I can't eat that, and the kids round my block can't eat it. They can't eat publicity, they can't eat gold medals. All they want is an equal chance to be a human being.'

The opprobrium heaped upon the athletes was immediate; Smith's prediction of vilification becoming true. Many in the crowd, once they found their voices, directed abuse at Smith and Carlos as they made their way from the podium back into the bowels of the Olympic Stadium. Most of the abuse was all too predictably racist in nature. As Carlos recalled, 'The fire was all around me.' Within days, the two athletes had been suspended. The *New York Times* correspondent at the Mexico Games, Joseph M. Sheehan, believed members of the American Olympic Committee were divided on how to deal with the black power protest from Carlos and Smith, some believing it did not warrant punitive action against the men. Yet the IOC made it clear action must be taken otherwise the rest of the US Olympic team would be on the plane home alongside them, bringing American participation in the Games to an end. Judging by the strength of the statement from the US Olympic Committee in condemning Smith and Carlos, their supporters, opposed to meting out any punishment, must have been in a minority of USOC members.

The statement read, 'The United States Olympic Committee expresses its profound regrets to the International Olympic Committee, to the Mexican Organising Committee and to the people of Mexico for the discourtesy displayed by two members of its team in departing from tradition during a victory ceremony at the Olympic Stadium on 16 October. The untypical exhibitionism of these athletes also violates the basic standards of good manners and sportsmanship, which are so highly valued in the United States, and therefore the two men involved are suspended forthwith from the team and ordered to remove themselves from the Olympic village. This action is taken in the belief that such immature behaviour is an isolated incident. However, if further investigation or subsequent events do not bear out this view, the entire matter will be re-evaluated. A repetition of such incidents by other members of the United States team can only be considered a wilful disregard of Olympic principles that would warrant the imposition of the severest penalties at the disposal of the United States Olympic Committee.'

As the statement more or less served as a metaphorical riot act for American competitors, it was read out to the other US athletes before they competed in the remaining events; notably Lee Evans and his compatriots in the 400 metres, Larry James and Ron Freeman. They took a clean sweep of the medals and settled for a low-key protest, opting to wear black berets on the victory podium. They removed them once the American national anthem struck up and the US flag was raised. Evans was asked at a press conference whether the wearing of the berets represented some form of private 'social message'. Evans responded with a smile, 'It was raining. We didn't want to get wet.' No action was taken against the runners. Nor was action taken against Bob Beamon, who had spectacularly broken the world long jump record. He went on to the podium with his tracksuit bottoms rolled up to reveal his black socks. Beamon told reporters he was 'protesting at what's happening in the USA'. As those athletes competed for medals and made their own subtle protests, Smith and Carlos were on their way home to be greeted as heroes by their supporters but unpatriotic villains by their detractors.

Time magazine summed up the anger felt by the critics of the black power protest with its front cover displaying the logo of the Olympic movement along with the words 'angrier, nastier, uglier' instead of the established motto 'faster, higher, stronger'. The *Los Angeles Times* criticised them for making a 'Nazi-like' salute. The *Chicago Tribune* accused them of heaping embarrassment upon their country. Avery Brundage was characteristically blunt, the man who once famously supported and promoted a Nazi Olympics claiming, 'They violated one of the basic principles of the Olympic Games: that politics play no part whatsoever in them.'

Support for Smith and Carlos was by no means unanimous among the black community. George Foreman, the boxing heavyweight gold medallist, expressed his disquiet with a hint of contempt. He dismissed the protest by saying, 'That's for college kids.' Sadly, those college kids were receiving death threats for making their protest. Carlos blamed the negativity towards him for the death of his wife, who took her own life. He bitterly recalled, 'One minute everything was sunny and

happy, the next minute was chaos and crazy.' Carlos went to the
Mexico Olympics as one of the world's best athletes yet came
back a sporting pariah. Smith, the Olympic champion and world
record holder, suffered the same.

As a pointed snub, president Richard Nixon left the
American track and field team off the list of Olympic athletes
invited to the White House; Foreman was among those who
did go. Years later Foreman admitted he regretted his decision
to belittle the black power salute protest as a gesture for 'college
kids'. Given the legendary status enjoyed by the two athletes
in the mists of time, Foreman probably had no choice but to
reassess. Supporters of Smith and Carlos had accused the boxer
of betrayal; something he said had brought him 'pain'.

Smith and Carlos were joined on the Olympic podium
for a memorable moment frozen in time by another man to
be shunned by his sporting and political establishment, Peter
Norman. Immediately after playing his part in the protest the
head of the Australian Olympic delegation, Julius Patching,
admonished him. Patching recognised everyone had a right
to express an opinion but said, 'When you are in another
country, you must not become involved in politics.' Despite
being Australia's best sprinter, Norman was left out of the
country's team to travel to Edinburgh two years later for the
Commonwealth Games and later for the Munich Olympics in
1972. Norman might well have won gold at both events. He
felt ostracised by the Australian establishment for making his
stand in support of Smith and Carlos even up to the staging of
the Sydney Olympics in 2000. His nephew, the documentary
film-maker Matthew Norman, said he suffered until the day he
died. It was a shocking act of spite from the leaders of a country
wrestling with its own racial problems in the 1960s.

Smith and Carlos both became lifelong friends of Norman
after their chance meeting in Mexico. They carried his coffin at
his funeral in 2006. Carlos saw Peter Norman as a hero, 'a lone
soldier'. Smith commented, 'He paid the price. This was Peter
Norman's stand for human rights, not Peter Norman helping
Tommie Smith and John Carlos out. He just happened to be a
white guy, an Australian white guy, between two black guys in
the victory stand believing in the same thing.'

As the years rolled by, Smith and Carlos, far from being pariahs, became heroes of the civil rights movement; both feted rather than ostracised by the American establishment. A gesture on the world sporting stage encapsulated the aims of a political and social movement; empowering and inspiring human beings suffering discrimination because of the colour of their skin. Thanks to being caught on camera, it is a moment in time not just symbolic of the American civil rights movement but ironically the Olympics; a movement in denial over the link between politics and sport. Just 15 years after Smith and Carlos were booted out of the Games in Mexico, Carlos was invited on to the organising committee for the Los Angeles Games to be held in 1984; a specialist adviser on minority affairs. By the nineties Smith returned to the fold of the American sporting establishment as coach to the US indoor track and field team. Both were honoured with 'men of courage' awards for making their stand; all a stark contrast to the bitterness and bile directed towards them in the immediate aftermath of their protest in Mexico City.

4

Cricket and Apartheid: The D'Oliveira Affair

AS an alternative sport for journalists and commentators in the media, knocking the International Olympic Committee and FIFA, the world governing body of association football, ranks quite high. Yet as South Africa faced mounting international condemnation for its apartheid policies during the early 1960s, both of these organisations responded by imposing a ban from international competition. As for the British colonial sports of cricket and rugby, it was business as usual. Their international ruling bodies maintained global sporting links; refusing to follow the example set by the IOC and FIFA. As far as the cricket and rugby establishment was concerned sport and politics must never mix; just ignore the racist policies of a member country of the International Rugby Board (IRB) or the International Cricket Conference (ICC), that member being South Africa.

For cricket, the lack of moral fibre and the hint of latent racism on the one hand and class snobbery on the other was brutally exposed during the autumn of 1968. One man was at the centre of the scandal, a mixed-race England Test cricketer born in South Africa. He was Basil D'Oliveira. Thanks to the dubious antics of members of MCC at Lord's cricket ground and the sickening obduracy of the South African president John Vorster, D'Oliveira became a *cause celebre*; his treatment eventually leading to the complete sporting isolation of South Africa and arguably the beginning of the end of the apartheid regime.

'No professional cricketer ever came to England with greater potential problems, of political and social adjustment, than Basil D'Oliveira.' Those were the words of broadcaster John Arlott, the man responsible for helping to bring D'Oliveira to England in the early 1960s. D'Oliveira had already earned a reputation as a prodigiously talented cricketer during the 50s, notching up 82 centuries in club and representative cricket, as well as captaining a black South Africa team and leading them on tour in East Africa. As a man from Cape Town deemed by the apartheid government as a 'Cape Coloured', playing Test cricket for South Africa was an impossible dream. D'Oliveira decided to try his luck elsewhere, England being his choice of destination and Arlott the man to facilitate the move. Years later, while in retirement, D'Oliveira admitted his best years as a cricketer were behind him when he wrote to Arlott requesting help. Arlott was only too happy to assist him, finding D'Oliveira a cricketing home at Middleton Cricket Club in the Central Lancashire League. It took him time to settle, not least because he had never come across a society in which whites and non-whites mixed together. Once he did so, Worcestershire offered him a contract to play first-class county cricket, England offered him the cherished opportunity to play Test cricket and D'Oliveira became a British citizen. Given that the calendar showed England were due to go on a tour of South Africa in 1968, alarm bells rang in the offices of South Africa's apartheid government led by John Vorster.

Britain's Labour government, despite discontent from some of its own supporters, was content with maintaining sporting links with South Africa though it foresaw a dispute in the event of D'Oliveira being selected to tour there for England. As early as January 1967, the sports minister Denis Howell warned that the planned tour of England to South Africa in the winter of 1968/69 would have to be cancelled if there were any moves to ban D'Oliveira. His comments were met with cheers by listening British MPs, and derision in the corridors of power in Pretoria.

Vorster warned former MCC president Lord Cobham that the tour would be cancelled if D'Oliveira was selected.

First of all though, 'Dolly', as he was affectionately known, would have to earn his place in the England side. It was to prove a little difficult. Colin Cowdrey, the England captain, dropped D'Oliveira from the team for the Lord's Test against Australia during the 1968 Ashes series. It was a curious decision given that Dolly was the only batsman to show any resistance in an opening defeat to Australia with 87 not out, the sole score of more than 50 by an England batsman. Cowdrey reasoned that he wanted to play an extra bowler and D'Oliveira was frozen out, his chance of going back to his home country as an England Test cricketer appearing remote. Throughout the summer it appeared as though the English cricketing establishment was doing its best to keep D'Oliveira out of the England side, seemingly determined to avoid any confrontation with South Africa. It was even suggested by MCC secretary Bill Griffith that D'Oliveira make himself available for his native South Africa; the oddest of proposals given South Africa's apartheid policies were at the heart of any potential dispute. Then the offer came from a tobacco company for a lucrative coaching contract, provided he refused to tour South Africa as an English international player. Frankly, it amounted to a bribe to keep him out of any England touring party. Dolly, naturally, turned down the 'offer'.

His chance to claim a place in the England touring side to South Africa came in the final Test of the Ashes series at The Oval when Roger Prideaux was forced to withdraw because of an injury. Despite being in relatively poor form in English county cricket, D'Oliveira was confident he would do well. He did so; a score of 158 making him in the opinion of fans a certainty to be called up for the forthcoming tour to South Africa. As he walked back to the pavilion at the end of his fine innings, he felt a sense of elation. Asked about his thoughts, he said they were simply, 'Yes! I am in there! I've done it now. It's all gone right.'

Cowdrey promised D'Oliveira that he would back his selection. The next day Cowdrey and his fellow selectors named their touring party to South Africa. D'Oliveira's name was missing from the list of players and the outcry was immediate.

MCC, the traditional bastion of the cricket establishment, had – to the critics – given in to apartheid South Africa.

For D'Oliveira himself there were just tears. County team-mates at Worcestershire tried to comfort him, including the England Test batsman Tom Graveney. Dolly recalled, 'As I waited in the dressing room at New Road after a Worcester v Sussex game, to hear if my name had been announced for the forthcoming tour to South Africa, I kept waiting and when it wasn't there I was dumbstruck. You could have heard a pin drop in the room. I don't know how long I stood there but the first thing I recall was Tom Graveney swearing bitterly and saying, "I never thought they'd do this to you, Bas." Tom saw the state I was in and took me into the physio's room where I broke down and sobbed like a baby. The stomach had been kicked out of me. I remember thinking, "You just can't beat the white South Africans," but I wasn't bitter. My mood was simply one of resignation and desperate sadness.' His sadness was felt by English cricket fans, the media and the Labour government, though the views of left-wing politicians were arguably of little concern to certain traditional establishment figures at the top of MCC.

Feelings of sadness turned into righteous anger, articulately summed up by D'Oliveira's mentor John Arlott. He wrote in *The Guardian*, 'MCC have never made a sadder, more dramatic or potentially more damaging decision than in omitting D'Oliveira from their team to tour South Africa. There is no case for leaving out D'Oliveira on cricketing grounds. No one of open mind will believe that he was left out for valid cricket reasons: there are figures and performances less than a week old – including a century yesterday – to refute such an argument.'

Warming to his theme, Arlott warned the scandalous omission of D'Oliveira went beyond sport and threatened a negative impact on race relations. He wrote, 'This may prove, perhaps to the surprise of MCC, far more than a sporting matter. It could have such repercussions on British relations with the coloured races of the world that the cancellation of a cricket tour would seem a trifling matter compared with an apparent British acceptance of apartheid. This was a case where justice had to be seen to be done.'

Starkly he warned that MCC, in arriving at its decision, had 'stirred the forces of good and evil'; powers in the opinion of Arlott it failed to understand. His views were backed by other cricket writers and journalists, Michael Parkinson writing in the *Sunday Times*, 'A group of Englishmen picked a cricket team and ended up doing this country a disservice of such magnitude that one could only feel a burning anger at their madness and a cold shame for their folly. The dropping of Basil D'Oliveira from the MCC team to tour SA has stirred such undercurrents throughout the world that no one but the impossibly naïve can any longer think that politics and sport do not mix, never mind believe it.'

Given the suspicion that the elite of the game of English cricket were more interested in soothing relations with apartheid South Africa than – in the words of John Arlott – 'justice', it was difficult to see them backing down. Regardless of whether or not Basil D'Oliveira toured it was controversial enough for England maintaining sporting links with South Africa in the first place, not just in cricket but also rugby. India, Pakistan and the West Indies refused to play the South Africans at cricket. Those countries demanded England, Australia and New Zealand, the 'white nations', did the same. Their pleas were consistently ignored up until the furore over Basil D'Oliveira. As far as their critics were concerned, the grandees of MCC saw nothing wrong in mollifying the Vorster government, so maintaining the narrative of Dolly being omitted from the England team 'on cricket grounds' proved all too easy for them. They were men from the days of Empire, comfortable with even the most despicable of regimes maintaining 'white rule' and openly discriminating against people of a different colour.

Quite possibly, they were unable to predict the fury unleashed by their decision to omit a man of mixed raced from a team to tour South Africa. It must have come as a shock. Their protestations of making a decision on sporting grounds alone 'rang hollow'. Doug Insole, England's chairman of selectors, insisted that D'Oliveira was not among the best 16 cricketers in England; an odd assertion given he had just finished the Ashes series with the highest batting average – albeit from two matches. Insole said he addressed his colleagues at the start of the selection meeting with the following words, 'Let's forget about South Africa. Let's pick a team to go to Australia. And that's what we did.' As the cries of outrage at Westminster and from the media grew, enlightened members of MCC began to resign in protest. Suddenly the cosy little world of the MCC elite was under threat. As unthinkable as it might have been of them wanting to find a way out of the mess they found themselves in, an opportunity presented itself.

As a classic piece of media opportunism, the *News of the World* had already stirred the proverbial pot by offering to take Basil D'Oliveira to South Africa. Its decision alone infuriated the Vorster government in Pretoria. Vorster sneered, 'Guests who have ulterior motives or who are sponsored by people with ulterior motives usually find they are not invited.' Worse was to follow, as far as Mr Vorster was concerned, with the staid and stubborn MCC dropping a bombshell. D'Oliveira's fledgling career as a pundit was to be short-lived. Remarkably D'Oliveira was back in the England squad; arguably the biggest and most duplicitous face-saving act from a group of team selectors in sporting history. Tom Cartwright, a bowler, told them he was injured and unable to tour. Their response – select a batsman, better still a batsman who can also bowl. Now, who's got Basil D'Oliveira's phone number? Naturally Dolly was delighted to take the call despite the original outrageous snub, recalling, 'I didn't care about the fact that the selectors were now choosing me as an all-rounder, that didn't matter anymore.'

The decision to recall him was met with delight by his supporters in England and the non-white community in his native South Africa. It was met with anger by the apartheid regime. Prime minister Vorster declared, 'It is not the MCC team. It is the team of the anti-apartheid movement.' On Tuesday 17 September 1968, the South African government announced it was not prepared to accept the England cricket team into the country on the grounds that a non-white player, one born in South Africa, was in the team.

It was shameful. It was inevitable. It changed the course of sporting history and arguably changed the course of South African history. In an era when the plight of Nelson Mandela, incarcerated on Robben Island, barely received any attention, the treatment of a mixed-race cricketer made global headlines. D'Oliveira later reflected, 'I felt very sad and sorry for everyone who was an innocent in this affair; the sportsmen, the spectators, the non-whites in South Africa who'd been so jubilant when they heard I was coming after all.'

He was also quite circumspect, believing whatever the outcome of this sad saga, only John Vorster and his apartheid government would be the short-term winners. He recognised it might have been better for MCC and the England cricket team to never have contemplated a tour of South Africa in the first place, commenting, 'I was now accustomed to the need to uphold dignity and sportsmanship as often as I could and I'd done my best therefore no one could surely reproach me. I realised that my original non-selection represented the best of both worlds for the Nationalist government. There was no chance of me becoming a national hero on the cricket field and the tour would implicitly put the seal of approval on their apartheid policies.'

His dignity helped to ensure the Vorster government and its apartheid successors would, in the long term, be losers. England were due to host South Africa's cricket team in the summer of 1970 but the tour was called off for fear of violent protests. England played a Rest of the World touring side instead. It would not be until the release of Nelson Mandela from jail and the end of the apartheid regime in South Africa that the two countries would play in an official Test series, although controversially there were rebel tours from English cricketers lured by lucrative South African contracts.

As far as Dolly was concerned, what became known as 'The D'Oliveira Affair' was a 'nightmare'. He reflected that he was the 'unwitting reason' for South Africa being banned from Test cricket and most international sport. Those views came long after his saga came to an end. D'Oliveira gained legendary status in the fight against racism, not by ranting and raving, not by making theatrical gestures, but simply doing what he did best – going out to bat in a cricket match. His century at The Oval could not eventually be ignored by an elite group of men suspiciously anxious to appease a racist foreign power. He quietly went about his work and allowed others to do the talking for him, not least the late and great broadcaster and writer, his old friend John Arlott.

In 1980, Arlott summed up Basil D'Oliveira's achievements, 'At times of stress – as admitted by the MCC establishment under fire for its abandonment of opposition to apartheid – he behaved with the utmost dignity. This happy conclusion – an honest man of high cricketing gifts against the forces of racism, his passage to freedom, taking his wife and children with him, and his example to millions of others has given me one of the greatest feelings of joy from any episode in my life.'

Those sentiments will be echoed by cricket lovers worldwide, indeed fans of other sports. Yet one sport seemed to ignore the furore over the South African government's insistence on influencing the choice of visiting sports teams on the grounds of race. This sport remains to this day a quasi-religion for Afrikaners. It is rugby union, a sport once loftily feeling itself above the politics of apartheid but eventually forced to join the rest of the international sporting community. Isolation in cricket was hardly a blow to the Afrikaans ego. Worldwide isolation in rugby union was quite another matter.

5

Rugby: An Afrikaans Religion?

AT the heart of the cricket and rugby establishments' argument to maintain sporting ties with apartheid South Africa was the curious notion of benevolence. Imposing a boycott, the narrative went, would do more harm than good. Cricket administrators at Lord's reluctantly abandoned this stance thanks to the row over the treatment of Basil D'Oliveira; a mess as much of their own making as the intolerable pressure being exerted by the South African prime minister John Vorster.

It became obvious to even the most blinkered conservative cricket administrator a policy of giving succour to a country selecting teams on the basis of the colour of a person's skin was unsustainable. Rugby union took a different view; stubbornly maintaining international ties with South Africa well into the 1980s. It provoked protests across the globe that were often violent, it forced players to examine their consciences as they became pawns in a political game rather than participants in a rugby match, and even prompted the mass boycott of African countries of the Montreal Olympics despite the sport of rugby union not even being played at those Games.

Anti-apartheid campaigners recognised the importance of rugby union as a sport to the Afrikaans psyche; to them it was akin to a religion. For those among the Afrikaans community promoting the politics of apartheid, the cutting of international ties in rugby union amounted to the work of the devil. On the basis sport must never mix with politics, the International Rugby Board refused to be cast in the role of the devil by white racists in South Africa. Instead, the IRB, its constituent unions, became the devil incarnate for those campaigning to bring an end to apartheid and fighting for social and racial justice in South Africa.

As the selectors of the English cricket team agonised over the prospect of taking Basil D'Oliveira to South Africa in the summer of 1968, a British and Irish sports team was already on tour there. Every four years rugby's 'home unions', England, Wales, Scotland and Ireland, put aside their tribal rivalries to combine in a British and Irish Lions team, taking on the southern hemisphere nations of New Zealand, Australia and South Africa. In 1968 it meant a trip to South Africa, a tour held despite protests and the growing movement to cast apartheid South Africa into the international sporting wilderness. Lions tours and reciprocal tours of New Zealand and South Africa were the most high-profile for the sport of rugby union and were also inevitably the most contentious.

It is a wonder the New Zealand Rugby Union maintained links with South Africa given a series of sleights over the decades. As far back as 1919 in the aftermath of the First World War, the outright racism of Afrikaners following their beloved Springboks rugby team was clear and evident. South Africa invited a New Zealand army team touring Britain to stop off on their way home for a much-anticipated six-week tour. There was just one condition. The South African Rugby Football Board made it clear that nobody with Maori blood, those belonging to New Zealand's indigenous population, would be welcome. New Zealand's rugby administrators complied with the demand, leaving out one of their best players, Parekura Tureia, and selecting a team with only those of European descent. Once the Kiwi touring squad was named, their South African hosts took umbrage at the inclusion of Ranji Wilson, a player with a white English mother and Afro-Caribbean father. As a result of the South Africans' racist objections, Wilson waved goodbye to his mates as they disembarked from the boat in South Africa and carried on with his voyage home to New Zealand.

A couple of years later it was South Africa's turn to tour New Zealand, another opportunity for Afrikaners to display their disdain for people of a different skin colour. After the Springboks beat a New Zealand Maori XV in Napier, one South African journalist wrote of the dismay of the South African team at seeing and hearing white spectators cheering on a non-white team. He exclaimed, 'Bad enough having to play officially designated New Zealand natives, but the spectacle of thousands of Europeans frantically cheering on a band of coloured men to defeat members of his own race was too much for the Springboks, who were frankly disgusted.'

Despite this display of outright racism sporting links were maintained for decades, even after state racism became established in South African law. Once the Afrikaner National Party secured a strong majority in a white-only Parliament, it began to introduce its Apartheid Grand Plan. In 1948 a series of laws were passed institutionalising racism. Still the British and Irish rugby home unions along with their New Zealand counterparts organised tours of the apartheid state, also inviting the fabled Springboks on tours to their own country. Even as first the Olympic movement in the guise of the IOC, then world soccer bosses at FIFA and even cricket began to ostracise South Africa on the global sporting stage, rugby stubbornly maintained links. Politics and sport must not mix, its rulers reasoned, though politicians had different ideas.

In 1960, New Zealand toured South Africa for the final time without their Maori contingent. It was the year of British prime minister Harold Macmillan's 'Winds of Change' speech and also the year of the Sharpeville massacre near Johannesburg. Scores of protestors were killed on 21 March 1960 when police opened fire on them, bringing international condemnation. New Zealand went ahead with their tour regardless of protests. For opponents of the tour, they had a simple mantra, 'No Maori. No tour.' More than 150,000 signed a petition calling for the tour to be called off but this was ignored. Yet by 1967 it became clear the practice of selecting a rugby squad to tour South Africa on the basis of race was untenable. New Zealand's prime minister, Keith Hollyoake, had declared, 'In this country we are one race.' Much to the dismay of Afrikaners, the All Blacks called off their tour. A year later British and Irish rugby faced the moral dilemma of whether or not to tour South Africa. Actually it turned out to be not much of a dilemma for those running the British establishment sport of rugby union. They went ahead with the tour.

Britain's Labour government opposed the tour but did little to stop it from happening. Sports minister Denis Howell, a former football referee, informed the Home Unions Tour Committee that he considered the Rhodesia leg of the tour to be 'against the public interest'. Rhodesia's all-white government had just unilaterally declared independence from the United Kingdom to stop the majority black population from gaining democratic power. Mr Howell also threatened in the House of Commons to cut the funding of sports bodies playing against teams from southern Africa selected on a racial basis. The British and Irish unions ignored the threat of sanctions, no doubt dismissing Mr Howell's threat as empty and hollow, especially as it was directed at organisations dripping in cash.

John Taylor, the Welsh loose forward, was among those touring South Africa with the Lions in 1968, believing the assurances of them being a potential force for good. He soon changed his mind and later refused to go on the subsequent Lions tour of South Africa in 1974. 'The moment I got there I realised it was a mistake. I'd had misgivings but I was desperate to play. I was 22. I wanted to be a Lion. I put all the misgivings to the back of my mind, believed all the twaddle about building bridges and that we weren't supporting apartheid and as soon as I got there I realised very much that we were,' Taylor explained in a newspaper interview. He went on, 'The night before we left, the high commissioner or the ambassador said something to the effect of, "Don't get involved in our politics; you won't understand them. But our rugby and our girls are great so go and enjoy them."

'And then, when we got out there and had our first night in a hotel in Stilfontein, a group of real Afrikaners came to our hotel and, without any prompting from us, launched into an aggressive defence of the apartheid system and how this was the only way to treat the blacks and so on and so forth. I thought, "Bloody hell! What have I come into?" I was injured in the first game we played, against Western Province, and really wasn't fit again on the whole tour and I had an awful lot of time to see what was really going on in South Africa. I got left behind by myself in a couple of places to get treatment and you saw the real South Africa as it was; not just the Lions' eye of it. It troubled me.'

On the decision of the 'home unions' to go back to South Africa in 1974 despite an avalanche of protests against the Springboks playing in Britain and Ireland during the intervening years, Taylor observed, 'I was absolutely convinced that the rest of the sporting world was right and that there was this sort of massive arrogance in rugby that the brotherhood of rugby, the fraternity of rugby, meant more than the brotherhood of man – that they couldn't be bad chaps because they played rugby. It was very much that sort of arrogance that I absolutely deplored in rugby. I had no doubts at all.'

As for the attitude of the men in blazers running New Zealand rugby, Taylor commented, 'It is still hard to believe that the New Zealand selectors just left out their Maoris for tours to South Africa until the 70s.'

Taylor's view, though, was a minority opinion in world rugby during the 1960s and 70s. His own team-mates, including legendary Irish figure Willie John McBride, strongly disagreed with him, pointing to sport's capacity to unite rather than divide people. McBride believed the Lions squad would serve as 'bridge-builders' in South Africa, ignoring editorials in British newspapers expressing the opposite view. The *Daily Mirror*, *Sunday Times*, *Sun* and *Guardian* had all stated that 'bridge-building' was 'fruitless' and that 'in sport, cause and effect, right and wrong, are now pretty clear'.

As the Lions touring party of 1974 gathered inside the Britannia Hotel near Heathrow Airport, hundreds of protesters gathered outside led by future Labour Party cabinet minister Peter Hain. Some invaded the lobby of the hotel but failed to disrupt a team meeting being held by McBride, a man deeply committed to going to South Africa. His view was simple, later recalling in his autobiography, 'All I felt was that rugby football would never have existed if we had allowed it to become embroiled in politics.'

Given that he was an Ireland captain and an Ulsterman from the Unionist tradition of Anglo-Irish politics this view was perhaps understandable. Rugby remained an all-Ireland sport in the 1920s despite political partition on the island. Football in Ireland had acrimoniously split. McBride in his autobiography recalled the meeting at the airport hotel with the Lions players. Ireland's Syd Millar, who was later to become the president of the International Rugby Board, and the tour manager Alan Thomas made the opening speeches. It was then McBride's turn. It was a melodramatic plea to his players, one based on a firm belief the 1974 Lions touring squad would even go as far as demonstrating the apartheid laws were in his words 'nonsensical'. McBride told his players, 'I know there are pressures on you and there must be doubts in your minds, but if you have any doubts, I would ask you to turn around and look behind you.'

He added, 'There, at the end of the room, two huge doors were then pulled symbolically open. Once that had been done, I spoke again, "Gentlemen, if you have any doubts about going on this tour, I want you to be big enough to stand up now and leave this room. Because if you do have doubts; then you are no use to me and no use to this team. There will be no stain on your character, no accusations if you do so, but you must be honest and committed." Not a soul moved. And I believe that was the moment when the 1974 Lions united and we became a special team.'

Indeed, in sporting terms the 1974 Lions tourists gained legendary status among rugby fans; admirably led on the pitch by McBride with his infamous '99 call'. McBride insisted the call was something of a myth but the determination to match the physicality of the South Africans, often with violence, was real. They went unbeaten. A controversial draw with South Africa in the final match served as the only blemish in the record book. However, the suggestion of there being a 'stain on the character' of anyone refusing to tour sat uneasily with opponents of apartheid South Africa and sporting links with the country.

Gareth Edwards, the Welsh scrum half, admitted to doubts in hindsight about touring in stark contrast to the zealous defence of the tour by Willie John McBride. He explained to the BBC, 'When you're young and you're inspired by sport, you tend to cloud issues which are around you and I must be perfectly honest, though we were aware of the political arena in South Africa, we were obsessed by wanting to play the sport and that sounds rather naïve now when you look back. And know exactly the way in which the Nelson Mandela story unfolded. We were made aware of some of the facts but of course as young aspiring sportsmen all we were really interested in, as I said maybe naively, was the sport itself and to play rugby against some of the best players in the world. Yes, it did play on our conscience but the call of the game, so to speak, was very, very strong.'

For the anti-apartheid movement in Britain, its failures to stop the tour came as an annoying blow, one compounded by the surprise decision of sports minister Denis Howell to welcome the Lions back to Britain along with the former Conservative British prime minister, Edward Heath. Howell justified his gesture as one to recognise their sporting achievements. The UK's Anti-Apartheid Movement ruefully noted in its annual report, 'Dr Piet Koornhof, South Africa's Minister of Sport, described the tour as a moral victory for South Africa, thus confirming the arguments that had been put forward against the tour.'

Rugby, in its view, was by the early 1970s the only major international sport maintaining formal links with South Africa. It should have come as no surprise. Campaigns for a rugby boycott in the intervening years between the 1968 and the 1974 Lions tour had ended in varying degrees of success. New Zealand's government stopped the South African rugby team from visiting its country in 1973, arguably for cynical observers to prevent a boycott by African countries of the 1974 Commonwealth Games to be held in Auckland. An original request from New Zealand's newly-elected Labour prime minister, Norman Kirk, to the New Zealand Rugby Union for it to withdraw the invitation to South Africa to tour was ignored. Undeterred, Mr Kirk cited public safety concerns illustrated by an arson attack on a stand in a rugby ground in Papakura, and blocked the Springbok players from entering his country. It was an unpopular move from Kirk in rugby-mad New Zealand.

Though anti-apartheid protests enjoyed strong support especially in urban areas, the majority of Kiwis wanted to welcome South Africa's rugby players to their shores. Kirk took a political gamble in stopping the tour, telling the NZRU he saw 'no alternative, pending selection on a genuine merit basis, to a postponement of the tour'. He recognised it was an unpopular decision but felt he would be 'failing in his duty' if he failed to order the postponement of the tour. At the following New Zealand general election he was out of office, his opportunist political opponents happily exploiting the unpopularity of his decision to cancel the Springboks' rugby tour.

Campaigns to stop other tours in the late 1960s and early 70s failed thanks to a curious air of moral superiority on the part of the rugby establishment; one firm in the view it was above politics. If anything their stance that the game must go on hardened among a wave of protests, many marred by violence both in Britain and New Zealand. Even disgust at Maori players only being allowed into South Africa on the basis they accepted being deemed 'honorary whites' did not prevent the All Blacks rugby team returning to the country in 1970. One of the tourists given the moniker of an 'honorary white', Samoan-born winger Bryan Williams, expressed his mixed feelings. Williams observed, 'All the publicity about the non-whites going to South Africa and the fear of apartheid and how we were going to be treated suddenly came to roost. For a few fleeting moments I thought I don't want to go through with this.'

He did go through with the tour though and offered a similar view to the 'building bridges' mantra of Willie John McBride, 'I never felt like an honorary white. I was a dark-skinned New Zealander going out to show what I could do on the rugby field, and also to show that dark-skinned people could compete very favourably with white-skinned people as well.'

Mass protests at rugby grounds throughout Great Britain and Ireland also failed to stop the Springboks from touring there, though it did arguably lead to the cancellation of a South African cricket tour in 1970. It seems odd given the fall-out from the D'Oliveira affair a cricket tour from the South Africans could be countenanced. Once Peter Hain and his anti-apartheid cohorts had engineered mayhem at rugby matches in England, Scotland

and Wales the powers that be at MCC rapidly withdrew their invitation to South Africa's cricketers. Hain recalled, 'The Anti-Apartheid Movement [AAM] had kept the flame of freedom flickering. Soon it was lit by our militant protests, which stopped white South African rugby and cricket tours in 1969/70. The country was forced into global sporting isolation. On Robben Island, brutal white warders, all fanatical rugby fans, vented their fury on Nelson Mandela and his comrades at the ostracism of the mighty Springboks, unwittingly communicating a morale-boosting message through the news blackout.'

Those militant protests in 1969/70, including an infamous pitch battle with police at Swansea's St Helens ground, failed, as Mr Hain suggested, to condemn South Africa to global sporting isolation. It was to come much later thanks to the stubborn determination of world rugby's rulers to ignore calls for a boycott.

New Zealand's Conservative prime minister Robert Muldoon and Britain's Conservative Party led by Margaret Thatcher also played their part in encouraging world rugby to maintain links with South Africa. Mrs Thatcher only requested the Lions call off their tour in 1980 because she had also called for a sporting boycott of the Moscow Olympics after the Soviet invasion of Afghanistan. To do anything else would have been blatantly hypocritical, even by the standards of the most cynical international politicians. Yet the request in the eyes of her critics seemed half-hearted, not least in the opinion of the Organisation of African Unity. William Tolbert, then the president of Liberia and chairman of the OAU, wrote to Mrs Thatcher imploring her government to do 'all in its power' to cancel the Lions tour of South Africa. He noted, 'At a time when certain Western Powers are waging a vigorous campaign against the Moscow Olympics we find it difficult to comprehend why the same rules should not be applied against a regime which definitely continues to pursue policies of suppression, oppression and blatant racism.'

Mrs Thatcher informed the OAU that British governing bodies were autonomous and added, 'Ministers do not have the power to direct them in their day to day affairs.' As will be discussed elsewhere, British athletes went to Moscow for the Olympics despite Mrs Thatcher's 'vigorous' objections. It was no surprise Britain and Ireland's rugby players went to South Africa during the same summer after coming under far less political pressure than their Olympian counterparts.

In the case of New Zealand, Muldoon thought he had a mandate to encourage links to apartheid South Africa. His National Party won a landslide victory in the 1975 New Zealand general election, campaigning 'to keep politics out of sport'. Given that the unpopular decision to cancel the 1973 Springbok tour was being brazenly exploited by Muldoon, this in itself smacked of hypocrisy. He declared the cancellation of the tour was 'one issue on which people will change their vote' and promised to back future tours 'even if there were threats of violence and civil strife'.

His stance attracted worldwide condemnation. Just as protests were being brutally quashed in the Johannesburg township of Soweto with hundreds killed, the All Blacks went to South Africa to play rugby. Politics and sport inevitably collided despite Muldoon insisting they ought to be kept separate. African nations demanded the withdrawal of the invitation from the IOC to New Zealand to compete in the Montreal Olympics of 1976. The IOC ignored the call. Rugby had not been played in the Olympics since 1924. The New Zealand Rugby Union was not even affiliated to the Olympic movement so the IOC presumably felt powerless to act. Rugby had nothing to do with them. New Zealand's athletes went to Montreal. African nations either kept their athletes at home or brought them back from Canada before they had the chance to compete. Rugby's determination to maintain links with apartheid South Africa had even managed to disrupt the Olympics, a global stage long departed by the sport.

In the aftermath of this mess, sporting contact with South Africa became centre stage at the Commonwealth Heads of Government meeting at the Scottish golfing resort of Gleneagles in 1977. Robert Muldoon was among those leaders of countries from the old British Empire to sign up to the Gleneagles agreement pledging to 'discourage' contact and competition between their sportsmen and sporting organisations, teams or individuals from South Africa. This pledge was put to the test just a couple of years later. The NZRU sent out another invitation to its Afrikaner friends to tour the country during the southern hemisphere winter of 1981, a decision first opposed by Muldoon's government. His deputy Brian Talboys wrote to NZRU chairman Ces Blazey, expressing dismay. Talboys believed it would be seen as condoning apartheid and have an impact on 'how New Zealand is judged in the international arena'. Yet with another election looming in 1981 and polls showing another showdown on the rugby field between the All Blacks and Springboks was popular among the electorate Muldoon did little to stop the tour. Instead, he did the opposite. He helped to facilitate the tour at enormous cost; describing white South Africans as 'our own kith and kin', citing New Zealand as a free and democratic country determined to keep politics out of sport. Presumably the irony of his desire to exploit sport for political purposes was lost on him.

For modern Kiwi historians, the 1981 Springbok tour managed inadvertently to expose fault lines in New Zealand society. Perhaps it is simplistic to describe those favouring the tour as representatives of the old order; men and women such as Muldoon and Blazey. They still believed in the British Empire, despite its collapse, and took pride in the country's sacrifices during two world wars. They were mocked by critics as 'Rob's mob'; older, male, blue-collar, mostly from rural areas and above all rugby supporters. Yet rugby fans were also among those opposing the tour; mostly young, from the cities, and more likely to be female rather than male. Effectively in this narrative of split in New Zealand society, it was 'Britain of the south' versus a modern vibrant independent Pacific nation. It also exposed New Zealand's own racial divide; European whites versus indigenous blacks. As far as keeping politics apart from sport, Muldoon for all his cynical protestations failed miserably.

It is estimated that more than 150,000 people took part in anti-tour protests at rugby grounds across New Zealand. Of those more than 1,500 were arrested for varying offences in a massive security operation ordered by the National Party government of prime minister Robert Muldoon. It failed to prevent anti-apartheid protesters forcing tour organisers to call off the opening Saturday fixture in Hamilton. Rugby Park was packed to the rafters with thousands of protestors outside, and crucially hundreds more inside determined to invade the pitch.

They succeeded. One recalled, 'Ripping down the fence took about ten seconds. It was very fast, the crowd on the bank pulled away from us and a flood of people went through and on to the ground. We ran under the goalposts into the middle. I remember the priests struggling with a bloody big cross.

'Police formed a cordon around this group, which had linked arms to form a solid block in the middle of the pitch. Police arrested about 50 of them over a period of an hour but were becoming increasingly concerned that they could not control the rugby crowd. Skirmishes broke out and objects were hurled at the protesters. It was terrifying, I don't know how big the crowd was, but they were clearly furious. Bottles and God knows what else were hurled at us, and people kept trying to get on to the pitch. The police looked vulnerable as they spread out around the whole ground.'

Eventually, to the fury of those wanting to watch some rugby, the game was called off and the protestors ushered off the pitch, being pelted with coins and bottles thrown by angry rugby fans. Quite what happened to the protesting priests with their crucifix is unclear. Predictions of civil unrest and mayhem were made by the former Labour prime minister Norman Kirk as he called off the planned 1973 tour by the South African Springboks. In 1981, this premonition of anarchy on the streets and rugby fields of New Zealand turned out to be correct. Worse was to follow.

As the world gathered around their television sets to watch the wedding of the Prince of Wales and Lady Diana Spencer at St Paul's Cathedral in London, the Queen's Kiwi subjects were mopping up thousands of miles away after a day of carnage in Wellington. It was the 'battle of Molesworth Street', a riot outside the New Zealand Parliament. More than 2,000 protestors had gathered there determined to march on the South African consulate. The police were equally determined to stop them. For the first time they deployed batons. As blood-spattered protestors staggered away in shock and confusion, the police justified their actions; describing the use of batons as a 'last resort' because they feared for their own safety.

One protestor, Karen Brough, who was a 16-year-old schoolgirl at the time, described being hit on the head by a baton and knocked to the ground before being repeatedly battered on her back, legs and arms. 'I could hear the pinging of batons on people's heads. There were a lot of injured people but there were no ambulances,' she remembered. Yet this was merely the start. For the next two months violence broke out inside and outside rugby grounds on a twice weekly basis as the South Africans made their way around the land of the long white cloud. It culminated in the final Test against New Zealand with a Cessna light aircraft flying over the Auckland stadium dropping flour and smoke bombs on to the pitch below. For the record New Zealand won the series by two matches to one.

It is difficult to argue whether sport, in the guise of rugby's Springboks and the All Blacks, was the winner or loser. Those opposed to apartheid saw it as the definite loser. It can be argued that Robert Muldoon's stance to maintain his pretence of sport being above politics also turned out to be a losing and costly cause. Estimates put the policing costs at some NZ$15m. The cost to New Zealand's international prestige by hosting a tour amid an orgy of violence is inestimable. One world leader monitored events thousands of miles away from his prison cell. Nelson Mandela remembered the moment he heard the game in Hamilton had been called off as 'it was as if the sun had come out'. South Africa and New Zealand would not meet on a rugby field until after Mandela was out of jail and the apartheid regime dismantled.

In defiance of public opinion, the Irish Rugby Football Union and the Rugby Football Union at Twickenham also countenanced matches between South Africa and England and Ireland during the early 1980s. To the fury of the then Irish prime minister, Charles Haughey, the IRFU had sent a team to South Africa before the Springboks flew out to meet New Zealand in 1981. It turned out to be grubby affair, though without a hint of embarrassment on the part of the Irish tourists' bosses at the IRFU's Lansdowne Road headquarters in Dublin. Mr Haughey had written to the IRFU warning of the dire consequences for Irish interests overseas, and urging them to call off the tour. His foreign minister Brian Lenihan reinforced the point by declaring, 'This is not a sporting event. It is, whether or not the players or organisers choose to regard it as such, a political act.'

Just in case the IRFU was in doubt about the depth of feeling in opposing their rugby tour, the Roman Catholic Archbishop of Durban, Denis Hurley, a man from the Irish diaspora, observed, 'Be quite clear about it. Both white South Africans and the black majority of people in South Africa clearly interpret the tour as an acceptance of the policy of apartheid.'

Yet the IRFU rather preposterously took the opposite view, claiming, just as the Lions had done before, their players' presence in South Africa might actually help to end apartheid. Such was the determination to go the players were asked to take separate flights to London before meeting up for their connection to South Africa. Given widespread opposition from politicians, trade unionists, the Catholic Church and student organisations, the IRFU feared protestors would stop them from leaving Dublin Airport en masse. Several Irish players refused to tour for moral reasons; namely Tony Ward, Moss Keane and Hugo McNeill. Their stance was supported by another Irish rugby international and a future Irish foreign minister, Donal Spring. In summing up his opposition to maintaining sporting links, or to be accurate rugby links, with apartheid South Africa, Spring said, 'Though I agree with the theory that sport and politics should be kept apart whenever possible, when the evil involved is so fundamental a part of society that it transcends all aspects of human life as in South Africa, one cannot hide behind a banner labelled sport, trade, tourism etc.'

Curiously one of the Irish rugby tourists did, as a broadcaster and a political activist, turn out to be a thorn in the side of the apartheid establishment. Scrum half John Robbie lost his job at Guinness Brewery for deciding in those days of amateur international rugby to take time off for the tour of South Africa. Robbie stayed on in South Africa, carving out a successful rugby career at provincial level and becoming a talk show radio host so acerbic in condemning apartheid that he received death threats. During hearings for South Africa's Truth Commission a policeman even alleged ministers had approved a plot to kill Robbie. Having played his part in opposing the bigots advocating apartheid, Robbie now regrets going on tour to South Africa, despite settling there and making it his adopted homeland. He reflected, 'I think about it all the time. I just wanted to play rugby and although obviously I knew what was happening, I felt there was nothing I could do. But when I think of it now, of how many people I hurt, it is something I'm deeply ashamed of. Given my time again, I would say no.'

Ireland lost both Tests against the Springboks but for the remainder of the apartheid years the IRFU, just like its Kiwi counterparts, would find it impossible to entertain matches with the South Africans. Just England toured, in 1984, with strangely enough John Robbie sitting on the bench for their Test matches as a replacement for South Africa.

Time was up though for the rugby establishment in its myopic desire to maintain the pretence of sport having nothing to do with politics. Time was also up for the sport in maintaining it was a bastion of amateurism and Victorian Corinthian values. Plans were afoot to organise a Rugby World Cup, along the lines of soccer's long-established competition, to give the sport a global platform and reach out to the wider international community. Inviting apartheid South Africa to compete in the inaugural Rugby World Cup in 1987 could hardly feature in those plans.

The South African Rugby Board remained a member of the International Rugby Board despite still being a sporting bastion of its country's apartheid regime. Yet suddenly, it found itself out in the cold and barred from competing in what was to become the sport's most prestigious competition. Quite whether this was a genuine policy decision on the part of the IRB is open to question.

Individual committee members from different countries openly embraced South African rugby despite its dubious role in being a totem for racists running the country. South African rugby administrators even voted on the merits or otherwise of whether or not to stage a World Cup. Yet by accident if not design the IRB struck a blow to the apartheid regime by refusing to invite the Springboks to compete in the World Cup. Finally, South Africa was left in complete sporting isolation, the last blow to Afrikaans pride. Within less than a decade the apartheid regime of South Africa had collapsed. Nelson Mandela was in power, leading a government of black majority rule.

6

Nelson Mandela and the Rugby World Cup

I N a collage of great sporting images, Nelson Mandela presenting the Rugby World Cup to Springboks captain Francois Pienaar, while wearing a replica of Pienaar's number six shirt, vies alongside the captured moment in time of Tommie Smith and John Carlos and their 'Black Power' salute as the greatest of all. South Africa's rugby Springboks, the pride of Afrikaners, had been embraced and supported by a man they had long despised and demonised. South Africa had come of age; the rainbow nation proudly taking a bow on the world stage. It was sporting triumph for South Africa mired in controversy solely for sporting reasons. It was also a political triumph.

As John Carlin, the author of *Playing the Enemy*, the basis for the Hollywood movie of the 1995 Rugby World Cup, *Invictus*, explained, 'Other politicians will pay lip service to sport and understand theoretically its value to them – but they lack the political intelligence to exploit it the way Mandela did. He had the political genius to transform a symbol of division – the Springbok jersey – into an instrument of unity, which is why he is the greatest political leader of our time.'

Mandela had an acute sense of political theatre. A global sport event provided the ideal stage. As the sport was followed with religious zeal by the Afrikaner people, a World Cup was ripe for exploitation. For once though, a politician, a world leader, was doing so as a force for good rather than evil. Just a year before the staging of the Rugby World Cup in South Africa, Nelson Mandela became president. At his inauguration he summed up his aims in uniting a divided nation by declaring, 'We enter into a covenant that we shall build a society in which all South Africans, both black and white, will be able to walk tall without any fear in their hearts, assured of the inalienable right to human dignity, a rainbow nation at peace with itself and the world.'

For him there was no better way of demonstrating those aims than by wearing the fabled Springbok jersey, once a symbol to blacks of Afrikaner and white racial supremacy, embracing the Springbok captain and presenting him with the Rugby World Cup. Of course there was just the important technical matter of the Springbok team actually going out and winning the tournament. They were hardly favourites to win as New Zealand were considered the best team on the planet. It would be far from easy.

Even staging the Rugby World Cup was a source of controversy for many black political leaders, those viewing the Afrikaner sport of rugby with suspicion. It was only three years since South Africa had been re-admitted into the international sporting fold, a far more fractious and tortured process for rugby than cricket or any other sport. Huw Richards, in his history of rugby union, *A Game for Hooligans*, commented on the dubious politics of some members of the International Rugby Board; men he described as unable to comprehend why South Africa had been isolated in the first place. He called the welcome given to South African officials and players at Twickenham in November 1992 from RFU president Peter Yarranton 'glutinous'. Yet once Mandela had walked out of jail in 1990 and his party, the African National Congress, had been legalised, putting them on the path to power, there needed to be a rapprochement between the ANC and South African rugby.

Contact had been made between ANC leaders and South African Rugby Board representatives in the Zimbabwean capital Harare and Zambian capital Lusaka a couple of years before

Mandela's release. Steve Tshwete, one of Nelson Mandela's fellow inmates on Robben Island, summed it up as 'a delicate process where the rugby talks are bound to influence the political process in the country and vice versa'. By January 1992 the 'white' governing body of the sport, the South African Rugby Board, and the multi-racial body, the South African Rugby Union, had merged to form the South African Rugby Football Union (SARFU). Almost inevitably the fabled New Zealand All Blacks were invited back to South Africa for the first game since the Springboks were sent into the international wilderness. Almost inevitably certain individuals, most of all the SARFU president Louis Luyt, almost conspired to send them back into the international wilderness with some cack-handed behaviour.

Luyt allowed the playing of the old South African anthem 'Die Stem' before the game at Ellis Park in Johannesburg; a provocative decision leaving the ANC infuriated. It put out a statement warning SARFU 'they can make rugby a reconciler of people, or they can use it as a ritual that celebrates conquest and domination of black people'. Luyt and his cohorts backed down, ensuring the playing of a further Test match against Australia and a subsequent tour to Europe for games against England and France. Though Luyt, somehow, managed to maintain cordial relations with ANC leaders, Nelson Mandela made his disdain for him clear, describing the rugby administrator and arch apartheid propagandist as 'a pitiless dictator'.

SARFU chairman Danie Craven was viewed more kindly by the ANC, which described him as a 'visionary' for instigating talks in the late 1980s despite the opposition of the then South African government. Yet many were suspicious he had failed to shed his own racist past, telling a former England rugby international, 'Black players should stick to soccer; that's their game. We don't want black players in our game.' Craven bid for South Africa's right to stage the Rugby World Cup in 1995. The IRB posthumously rewarded him by approving the bid in January 1993 just after he'd died.

Even then the staging of the tournament in South Africa remained in serious doubt. Insurers refused to back the event because of the threat of political unrest with full democratic elections yet to be held and the white supremacist National

Party hanging on to power, creating doubt over what the future held for South Africa's racially-divided people. It was also just plain expensive to stage a Rugby World Cup at a time of great economic hardship. Additionally, once Mandela was eventually elected as South Africa's first black president, there was the threat of terrorism from right-wing extremists angered by the end of apartheid and being ruled by a man they deemed themselves as a terrorist. The IRB drew up contingency plans for the staging of the 1995 finals in either England or France. Yet for all the doubts, not least from some of his own ANC colleagues in government, Mandela eyed an opportunity. It was a heaven-sent chance to showcase his 'rainbow nation' and bring it together in support of the Springboks, which had been unthinkable to the black and mixed race population during the apartheid years.

South Africa captain Francois Pienaar recalled meeting Mandela for the first time ahead of the tournament, 'When he became president and I got the call to go and see him, you can imagine how nervous I was. I sat outside his office at the union buildings and I could hear his booming voice, and as he walked towards me what struck me was his size – as an athlete and a boxer he's a big man. The first thing he said to me was in Afrikaans, and most of our conversation was in Afrikaans. I tried to switch to English, which was not a great thing for me to do, and he kept steering back to Afrikaans, so we had an hour's chat which was very special.'

On Mandela's death, Pienaar admitted he didn't realise 'just how special' the meeting was to him. He had grown up in a typical Afrikaans family, one demonising Nelson Mandela as public enemy number one. It was feared on Mandela's release their country would descend into anarchy and even civil war. Yet it never happened. Instead Mandela sought reconciliation for the people of South Africa and embraced the Afrikaners' precious sport of rugby. Although rugby enjoys nowhere near the worldwide profile of its rival footballing code of soccer, this was also an opportunity to make a statement to the international community and illustrate harmony and unity in contrast to decades of racial and social division. It was almost as though sport was of a secondary concern.

After progressing through the tournament with steady progress, beating England in the group stages to guarantee avoiding favourites New Zealand until the final, South Africa met France in a semi-final dripping in controversy. It was first of all played in appalling conditions with torrential rain making the pitch in Durban almost unplayable. Kick-off was delayed by more than an hour as hapless ground staff tried to sweep away standing water. They were joined by the South African military, deploying a helicopter, and a willing army of black women with mops. As the tournament progressed, the players noticed more and more of the black population were offering their support. Suddenly rugby was more than just a game. For once the cliché was true not for commercial matters as often in sport but for social and political reasons. South Africa were in danger of going out of the tournament at the semi-final stage without a ball being kicked thanks to the weather. If the referee called off the game then France would progress to the final under competition rules because of a better disciplinary record. Eventually, Welsh referee Derek Bevan was persuaded that the pitch was fit to play on, despite conditions being more suited to a game of water polo.

Once the match was under way, the Springboks established a fragile lead until coming under fierce pressure from the French in the final minutes. From five metres out the French forward Abdel Benazzi drove for the line to score what looked to be the winning try. Controversially, it was disallowed by Bevan who, inexplicably, ruled that Benazzi had been held up short of the line and awarded a five-metre attacking scrum to the French rather than a try. Despite further French pressure, South Africa's defence held out until the final whistle. South Africa celebrated and were in the Rugby World Cup Final. For his part, Bevan was presented by a grateful Louis Luyt with a gold watch at the post-tournament dinner. The Welshman had the good sense to turn it down and walked out in disgust. Independent analysts, not just the frustrated and dejected French players, felt the try was wrongly disallowed. For them, Benazzi had clearly scored. Bevan insisted it was an honest decision even if others were to call it wrong. As a result of his controversial call, history beckoned.

For the South African players, the pressure was enormous. 'Pressure' is an overused word in sport to describe the travails of an athlete performing at the elite level. Yet for the Springboks the enormity of the occasion, a World Cup Final on home soil with an expectant nation and people of all races united in support, merely heightened the sense of nervous tension in the camp. Francois Pienaar admitted that he endured a sleepless night before the game. In the dressing room it was his job to make sure his team-mates were relaxed and focused to play 80 minutes of rugby, the biggest game of their lives. He recalled, 'We had a sense of what it meant to South Africa.' Then came a knock on the door and president Mandela walked in to give them one final rallying call. It was not what he said which mattered. It was what he wore. For Nelson Mandela there was to be no finely-tailored suit. He stood before the South African rugby team wearing a replica of their iconic green and gold jersey and the Springbok, for long a symbol of apartheid, on his chest.

Pienaar explained, 'When he walked into the dressing room wearing a Springbok on his heart, it was just "wow". You bite your lip and I walked over to him and actually I didn't even get to him and he said "good luck boys" and he turned round and my number was on his back. And that was me; I couldn't sing the anthem because I knew I would cry. I was just so proud to be a South African that day.'

Despite playing on home soil, the South African players were still slight underdogs. New Zealand had demolished England in the semi-final; their giant wing Jonah Lomu proving to be unplayable, as he had done throughout the tournament. Lomu helped himself to four tries, scattering hapless English defenders across the park in a 45-29 victory with the final score flattering England thanks to the All Blacks easing up in the final minutes.

Once the anthems were over, the task for the Springboks was to focus on the rugby rather than sporting and political theatre and stop Lomu. If Lomu produced another rampant performance, the Rugby World Cup was going back across the Indian Ocean on its way to New Zealand. Yet somehow South Africa were able to deal with Lomu in a game of unbearable tension. Neither side was able to produce their best rugby with Lomu at times a frustrated spectator on his wing. As a game of rugby, it was hardly a sporting classic with both defences dominant and it went into extra time at 9-9 without a try being scored. After an early exchange of penalties, Joel Stransky stepped up to score the winning drop goal in a 15-12 victory and sent a nation into ecstasy.

As is the modern tradition, the trophy ceremony took place out in the middle of the pitch. Mandela walked out in his Springbok rugby jersey and still wearing a supporters' baseball cap. Pienaar emotionally recalled the presentation in an interview with the BBC, 'That was incredible. Incredible when I walked up to the podium and Mr Mandela stuck out his hand and said to me, and I still can't believe to this day that he said it, "Thank you Francois for what you have done for this country." I wanted to jump over and give him a hug but I said to him, "No sir, thank you for what you've done for this country."'

It is Pienaar's belief his country changed forever on the blow of the final whistle at the Rugby World Cup Final in Ellis Park, Johannesburg, on 24 June 1995. Few would disagree. A crowd of 63,000, mostly white and mostly Afrikaner, had been chanting 'Nelson, Nelson' in praise of their president. They were supporting the Springbok rugby team, a totem pole for an Afrikaner people once intent on subjugating the non-white population of South Africa. They were also hailing, as a hero, their first black president.

Also among the crowd was the French rugby team, defeated by Pienaar's men in the semi-final. John Carlin offers the story of Abdel Benazzi coming across the South African forward Morne du Plessis some years later. Benazzi apparently told du Plessis, 'We cried like hell when we lost to you guys. But when I went to the final the following weekend I cried again, because I knew it was more important for us not to be there, that something more was happening before our eyes than victory or defeat in a game of rugby.'

In the immediate aftermath, All Blacks captain Sean Fitzpatrick displayed noble magnanimity, refusing to blame their defeat on a mystery illness sweeping the team hotel in the build-up to the game. It led to suspicion from New Zealand fans of a plot to nobble their players. Some were clearly ill but there is no evidence of a plan by the South Africans to poison their opponents.

The Kiwis' mood was hardly helped by the crass and boorish behaviour in the post-match celebrations by Louis Luyt, a man incapable of matching the levels of dignity of Mandela. Aside from trying to present Derek Bevan, the semi-final referee, with a gold watch, Luyt stood up to question the validity of New Zealand and Australia's World Cup victories in 1987 and 1991 given the absence of South Africa because of apartheid. It led to a walk-out from the New Zealand, England and France teams present.

One of the Kiwi players apparently gave Luyt a parting shot questioning the Afrikaner's manners in the plainest of Anglo-Saxon vernacular. Just as the Olympic movement up until the 1970s had its bogeyman in the guise of Avery Brundage, South African rugby had a similar figure from the apartheid era in Louis Luyt. As an entire nation celebrated becoming world champions in rugby he little realised he was a dinosaur; a relic of the past.

For all this lingering sporting controversy, the game, the occasion, stands out for the political leadership of Nelson Mandela. Debates over how and why South Africa progressed to the 1995 Rugby World Cup Final and eventually beat opponents weakened by illness paled into insignificance compared with the political impact. For once sport was being manipulated by a world political leader with benevolent rather than evil intent. Mandela's recognition of how sport can be embraced as a force for good by society at large is illustrated by these comments from him, 'Sport has the power to change the world…it has the power to inspire. It has the power to unite people in a way that little else does. It speaks to youth in a language they understand. Sport can create hope where once there was only despair. It is more powerful than government in breaking down racial barriers.'

7

The Football War

ENGLAND'S public schoolboys played with the quaint notion of sport being an alternative to war, their masters even seeing football as preparation for hostilities. As they codified the game, bringing the world the separate footballing disciplines of association (soccer) and rugby, no one probably envisaged football would lead to an actual war. Yet in the late 1960s a series of matches did inadvertently lead to conflict and bloodshed; a series of World Cup qualifiers seemingly being used as a pretext for going to war.

The Central American states of Honduras and El Salvador had been at loggerheads for years. The staging of games between those countries to qualify for the 1970 World Cup finals in neighbouring Mexico have long been viewed as a spark for the declaration of hostilities. Of course it has become all too easy in popular culture to blame football for the war between Honduras and El Salvador, fought over just a few days in July 1969. It is the ideal trivia question to answer correctly for the smug football fan. Inevitably far more important factors were in play than football rivalry. As with most wars, fervent nationalism, jingoism and xenophobia were to blame; football's ritual habit of unwittingly feeding those triple poisons hardly serving as a recipe for peace and reconciliation.

Honduras is geographically the larger of the two nations and is five times as big as El Salvador. Yet estimates in the late 60s show that El Salvador, a country with limited natural resources boasted a far larger population, roughly three million to just over two million in Honduras. Basically, El Salvador was overcrowded. A large proportion of the Honduran population were either Salvadoran immigrants or of Salvadoran descent. For the early decades of the 20th century hundreds of thousands of Salvadorans had fled the poverty of their own country, lured by the promise of cheap land in Honduras. They also escaped a succession of dictatorial military rulers imposing their will on the people with savage brutality. Yet for those migrant Salvadorans, Honduras was hardly the land of 'milk and honey'. Their presence was deeply resented by the native population; people struggling to survive economically and under the political cosh of their own military dictatorship.

General Lopez Arellano took power in Honduras as head of a military junta in October 1963. Just a few years later he was struggling to keep a grip on power with the country beset by social and political unrest. For the solution to Arellano's problems, the answer was simple – blame the immigrant Salvadorans. Already, wealthy landowners had formed a group known as the National Federation of Farmers and Livestock Farmers. It became a powerful and influential lobby group, eagerly embraced by the military regime desperate to deflect attention away from its failure to run the country properly.

Immigrant Salvadorans occupying Honduran land were targets in an increasingly violent campaign. Crucially, the junta decided to meet the demands of the seemingly xenophobic National Federation of Farmers and Livestock Farmers by passing a Land Reform Act in 1967. It confiscated land occupied by Salvadoran immigrants, a population estimated at some 300,000 in the mid-60s, and redistributed it among Hondurans. Naturally, El Salvador was enraged by the actions of Honduras, not least because the overcrowded and impoverished country was now struggling to accommodate the returning migrants. El Salvador even took the step of declaring sovereignty over land once occupied by its citizens so they could go back, a declaration it was unable to enforce without invading Honduras. In a perverse sense both dysfunctional military governments played into the hands of each other by fuelling xenophobia with both regimes anxious to deflect attention away from their disastrous economic plight. Stoking up nationalist fervour suited the despotic governments of Honduras and El Salvador. Conflict appeared inevitable. There was just in the meantime the smaller matter of getting a series of World Cup qualifying games between the two countries out of the way. Sadly and perhaps inevitably, it turned out to be anything but a small matter.

Honduras and El Salvador had topped their qualifying groups for the right to meet in the CONCACAF (Confederation of North, Central American and Caribbean Association Football) World Cup qualifying semi-finals. Honduras had seen off Jamaica and Costa Rica while El Salvador were too good for Surinam and the Dutch Antilles. Just to complicate matters and potentially make the tie politically even trickier, the semi-final over two legs was not subject to the traditional system of aggregate scores. Points were awarded instead; two for a win, one for a draw and goal difference did not count. Both teams won their respective home ties, necessitating a replay on neutral territory in Mexico and prolonging the antagonism and tension over a mere football contest.

Honduras had the honour of staging the opening semi-final leg and duly made life as difficult as possible for the visiting El Salvador team. Hostile fans camped outside the team hotel overnight in the capital Tegucigalpa, causing as much of a din as possible, a fairly common disruptive practice in central and South America. It was just that the Hondurans took their particular fan vigil on this occasion to new levels. It was viewed by observers at the time as not just hostile but positively menacing. There were few independent chroniclers of the game, most of the world paying little attention to a match between two of the lesser powers of international football – let alone the grim possibility of the tie leading to war between the two countries. El Salvador's footballers appeared to have acquitted themselves quite well in the match despite a nerve-jangling and sleepless night before. It was not until deep into injury time that Honduras managed to score through Roberta Cardona and secure a 1-0 victory.

It meant that Honduras had a slight advantage going into the return game, a state of affairs one Salvadoran fan found far too traumatic with tragic results. According to the Salvadoran media, teenage girl Amelia Bolanos was so upset by watching the agonising defeat on television that she shot herself in the heart after the referee blew the final whistle. The following morning, Miss Bolanos was raised to the curious status of a national martyr. Her suicide was used to whip up yet more nationalistic fervour with tensions already inflamed. One of El Salvador's newspapers, *El Nacional*, wrote, 'The young girl could not bear to see her fatherland brought to its knees.'

El Salvador had merely lost a football match, not a war. Given the colourful rhetoric from both sets of media it was no surprise that both countries would eventually be at war. Such was the hype over the circumstance of her death, Amelia Bolanos was given a state televised funeral. El Salvador's players broke off their training to walk solemnly behind her flag-draped coffin along with the country's president. Salvadoran fans demanded nothing less than victory and sporting revenge in the forthcoming football match.

Polish journalist Ryszard Kapuscinski gave the most authoritative account of the game in his book *The Soccer War*. He described the build-up by writing, 'It was the Honduran team that spent a sleepless night. The screaming crowd of fans broke all the windows in the hotel and threw rotten eggs, dead rats and stinking rags inside.' Remarkably, those riotous scenes outside the Honduran team hotel were apparently orchestrated by the Salvadoran military, with the man allegedly leading the country's notorious right-wing death squads, General José Alberto Medrano, prominent in whipping up the fury. Eventually, during the night, the Honduran players were ushered out of the hotel to take refuge in their country's embassy.

As the players were driven to the match in armoured vehicles, fans lined the streets holding up portraits of their new national martyr Amelia Bolanos. Inside the stadium everything possible was done to provoke Honduran outrage. Of the playing of the anthems Kapuscinski wrote, 'Instead of the Honduran flag – which had been burned before the eyes of the spectators, driving them wild with joy – the hosts ran a dirty, tattered dishrag up the flagpole.' Once the game kicked off it turned out to be an easy victory for El Salvador, one the Honduran coach was apparently all too keen to grant them. Mario Griffin commented, 'We're awfully lucky that we lost. Otherwise we wouldn't be alive today.' For the record, the game ended 3-0 to El Salvador with goals from Juan Ramon Martinez, Elmer Acevedo, and Rodriguez. It led to wild celebrations.

It also led to an orgy of violence in San Salvador with two Honduran fans killed and many others injured. Revenge attacks on Salvadoran immigrants in Honduras soon followed. Gangs roamed Salvadoran ghettos in Tegucigalpa, aiming to drive them out, burning their houses to the ground. The violence led to thousands of Salvadorans fleeing Honduras to safety and the drumbeat of war was being sounded by El Salvador's media. One newspaper declared, 'El Salvador should civilise Honduras by force.' Intriguingly, declassified CIA documents show the American spy agency was beginning to take the danger of a looming war seriously; issuing warnings to the White House. Before hostilities would commence, one more football match needed to be played.

The respective victories on home soil for Honduras and El Salvador meant a third game would have to be held to decide the tie, this time on neutral territory in Mexico City. Before heading for Mexico, El Salvador's footballers and coaching staff were summoned to the presidential palace. Their Argentinian manager, Gregorio 'Goyo' Bundio, remembered the uncompromising message of encouragement from president Fidel Sanchez Hernandez, 'He gave us some sweet bread and soft drinks and told me that "as a foreigner" I had to defend the national colours, because this match was for our national dignity.' Bundio knew defeat for either side was unthinkable. It would hardly be worth returning home from Mexico.

At least the players were able to prepare in a little comfort in Mexico City. It was a far more civilised affair than in the build-up to the two previous encounters. However the game itself still required the presence of 5,000 Mexican riot police to deal with any hint of trouble from the rival sets of fans. Although the cold, rain and altitude might have been a hindrance to the players, those unfavourable conditions probably also served to alleviate any security concerns, quietening down and physically taxing the more raucous fans.

This time the fans looked on as the two sides played out a draw, needing extra time to separate them to earn a place at the finals of the 1970 World Cup. El Salvador twice took the lead but they were pegged back, Juan Ramon Martinez opening the scoring in the eighth minute only for Jose Enrique Cardona to equalise for Honduras in the 19th minute.

No World Cup tie involving Latin American teams, whether in the finals or qualifying, can go without a star player being kicked all over the pitch. Cardona, who played his club football for Atletico Madrid, was the man being targeted throughout this series of matches by his opponents from El Salvador. He recalled, some years later, 'They kicked me off the pitch! I got a boot right in the chest. I've played in Spain, in England, in Ireland, and it's never happened to me since.'

Those brutal tactics helped them to gain a 2-1 half-time lead with Martinez putting them back ahead. An equaliser from Rigoberto Gomez ensured this match, a bizarre prelude to war, would go to 30 minutes of extra time. It was settled in the 101st minute with Jose Antonio Quintanilla scoring the winner. It marked the end of footballing hostilities, not the end of outright animosity between two countries serving in the late 1960s as the ultimate stereotypical 'banana republics'.

El Salvador's government barely waited to celebrate its football team's victory and qualification for the 1970 World Cup finals, instead sounding the drumbeat for war. Within hours it broke off diplomatic relations with Honduras. The Hondurans responded likewise. El Salvador declared, 'The government of Honduras has not taken any effective measures to punish these crimes which constitute genocide, nor has it given assurances of indemnification or reparations for the damages caused to Salvadorans.' As for any student of Spanish wishing to brush up on insults, a trawl of the Honduran and Salvadoran newspapers in the aftermath of his World Cup qualifier might prove worthwhile. 'Nazis', 'dwarfs', 'drunkards', 'sadists', 'spiders', 'aggressors' and 'thieves' are just a few of the words being used to describe someone of a different nationality. Football had helped to fuel jingoistic fervour as two countries went to war, though it was a fortnight after the final game in Mexico before real battle began.

Initial skirmishes along the border broke out on 11 July 1969. CIA operatives in declassified documents warned their bosses in Washington, 'Fighting has broken out along the border and there is concern in Honduras this might be the prelude to an invasion.' They reported that four troops had been killed; the first casualties in clashes between the troops of Honduras and El Salvador since the breaking off of diplomatic relations. Three days later it became an all-out conflict and the 'Football War' had begun. Just as football coaches might learn little from the encounters between El Salvador and Honduras on the pitch, military strategists might avoid an examination of the tactics in the war between these countries, apart from the use of air power which was almost a throwback to the colonial conflicts of the 19th century.

It was brutal and quick, claiming thousands of victims in just 100 hours of fighting. It was the last war to be fought using propeller prop aircraft thanks to an arms embargo on both countries forcing them to use ancient warplanes. At times, the conduct of the war from both sides was also something of a tragic shambles.

Salvadoran warplanes began the air offensive bombing and strafing Honduran military positions along the border and also attacked the main airport in Tegucigalpa. A ground invasion involving an estimated 12,000 men soon followed with rapid victories for the Salvadoran forces. CIA monitors sending despatches back to Washington noted a sense of 'tremendous euphoria' among officials in El Salvador. In contrast there was an initial assessment of desperation among the Hondurans with one radio network exhorting 'civilians in the western highway area to grab machetes or other weapons and move to the front to assist the army'. Those civilians with machetes failed to halt the swift advance of Salvadoran ground forces as they captured nine Honduran cities within hours of crossing the border. Superiority on the ground, though, was not matched in the air. El Salvador's early air strikes were far from decisive, allowing the Hondurans to counter-attack with their own sorties deep into Salvadoran territory. El Salvador had no radar coverage and the element of surprise for the Hondurans allowed them to attack airfields and oil facilities at will.

Once key strategic facilities in El Salvador were disabled, the Honduran air force, under orders from the country's president, concentrated solely on support for the beleaguered ground forces. Advances from El Salvador's army ground to a halt within days of the invasion, hampered by a lack of fuel, dwindling supplies of ammunition, inclement weather, and crucially fierce resistance from Honduran troops and civilian militia. Honduran air superiority turned out be significant in countering El Salvador's advances on the ground as they were able to secure more warplanes from the USA in a covert deal despite an arms embargo officially being in place. All through the war, the Organisation of American States tried to broker a ceasefire, the CIA in its assessment optimistic the Salvadorans would settle for peace. It was less optimistic the Hondurans would agree to a deal given their loss of territory. Yet after 100 days of war, a ceasefire was agreed. The fighting came to an end, the guns fell silent but tensions lingered with El Salvador stubbornly refusing to withdraw its troops from Honduras.

Hostilities ended with estimates of more than 2,000 dead on both sides, many of them civilians. Around 100,000 Salvadorans were left homeless, placing further pressure on the immensely fragile economies of both countries. One Honduran soldier summed up the futility of the Football War, 'We soldiers didn't have a clue. We went to war not knowing what we were fighting for or why. They just told us to defend the national sovereignty.'

Despite the efforts of the Organisation of American States, which eventually declared El Salvador 'the aggressor' in the dispute, the diplomatic impasse lasted for decades. In October 1980, Honduras and El Salvador signed a peace treaty, 'agreeing to continue negotiations on the final demarcation of the border'. Those negotiations dragged on for another dozen years; the World Court at the Hague in the Netherlands coming up with a solution to divide up territory between El Salvador and Honduras.

Football as a sport, and its greatest tournament the World Cup, was never to blame for the conflict. Yet the political climate during a series of qualifying games between Honduras and El Salvador for Mexico 1970 is the bloodiest illustration of how politicians can use sport to whip up nationalist fervour for their own dubious ends. Ever since the fighting ended on 18 July 1969 El Salvador has been beset by civil war and social unrest. Honduras has also endured more than its fair share of social and political unrest. It remains one of Latin America's poorest countries and 15 per cent of the population can't read and write. It also has the world's highest murder rates. Football can be a release for the people from the grind of daily life. The people's love of football, their sense of patriotism in support for the national football team, can also be manipulated by their rulers with disastrous consequences. The Football War between El Salvador and Honduras is arguably the most tragic example.

8

World Cup Final 1954: 'The Miracle of Bern'

ASK any England football fans about their favourite chant and often the politically incorrect little ditty 'Two world wars and one World Cup' is trotted out. It is a dubious fusion of sport and politics supposedly meant in the spirit of jovial banter; a reference to a football match in July 1966 and the great conflagrations engulfing the planet in the early and mid-20th century.

Germany emerged from the horrors of the Nazi regime a beaten nation in war, a divided nation and one in the paroxysms of its people suffering shame and humiliation. Football changed the German people's self-image. England's victory over West Germany in the 1966 World Cup Final was a rare success for the English. West Germany and then a re-unified Germany became a dominant world footballing superpower during the post-war decades, a success story reflecting its immense social and economic recovery over the same period.

Arguably it all began in neutral Switzerland. It began with a game still laced with controversy, the German players lining up for the 1954 World Cup Final, men allegedly doped with drugs, in what became known as 'The Miracle of Bern'. It was West Germany 3 Hungary 2. In the most popular team sport on the planet, the Germans, against all expectations at the time, were world champions. It meant for the first time in a generation the German people, whether from the west or east, felt able to celebrate and take pride in a country with its self-respect restored after the ravages of war. Just under a decade after the guns fell silent across Europe and the defeat of Nazi Germany, German flags were being waved with pride once again. The feeling of the German people in celebrating an unexpected World Cup triumph was summed up by the phrase 'Wir sind wieder wer'; or roughly in English, 'We are somebody again.'

Going into the final against Hungary, the West Germans were the firm underdogs. The Hungarians were by far and away rated as the best team in the world and were unbeaten in five years. Their star player Ferenc Puskas was being feted as the best footballer in the world, perhaps the best ever. They had unceremoniously demolished England 6-3 at Wembley a year earlier, ending lingering deluded English notions of footballing supremacy. Frankly, it seemed to the pundits of the day all the Hungarians had to do to win the trophy was turn up. No other team would be able to compete with them.

It was even a surprise for West Germany to make the final because the players lacked international experience. German teams had been banned from the 1950 World Cup in Brazil. The snub to a country defeated in war mattered little to the Germans. Re-establishing professional football was hardly a priority as rebuilding began in the ruined cities of a divided nation in which its people had almost lost their national identity. As the news magazine *Der Spiegel* put it, 'In short, Germany was divided and defeated in so many different ways that people were no longer keen to be identified with being German anymore.' To many in the outside world being German still equated to being a Nazi.

Prior to the 1954 World Cup, conveniently held in a country which had been neutral for the duration of the war, there was little hope of a German triumph let alone expectation. This German team, in stark contrast to their multi-millionaire successors, was largely amateur with their ranks boosted by returning prisoners of war from camps in England. Just avoiding a humiliation at the hands of professionals from South American and European nations seemed a reasonable aim. As for facing an Eastern Bloc nation such as Hungary, with the communist regimes there exploiting sport as a means of promoting the 'superiority' of their economic creed, defeat seemed inevitable given the vast gulf in resourses.

East Germany, incidentally, did not enter the competition with political turmoil there as citizens protested against the pro-Soviet rulers. West Germany qualified for the tournament in Switzerland by easily beating fellow German side Saarland, a statelet run until the mid-1950s by the French. A victory and a draw with Norway, the only other team in the group, was enough to see them through to meet their footballing destiny.

After a comfortable 4-1 victory over Turkey in the opening game of the finals, the next match against Hungary hardly served as a confidence booster for the West German players as Hungary thrashed them 8-3. They might have felt it was better to pack their bags and go home. A few of the better German players had been rested but this was a humiliating result. Admittedly though very few other countries fared any better at the time against the Mighty Magyars. The Germans did strike one crucial blow against their opponents – an act of physical violence against Ferenc Puskas. Centre-half Werner Liebrich kicked the man rather than the ball in an act of thuggery, forcing Puskas off the field with an ankle injury. He never physically recovered for the rest of the tournament. In the slightly bizarre format of the 1954 World Cup, West Germany and Turkey were forced to play off for the right to claim a quarter-final place, a match ending in a 5-2 German victory. There were then comfortable victories over Yugoslavia and then Austria in the semi-finals. Against the odds, they had made the final.

As for Hungary, their path to the final was not quite as serene. Their quarter-final against Brazil became dubbed the 'Battle of Bern'. Brazil were still smarting from losing at home to Uruguay four years earlier in the World Cup Final. Against theoretically the best side Europe had to offer, the Brazilians engaged in a kicking contest, against man not the ball. Two Brazilians and a Hungarian player were sent off. Amid the mayhem, Hungary managed to win 4-2. They qualified for the final thanks to an extra-time victory over the holders Uruguay, again 4-2.

Most observers felt the trophy was theirs to take back to Hungary given the drubbing they meted out to their final opponents earlier in the tournament. West Germany, to the joy of a spellbound nation, had other ideas. As an indication of the growing interest in their progress to the final, sales of television sets in West Germany served as a good indicator. This was the first World Cup to be televised live. At the beginning of 1954 it is estimated there were 11,000 TV sets in West German homes. By the end of the year the figure had risen to 84,000. Most of the growth in sales came during the World Cup with factories and shops selling out as the tournament wore on.

Until West Germany progressed to the final, international sport, thanks to the antics of the Nazis at the Berlin Olympics, was a source of embarrassment and shame for most German people. But, out of nowhere, a bunch of 'no-hope' amateur footballers were beginning to restore their faith in sport and their pride in a German identity. At the time there were no dark allegations of doping among the players. Tales of drugs being used as stimulants to boost performance were yet to come. This was a likeable bunch of young men to be cheered on hopefully to victory.

On 4 July 1954, West Germany and Hungary lined up in a deluge for the World Cup Final in Bern's Wankdorf Stadium. As the game began memories of the 8-3 thrashing at the hands of the Hungarians returned to pessimistic German fans. Ferenc Puskas scored from a long-range shot after just six minutes, then just a couple of minutes later Zsoltan Czibo pounced on a mix-up between goalkeeper Toni Turek and defender Werner Kohlmeyer to make it 2-0. Even at this early stage victory seemed assured for Hungary. Yet remarkably West Germany recovered and did so quickly. Their morale remained intact despite the setback.

In his biography, captain Fritz Walter recalled, 'Dismayed, we looked around at each other, but there was no criticism of "Kohli" or Toni. As soon as we got the ball ready for the restart, Max Morlock did his best to rally the troops. "It doesn't matter," he cried.' Walter also mentioned how another player, his namesake, Ottmar Walter, came up to him and whispered, 'Fritz, keep going, we can still do this.'

Just moments later they were back in the game. Helmut Rahn's shot on ten minutes was deflected by Jozsef Bosik into the path of Max Morlock, who poked the ball into the net. As the heavy rain began to soften up the pitch into something of a mud heap, the conditions seemed to be favouring the West German players with their impressively high levels of energy. Puskas was increasingly looking a passenger on the Hungarian side and was still suffering from the ankle injury inflicted during the previous game between the two sides. It was not long before West Germany had equalised and the first murmurings from observers of possibly witnessing an upset surfaced. On 18 minutes, Fritz Walters took a corner with the ball somehow sailing over the Hungarian defenders and goalkeeper Gyula Grocsis for Rahn to pounce at the far post. Fresh from being tested against the reigning world champions Uruguay, the Mighty Magyars were fighting not just for a chance to be crowned world champions but also their reputation as the invincible masters of 1950s football.

The post prevented them from retaking the lead just before half-time. At the break though, the sides remained level and West German coach Sepp Herberger was upbeat. According to the official FIFA website, Herberger told his players during the interval, 'Lads, you've done brilliantly so far. Don't give them an inch in the second half.' What FIFA fails to mention is the accusation that something more sinister was going on in the West German dressing room rather than just a half-time pep talk from the coach and a few sips from a cup of tea. Were the players given performance-enhancing drugs?

It is not in dispute that the West German players were given injections by the team doctor. As far as the West German camp was concerned they were being given nothing more sinister than a boost of vitamin C. It was a defence made in response to allegations made on the 50th anniversary of the game from the groundsman at the Wankdorf Stadium, Walter Brönnimann. He told the German television station ARD that he found syringes under drainage gates. Confronted by the revelation, West Germany's team doctor Professor Wilhelm Schänzer insisted the substance he injected the men with was vitamin C. He explained, 'I injected the men with vitamin C because it was supposed to raise their stamina levels. You cannot measure the effect it has, but the players believed in it.'

German football fans were willing to believe his version of events. Unfortunately for them, details from a doping investigation carried out by Humboldt University in Berlin and the University of Münster into doping in German sport from the 1950s onwards shows the players may have been given pervitin, an amphetamine commonly known as 'speed' and refined by Nazi doctors during the Second World War, earning the drug the nickname 'Panzer Chocolate'. Luftwaffe pilots and Wehrmacht soldiers were chemically enhanced by the drug to allow them to fly or to fight for longer. In boosting footballers' stamina levels it would certainly have been more effective than a dose of vitamin C. How much the alleged subterfuge worked to ensure a dogged and remarkable second-half performance from the West German team in the 1954 World Cup Final is open to question. If the players had been doped with pervitin, it seemed to work.

Hungary were fired up after the interval, perhaps not by drugs but certainly from a few choice words from their coach. It was imperative that they quickly restored their lead and then killed off the game. Puskas, Czibor and Nandor Hidegkuti posed a constant threat with the ball yet again striking the post and the crossbar and a succession of goal-line clearances kept the scores level. The Hungarians, for all their renowned skills, were unable to break the German defence.

As time was running out and with extra time beckoning the crucial strike came and West Germany took the lead with just six minutes left to play. These are the words of the German radio reporter Herbert Zimmermann describing the winning goal, 'Germany, down the left with Schafer. Schafer's ball to Morlock is blocked by the Hungarian defence – Boszik, still Boszik on the ball, the Hungarian right winger. He loses the ball this time to Schafer – Schafer crosses into the middle – header – blocked – Rahn has to shoot from distance – Rahn shoots! Goal! Goal! 3-2 to Germany!'

Rahn's low shot driven past the goalkeeper had secured victory but not before one last scare. Puskas thought he had equalised only a couple of minutes after Rahn had put the

West Germans into the lead. Years later, in David Goldblatt's history of football, *The Ball is Round* – a term credited to West Germany's coach in 1954, Sepp Herberger – a scene is depicted of Puskas ruefully summing up his feelings about the controversially disallowed goal. He moaned it took an age for the Welsh linesman Sandy Griffiths to raise his flag and alert the English referee William Ling, who appeared originally to award the goal. For the Hungarians it was some sort of odd British Cold War conspiracy. In Goldblatt's narrative Puskas moaned, 'We gave two silly goals away. We should have pressed on then looking for the third to kill the game off. I got an equaliser right at the death but that Welsh linesman Griffiths disallowed it for offside. Even the English ref Billy Ling had given it.'

It is estimated that 60 million Germans were glued to their radio sets, along with the tens of thousands enjoying what was then the novelty of television, nervously awaiting the end of the game. Zimmermann's words in his radio broadcast cued national celebrations, 'Over! Over! Over! The match is over! Germany are world champions, beating Hungary 3-2 in the final in Bern.'

It is worth noting Zimmermann chose to use the words 'Germany are world champions' rather than 'West Germany', then a fledgling state at the beginning of the Cold War with the Berlin Wall yet to be erected. Much to the disgruntlement of the communists in East Germany, this was a national victory for all Germans regardless of political or geographical divide and a chance to take pride in the country after years of ignominy. For the first time in nearly a decade the German nation felt in party mood, celebrating victory in the World Cup with skipper Fritz Walter proudly lifting the Jules Rimet Trophy.

After the final whistle, the Berlin correspondent of the *Manchester Guardian* filed this report, 'There was wild cheering and people started dancing on the pavements. Crowds had gathered inside and outside cafes all over the city to listen to the radio commentary. Knots of excited people danced beside taxi cabs which had their radios on full blast.'

In echoing the words of Zimmermann, West Germany's half-back Horst Eckel summed up the national mood for *Der Spiegel*, 'People didn't say that the national team players were world champions. They said, "We are world champions." The feeling of togetherness of the Germans was suddenly there again.'

Millions of people turned out to welcome the team back across the Swiss border. Over-enthusiastic fans stood on the railway tracks blocking the train for a time as it tried to make its way towards Munich, where hundreds of thousands of people turned out in the main square. Wild scenes of celebration were repeated from village to village and town to town, before the team finally arrived in Berlin for the biggest celebration of all. Eckel recalled in *Der Spiegel*, 'We really had no idea how important it was or what was waiting for us back in Germany. We only realised when we returned to Germany – as soon as we crossed the border.'

As for the esteemed news magazine itself, *Der Spiegel* notes the importance of the World Cup victory as a seminal moment in its country's history. It opines, 'Every nation has a founding legend. For modern Germany it is the 3-2 victory over Hungary in the 1954 World Cup. After World War II, the championship became a sign of being accepted by the world again. Germany has the World Cup. Specifically, the global football championship of 1954 held in Switzerland. The Miracle of Bern. In one 90-minute match against Hungary, modern-day Germany was born.

'Germany was divided and defeated in so many different ways that people were no longer keen to be identified with being German anymore. Until the evening of July 4, 1954 when the final whistle blew with West Germany holding a 3-2 lead over a team that, at the time, was just as feared as Brazil is now. An entire nation went berserk.'

The notion of 'acceptance' from the world at large in 1954 is more than a little overstated. There's no doubt though the German nation went berserk.

British and French editorial writers in their countries' newspapers recoiled in horror at events in Bern and the subsequent outpouring of joy from the German people. Their ire was further provoked by some ill-judged comments from the German Football Federation's president Peco Bauwens in a speech made in a Munich bierkeller, carried live on Bavarian radio. Bauwens, perhaps fuelled by too much alcohol, embarked on not just a nationalistic but a brazenly jingoistic rant, moaning about the ban on the use of the opening verse of the old German anthem, criticising neighbouring nations with their Latin-based languages, invoking Wotan, the ruler of the Norse gods, and asserting the West Germans had benefited from the discipline of 'Derfuhrerprinzip' or in English, the Fuhrer Principle. It was astonishing stuff, hardly diplomatic less than a decade after the defeat of the Nazis.

Mysteriously, though not surprisingly, the broadcast was cut short and tapes of the recording of the speech were conveniently lost. Nevertheless his comments were noted down and chronicled in the next day's press. Additionally to the quasi-Nazi rantings of the boss of the West German football federation, sports journalists from the victorious nations of the Second World War reported that the German fans at the World Cup Final in Bern sang the banned verse of the national anthem at the presentation of the trophy. Britain's newspapers made as much of German victory in the French Grand Prix with Mercedes Benz as its triumph in the World Cup. The *Daily Mirror*'s legendary columnist William Connor, under his byline Cassandra, dryly remarked, 'Even in football – not a noticeable German sport – they wiped up the Hungarians at Bern in the World Cup series. The Hungarians had not been beaten for four years.' Cassandra concluded, 'Nothing can stop these unlovable people.'

In France, *Le Monde* accepted winning a football match or a Grand Prix was an innocent event but went on to comment darkly, 'The "innocent" Weimar Republic had given birth to Hitler.' The controversial comments from the president of German football perversely came as a relief to East Germany's communist rulers. It gave them the propaganda they needed to denounce their western counterparts as still the dangerous embodiment of fascism.

What few of the critics realised at the time, perhaps even the Germans themselves, was that the victory marked for some historians the beginning of at first West Germany's, then Germany's rise to pre-eminence and dominance in world football, one mirrored by the nation's recovery from the ruins of defeat in war to becoming an industrial powerhouse. One of those to benefit from the commercial revival was a member of the backroom staff, Adi Dasler, founder of Adidas and inventor of the removable stud, an innovation credited with giving the German players something of an advantage on a mud-bath of a pitch. Few, until the ugly stories emerged, realised the players' performance may well have been boosted by drugs.

For Germans looking back misty-eyed to July 1954 this awful subplot to the Miracle of Bern threatens to diminish its importance in the pantheon of sport. Yet there is no doubting the political landscape of the time, for once not engineered by politicians. If anything, there were attempts to dampen down the fervour. West Germany's president Theodor Heuss admonished the man he called 'the good Bauwens', informing the boss of German football and other like-minded people 'a good kicking does not make good politics'. Yet though the political establishment of the day was largely successful in keeping a lid on the more extreme nationalist interpretations of a World Cup victory, foreign observers noted a discernible boost in national morale. The people cared little for any diplomatic sensibilities.

As the *Manchester Guardian*'s Berlin correspondent put it on the day of the triumph, 'To understand this joy one must remember both the giant load of bewilderment beneath which this nation has been staggering since one type of German pride came to its catastrophic fall nine years ago, and also, especially in Berlin, the zeal for an emotional release to lift minds out of the ever present spectacle of surrounding ruin.' The sense of pride lingered, lifted a nation, with the possibility the players were drugged serving half a century later to sully a cherished memory.

As far as the players were concerned, they were not doped despite taking injections. Given that the doctor insisted the doses he gave them were innocent, merely vitamin C, this is hardly surprising. Winger Hans Schäfer said, 'Everything our doctor said is right. He gave us things to build us up so that we'd remain fresh. We were not doped and I don't have a bad conscience.' Yet several players suffered severe health problems in the months after the final, possibly as a result of being injected with a purely sterilised shared syringe. Three suffered from jaundice, one contracted black fever, and two more later died of cirrhosis of the liver, one of them a teetotaller. On being presented with the evidence of doping from the academics at the Humboldt University in Berlin and the University of Münster, the president of the German Olympic Committee, Thomas Bach, declared it 'a good day for the fight against doping'.

Yet these revelations had relevance beyond the modern-day fight against the use of performance-enhancing drugs in sport. Suspicions were cast on decades of German sporting performance from the 1950s and the Miracle of Bern onwards. It had always been accepted that communist East Germany had systematically doped athletes. Now it appears West Germany may have done the same, even chemically enhancing its fabled footballers from the 1954 World Cup. They did help to raise the spirits of a nation but it came at a personal price to those men. As the historian Guido Knop concluded in a German television documentary outlining the allegations of doping, they were 'victims of the politics of sport'.

For the defeated Hungarians there was an ignominious return to Budapest and a disgruntled, agitated sporting public unhappy at its own social and economic plight under dictatorial rule from a Soviet puppet government. Not only did Hungarian football go into decline but in the eyes of some observers the World Cup defeat served to light the blue touchpaper for the 1956 uprising, which was ruthlessly crushed by the Soviet Union. One of those sharing this view happened to be the goalkeeper Gyula Grosics, a man blamed by many fans for the defeat. Grosics stated, 'The reaction in Hungary was terrible. Hundreds of thousands of people poured into the streets in the hours after the match. On the pretext of football, they demonstrated against the regime... In those demonstrations, I believe, lay the seeds of the 1956 uprising.'

Germany was on the rise. Hungary was in decline, on the brink of revolution. For an oppressed people with thousands killed as the Soviets crushed their uprising against dictatorial communist rule, their sporting heroes became a group of young men in an Olympic swimming pool; blood in the water and a clash of sport and politics. This time, unlike the Miracle of Bern, was no accident of history.

9

Melbourne 1956:
'Blood in the Water'

HUNGARIAN footballers consoled themselves for their World Cup Final defeat by going on to win the Olympic gold medal at the Melbourne Olympics of 1956, a Games tainted because of the absence of professionals from western Europe and South America. Football in Hungary though was on the wane. The Hungarian people were about to adopt a different set of sporting heroes in the midst of a bloody revolution. There would even be blood spilt in a proxy war fought in an Olympic water polo contest between Hungary and the Soviet Union. It was the blood of star player Ervin Zador, the image of him dazed and nursing a deep wound just below his right eye adding to the catalogue of iconic Olympic pictures.

As protesting students triggered the uprising in Budapest on 22 October 1956, the Hungarian water polo players were holed up in a hotel on the outskirts of the capital under the watchful eye of Soviet minders. Much to their chagrin the Soviet water polo team had set up home in Budapest to use the Hungarians' pool facilities and tap into their considerable expertise. Hungary were reigning Olympic champions, by far and away the number one team in world water polo. As both teams began the long journey to Australia, the outcome of the revolution remained uncertain. Hungary's reformist prime minister Imre Nagy, who had been sacked a year earlier, was returned to power on 24 October; a Soviet move to try to restore calm after secret police had opened fire on crowds of protestors taking to the streets of the country. Nagy successfully persuaded the Soviet Union to withdraw its forces, introduced democracy, established free speech and freed from prison the leader of the Roman Catholic Church in Hungary, Cardinal Mindszenty. He also proudly despatched his country's Olympic team to Melbourne as representatives of a free Hungary. Freedom didn't last longer than five days.

Once the Hungarian Olympians had arrived in Australia the Soviet tanks had rolled back into their homeland. Nagy announced on 3 November 1956 that he was pulling his country out of the Warsaw Pact, leaving the Soviet leader Nikita Khrushchev infuriated. He ordered the Soviet tanks back into Budapest, ruthlessly crushing the revolution, leaving more than 4,000 Hungarians dead. Appeals to Western nations for help fell on deaf ears. They were already bitterly divided at the United Nations over the Suez Crisis and powerless to act against the rampant Soviet military machine. France, Great Britain and Israel had begun their botched invasion of Egypt on 30 October, the same day that the Hungarian water polo players had set out for Australia. The British and French imperial adventure could not have been worse timed as far as the Hungarian people were concerned as they tried to stand up to Soviet aggression from the east. It was left to Hungary's Olympic athletes to restore honour and national pride with their own proxy war at the Games of the XVI Olympiad in Melbourne.

At one point the Suez Crisis and the political turmoil behind the 'iron curtain' put the staging of the Melbourne Games in doubt. For many, it seemed inconceivable an international sporting festival could go ahead at a time of global political tension. Avery Brundage, of course, resisted, ensuring that the Games went ahead. Ignoring the lessons from Hitler's Games in Berlin a couple of decades earlier, indeed ignoring the rampant nationalism of competing nations at any Games, Brundage stubbornly stuck to his mantra of the Olympics being above politics. He declared, 'Every civilised person recoils in horror at the savage slaughter in Hungary, but that is no excuse for destroying the nucleus of international co-operation. The Olympics are contests between individuals and not between nations.'

The Hungarian water polo team took a different view. This was not a collection of individuals. They were a team; one intent on winning gold and humiliating their Soviet nemesis.

On arrival in Australia, the Hungarian team was desperate for news of the revolution at home, worried for the plight of loved ones left behind. Just one of the players, Miklos Martin, spoke English. He grabbed a newspaper with his team-mates huddled around him and began to translate the grim contents, with reports of the revolution being ruthlessly crushed and thousands being killed. Many of the team decided there and then they would not be returning to Hungary and instead would seek to claim political asylum in Australia. Zador summed up his thoughts in an interview decades later. He remembered, 'We were in the restaurant, waiting to change planes, when we heard that the Russians had taken care of the Revolution. I stood up with a glass of whatever I was drinking and announced I was not going home. It had been bad before. Now I felt it was going to be much worse, and that the Russians would never leave. Normally such a statement would have meant no Olympics for a player.

'But the team officials were still unsure of how things would turn out back home and so I got away with it. Even today I am shivering thinking about the risk I took. Other players felt the same way, but didn't say so out loud. By the time we got to Melbourne we just wanted to get the job done that we had worked so hard for. But we were very afraid that we were out of shape because we hadn't been in the water for almost a month.'

They also decided in a token act of defiance to tear down the communist flag of Hungary in the Olympic village, replacing it with the flag of a 'Free Hungary'. The draw meant there was a strong chance of meeting their Soviet oppressors in the water polo pool. The scene was set for one of the most brutal contests in Olympic history, Hungary versus the Soviet Union. As one player, Gyorgy Karpati, later recalled, 'In the strained political situation we were in, it was a body-to-body encounter with our opponents. We were from a small country battling the huge Soviet Goliath.'

They had done little training in the build-up to the Games so the players decided to come up with a tactical plan to see off potentially fitter opponents, based on a zonal defensive system. Zador explained, 'We had travelled all over the world and people didn't expect us to play like that. Our opponents didn't know how to handle it. We double-marked the most dangerous opponent and chose one player to leave free. We shouted to him, "Okay. Go ahead and shoot." No one expected to be given the choice to shoot against us. But we had a very good keeper, and these players became nervous, and then they were never going to score. It was totally a mind game.'

It worked. They cruised through to the semi-finals, thrashing Great Britain and the United States 6-1 and 6-2 respectively, before beating Italy and Germany by the same 4-0 scoreline. Lying in wait, as expected, was the 'Soviet Goliath'.

For the benefit of their Russian rivals, the Hungarian players came up with what might be described as a slightly more nuanced psychological game plan – verbal abuse, or as Zador more diplomatically put it in a BBC interview, 'verbally agitating' their opponents. He reasoned, 'We figured if they get angry, they'll start to fight. Once they fight, they won't play well. If they don't play well, we'll beat them – and if we beat them, we'll win the Olympics!'

Given that they were all brought up in the Soviet system and taught Russian to the extent they were fluent, it was not difficult to verbally wind up their opponents. The abuse meted out on both sides in a fevered atmosphere was more than just verbal. As Zador and his team-mates happily accepted, it was also going to be physical. A raucous capacity crowd, swollen by members of Melbourne's large Hungarian community, stoked up the atmosphere. 'The Hungarians there were so charged, and there was such deep hostility for all the things they did to our country since 1945, that all these people in Australia just went absolutely berserk,' remembered Zador.

The crowd and the players were all fired up for a game of water polo. It was 6 December 1956, less than a month after the Soviet tanks had crushed the Hungarian revolution. Hungary's

Istvan Hevesi recalled the curious lust in a water polo match for revenge for the deaths of their compatriots, just weeks earlier. He said, 'They began to shoot us, those bastards. The fire inside us was beating so strongly. God help us, we'll beat them for sure.' As the crowd was on their side, there were suspicions a biased referee was on their side, and quite frankly they were far more talented than their opponents anyway, so victory was assured. It came in an orgy of gratuitous violence, with arguably less blood spilt in the nearby boxing venue.

As the Hungarians anticipated, the Soviets responded to the verbal aggression with their fists, one of their players ending up in the penalty box – sin bin, effectively – with less than a minute played. The atmosphere became more febrile as Hungary opened the scoring, the captain Dezso Gyarmati with a twice-taken penalty and contriving to catch a Soviet player's chin with his fist in the process. It sent the crowd wild, not in anger at an unsporting act of violence but absolute delight. As the game came to a close with Hungary winning comfortably 4-0, five players had already been banished from the pool by the referee; three Russians, two Hungarians.

Ervin Zador, who had scored two of the goals, then had what he called a 'horrible' lapse in concentration. Throughout the game he maintained the verbal abuse and exchanged blows in between playing some water polo. 'We were yelling at them, "You dirty bastards. You come over and bomb our country." They were calling us traitors. There was fighting above the water and fighting beneath the water,' he later explained.

As the clock ticked down, Zador was asked to mark the Soviet captain Valentin Prokopov and was more than happy to oblige. Prokopov's marker Antal Bolvari had taken a blow and feared he had ruptured his ear drum. Zador swam over to Prokopov and introduced himself with a volley of verbal abuse which must have by then been familiar to his Soviet opponent. 'I looked after Prokopov for the last few minutes, and I told him that he was a loser, and that his family were losers and so on,' he said.

On the shrill blast of the referee's whistle Prokopov took the opportunity to deal with his young tormentor with a volley of blows. Zador had fatefully taken his eye off the Russian, looking across to the referee to see what the whistle had been blown for. Zador ruefully remembered, 'The moment I did that, I knew I'd made a horrible mistake. I turned back and with a straight arm, he just smacked me in the face. He tried to punch me out.' Prokopov did more than try. He succeeded.

In an interview decades later Zador graphically recalled, 'He had his full upper body out of the water and he was swinging at my head with an open arm. I could imagine he wasn't very happy because the game was won and lost. All he had was anger. After he hit me I was seeing about 48 stars. Man, oh man, I was just like a stuffed pig.' A wound soon opened up below his right eye and blood gushed out on to the water, leading to uproar among a pent-up crowd already in a state of frenzy. Spectators jumped over barriers to try to exact their own revenge on the Russian players but were swiftly stopped by police stationed at poolside. Security officials predicted trouble and sadly they were proved right.

Amid the mayhem, the Swedish referee blew the final whistle a minute early, presumably wanting to rush to the sanctuary of the dressing rooms as quickly as possible. Given the noise inside the stadium it was difficult to hear his whistle and there was little chance of the game going on any longer given the unfolding anarchy, with the public address announcer pleading for the restoration of calm. Melbourne police officers escorted the Soviet players and officials away to safety as witnessed by the *Sydney Morning Herald*'s special correspondent in a poolside dispatch, 'A fierce water polo match between Hungary and Russia ended in the ugliest scene of the Olympic Games after a Russian player punched a Hungarian player in the eye. Many angry spectators jumped on to the concourse beside the water, shook their fists, shouted abuse and spat at the Russians. Only the sudden appearance of police, who had obviously been waiting out of sight, prevented a riot. The police shepherded the spectators away and had to restrain only one of them forcibly. The incident occurred late in the second half, and above the noise the announcer's voice could be heard declaring the match finished, with Hungary winning by four goals to nil. This prevented the trouble from becoming more serious.'

Doctors treated Zador for his injuries by the side of the pool as photojournalists captured his battered visage on film for posterity. They gathered around Zador and chronicled his feelings. He told them, 'We were playing not just for ourselves but for every Hungarian. This was the only way we could fight back. The Russians should not be allowed to play in the Games. It was not water polo out there, it was pure boxing in the water.'

He was backed up by Desmond Gyarmati, who was more than happy to condemn Russian violence in and out of the pool. Gyarmati, who of course failed to mention the Hungarians' own dubious tactics, revealed that the Russians had tried to apologise for their behaviour and ranted, 'In Hungary, many people die, and then the Russians say they are sorry. Our coach, Bela Rajki, told us we must win, but to play clean polo. The Russians started very dirty tactics when we led 4-0. The two players mainly concerned were Markarov and Prokopov. During the match these two kept calling us fascists. I myself received a terrific kick in the stomach.'

The Hungarians had adopted the moral high ground and, in the context of the horrific events in Budapest a month earlier, they were given a sympathetic hearing. Possibly in hope more than expectation the Soviet Union demanded a rematch because the game had been abandoned. Olympic officials had no stomach for such an event and ruled that the 4-0 score, with a minute left on the clock, stood as the final result. Hungary had their victory over the bitterest of enemies. They still, though, had to win the Olympic gold medal, and the final awaited against Yugoslavia.

Zador, despite his eye injury, was desperate to play in the final but the Hungarian team doctors ruled him out. It was too badly swollen and he was forced to watch from the stands as his team-mates eked out a 2-1 victory and secured the gold. A relieved Zador remembered, 'Watching was agony. I was sure we were going to lose the Olympics because I wasn't there. So when we won, it was awesome.'

Along with Zador, more than half of the Hungarian Olympic delegation in Melbourne sought political asylum after the Games and defected to the West. For Zador, as a 21-year-old Olympic gold medallist with his future secure in communist Hungary, it was something of a sacrifice. It was one he never regretted, settling in the United States and becoming a swimming coach. His greatest protégé just happened to be a certain Mark Spitz, one of the great all-time Olympians. Zador explained his decision to defect after the Melbourne Olympics of 1956, 'Freedom is like breathing; breathing openly.' It was something he was able to do with a gold medal in his pocket despite feeling the clunk of a Soviet fist in an Olympic swimming pool.

10

Black September: Munich 1972

THIRTY-SIX years on from the 1936 Olympics the German people welcomed the world's youth to their shores once again in a celebration of sport. This was to be redemption. These were to be the Games of 'peace and joy'. Adolf Hitler's Games had been a propaganda vehicle for the evil Nazi regime. Now in a country divided in the aftermath of the war fought to rid Europe of Hitler and his Nazi tyrants, West Germany had the chance to showcase a friendlier, warmer face to the world.

Once again, as in Berlin 36 years earlier, state-of-the-art facilities were constructed, this time in the Bavarian capital Munich. Its Olympic Park was a 'futuristic' architectural showpiece typical of the late 1960s and early 70s. Friendliness and openness were seen as key to the success of the Games. Security was conspicuously low key. Athletes were to take centre stage, not security barriers with men and woman toting guns.

In the late summer of 1972, Russia's diminutive gymnast Olga Korbut, the American swimmer Mark Spitz and in the UK Belfast's 'golden girl' Mary Peters became household names. The athletes played their part in trying to make the 20th Olympiad in Munich memorable. Tragically, terrorists would play a greater part in the darkest hours of the Olympic movement, turning the Games of peace and joy into violent death and tragedy. Shamefully, as murdered Israeli competitors were being taken home in coffins, Avery Brundage, as IOC president, uttered the most immortal and infamous words in the tortured history of sport and politics, 'The Games must go on.'

It was the early hours of the morning on Tuesday 5 September as Israeli athletes, coaches and officials slept in their beds that terrorists from the Palestinian Liberation Organisation's Black September movement struck. Security was all too lax. They were easily able to reach their target, scaling a six-foot-high perimeter fence around the Olympic village before making their way unchallenged to 31 Connollystrasse, the Israeli team's headquarters. Armed with assault rifles and grenades, they took Israelis hostage in two apartments with officials and coaches Yossef Gutfreund, Amitzur Shapira, Kehat Shorr, Andrei Spitzer, Jacov Springer and Moshe Weinberg in one, and weightlifting and wrestling team members Eliezer Halfin, Yossef Romano, Mark Slavin, David and Zeev Friedman in the other.

Despite being taken by surprise while in their sleep, the Israelis fought back. The Palestinians had no hesitation in opening fire. Romano and Weinberg were shot dead while the rest were subdued by the terrorists. It was then for the Palestinians to reveal their demands to the world; the release of 234 prisoners being held in Israeli jails and a safe passage out of Germany. A deadline was set for noon Munich time; otherwise the remaining nine Israel hostages would be shot dead.

The resulting siege gripped the watching world with almost a billion people able to view on TV, thanks to relatively new satellite technology, the shadowy figures from Black September as they gestured to German security forces from balconies in the Israelis' accommodation block. Astonishingly, despite the deaths of two Israeli athletes, the IOC decided to allow competitive events at the games to carry on and many athletes were oblivious to the unfolding hostage crisis. Not until almost 11 hours after the Palestinian terrorists had burst into the Israelis' rooms did the IOC relent to international pressure and suspend competition.

Among those sports journalists suddenly covering a news event of geo-political significance rather than just a sporting jamboree was the distinguished American writer Walter Wellesley 'Red' Smith. In his coruscating criticism of the IOC he observed, 'Not until 4pm did some belated sense of decency dictate suspension of the obscene activity, and even then exception was made for games already in progress. They went on and on while hasty plans were laid for a memorial service. The men who run the Olympics are not evil men. Their shocking lack of awareness can't be due to callousness. It has to be stupidity.'

TV viewers, no longer able to view the sport, watched instead a tense terrorist siege unfold, a ghoulish and mawkish spectacle. As the first terrorist deadline to meet their demands passed at noon, Peter Jennings of the American TV network ABC speculated on the outcome of the stand-off. 'With this first deadline passing and the next one four hours away, my guess would be that this operation of theirs is more likely to fail than to succeed,' Jennings told his viewers and listeners. He added the caveat, 'That, however, is pure speculation.'

More deadlines came and went as the Germans stalled for time to try to put together with seemingly increasing desperation a viable security and rescue operation to counter the terrorists. During the afternoon, they cobbled together 'Operation Sunshine', a plan to storm the apartment complex with police and border guards dressed in athletes' tracksuits apparently in an attempt to make them look less conspicuous. As the assault team gingerly made their way through alleyways and across rooftops, the world looked on anxiously thanks to extensive TV coverage. West German TV opted not to show the live coverage for fear of compromising the operation. East German TV had no such compunction. Its signal could be picked up in Munich so the Palestinians also had an armchair seat and were able to watch the build-up to a 'surprise' attack.

At the last minute, Operation Sunshine was called off. One of the commanders of the rescue operation admitted it would have been 'suicide' to go ahead. Far from just casually watching on TV, the terrorists were lying in wait. It later emerged that some of this assault team had no firearms training. The inability to mobilise trained German military units because they were constitutionally prevented from operating on home soil further hindered any attempts to execute a successful rescue operation. As the ITN correspondent Gerald Seymour put it, the myth of German efficiency was shattered.

Protracted negotiations and a farcical attempt to carry out a rescue operation did not at first give the terrorists holed up inside 31 Connollystrasse with their hostages much to worry about. After all, they had secured the worldwide propaganda stage they craved. One-off bomb attacks, plane hijackings and gun attacks in the late 1960s and early 70s had gained the PLO what the future British prime minister, Margaret Thatcher, would term for terrorists the 'oxygen of publicity'. In terms of impact through media coverage though, this assault on the Olympic village and subsequent exposure was on a different and unimaginable scale than any previous atrocities. They had gripped the attention of the entire world thanks to the global reach of the Olympics. It served as a propaganda tool and every second, every minute, every hour of chatter and speculation concerning the motives of the Palestinian guerrillas counted.

Eventually though, the Palestinians lost patience. In the evening of 5 September, their leader 'Issa' reiterated not only his demand for safe passage out of Germany but also for a plane to take his men and the Israeli hostages to a destination in the Middle East, namely the Egyptian capital Cairo. The German authorities appeared to comply with his demand.

Watching on, Howard Cossell of America's ABC News gave his account of the unfolding chaos as the German police began preparations to escort the Palestinians and their hostages by helicopter to a waiting Lufthansa plane at a nearby military airport, Fürstenfeldbruck. Cossell reported, 'We have a flurry of action here. Suddenly in the whole area between 20 and Building 12 they have been clearing out cars. Police officers in almost platoon-like numbers have been running past us and are now staging in front of us. We are building up to a climax, I think.'

In this climax, the Germans had planned a surprise ambush once the helicopters landed at the airfield. The waiting Boeing 727 had no pilot. It was flying nowhere. German sharpshooters waited for the terrorists and their hostages to arrive. Scandalously, though the Germans were woefully as lax in their preparation for this rescue operation as they were in providing security for Olympic athletes and officials in the first place.

Among the anxious observers was the head of the Israeli security service Mossad, Zvi Zamir. In the Oscar-winning documentary *One Day in September*, Zamir recalled the shambolic nature of the rescue operation, 'When we got to Fürstenfeldbruck, it was very dark. I couldn't believe it. We would have had the field flooded with lights. I thought they might have had more snipers or armoured cars hiding in the shadows. But they didn't. The Germans were useless; useless, all the way.' Mysteriously, German policemen aboard the waiting Boeing 727 decided to abandon their positions just as the helicopters with their grim human cargo of terrorists and hostage were landing. It meant only five German gunmen were left to take on eight heavily-armed Palestinian guerrillas. The result was catastrophic.

At 10.40pm the helicopters landed and the Palestinians quickly realised they had been duped, before a firefight ensued. It ended in stalemate and yet another stand-off with the odd sporadic gunfire interspersing an hour of tension before German reinforcements lumbered on to the airfield in armoured cars. That was the cue for the Palestinians to panic. One of them shot four of the hostages inside a helicopter as another tossed in a grenade, rupturing the fuel tank to further compound the force of the explosion. Another terrorist shot dead the remaining hostages in the second helicopter. Eleven Israelis, five Palestinians and a German police officer died in the Munich tragedy of 5 September. Three Palestinian terrorists were captured in the botched rescue operation only to be released in dubious circumstances some months later.

They were marked men. Israel's prime minister Golda Meir ordered them to be tracked down and killed in 'Operation Wrath of God'. Not only did she want them dead but also those allegedly responsible for helping them. Dozens of Palestinians were killed over those next couple of decades in political assassinations carried out by Israeli agents. Allied to these operations, Israeli warplanes carried out attacks on Palestinian camps in the immediate aftermath of the Munich massacre. Militant Palestinians were killed but also hundreds of Palestinian civilians lost their lives, including children. It was a brutal response to what many modern historians consider to be the 9/11 of the 1970s. Yet the attack on the Israelis living in Munich's Olympic village perhaps could and should have been prevented. There was mind-numbing complacency from the German authorities and above all from the Olympic movement itself; one in conspicuous denial at the time of the tragedy befalling the Munich Games.

In terms of the security operation, it's now known that the Palestinian guerrillas were hardly the hardened crack force of terrorists portrayed at the time. Leading German newspaper *Der Spiegel* has found documents not only disclosing the incompetence of police and security forces, but also attempts to cover up their failings. Portraying the Munich terrorists as the elite of the Palestinian Liberation Organisation helped to hide the truth. They were so shambolic that they struggled to find a hotel room in Munich in the days leading up to the attack because they had left it too late. As for this being an attack carried out with 'precision', as claimed by the German federal and Bavarian state authorities in 1972, it has now been revealed the terrorists only carried out a limited reconnaissance mission, some of them being given last-minute accreditation to the athletes' village by alleged East German competitors.

As for security preparations, clear warnings of the possibility of a terrorist attack from Black September were ignored. A German official working at the country's embassy in Beirut warned in April 1972 that 'an incident would be staged from the Palestinian side during the Olympic Games in Munich'. Even journalists and not just intelligence officers got wind of the possibility of an imminent attack. Just three days before the Palestinians scaled a relatively low perimeter fence and marched into the Israeli quarters to seize their hostages, the Italian publication *Gente* wrote of Black September planning a 'sensational act during the Olympic Games'. Furthermore, *Der Spiegel* later asserted that a police commissioner seized documents shortly after the Munich Games outlining crisis scenarios, including a terrorist attack by Palestinians at the Olympic village. He did so to keep them out of the public domain and erase any evidence of security failings.

In its official report of the Munich Games the International Olympic Committee appeared remarkably blasé about the security failures. The report declares, 'The Games of the XX Olympiad should have proceeded in a serene, unconstrained and peaceful fashion. The architecture, the visual configuration and the organisation expressed this idea. The security conception also had to adjust itself to this idea, although its planning provided that its effectiveness would not thereby be impaired. This was no place for an absolute priority to be given to every conceivable aspect of security or for a total presence of heavily armed police. Barbed wire and machine guns would not have been appropriate for the creation of a peaceful atmosphere of international encounter at the Olympic contests, nor could these give the world at large a true picture of the Federal Republic of Germany.'

It goes on to claim, 'No concrete indications of any sort concerning disturbances or assassination plots against Israeli sportsmen or visitors were evident.' Decades later, thanks to the emergence of declassified German documents, the latter assertion from the IOC appears not to be true. There were warnings; one seemingly a reliable intelligence warning from Beirut. Frankly to hide behind the words 'concrete' and 'specific' in relation to word of any plots and fail to respond by putting in place adequate measures was irresponsible and ultimately tragic. As for 'no place for an absolute priority' to be given to security, the modern IOC, now a more reformed and grounded organisation than its 1970s counterpart, thankfully takes the opposite view.

For all the criticism of the inept security operation at the Munich Olympics, the true people to blame were of course the terrorists themselves. However, it can only add to the pain of the victims' families for there to be a cover-up of the security failings leading up to the attack and indeed during the siege of the Olympic village and the subsequent firefight at Fürstenfeldbruck airfield. The handling of the hostage crisis by the International Olympic Committee further served to compound matters. Once the botched rescue operation had ended in tragedy, the response of the IOC and its notorious godfather, Avery Brundage, plumbed new depths with a speech of breathtaking crassness.

Contemporary news agency reports suggest Willi Daume, the chairman of the organising committee, was in favour of calling off the Games. He was over-ruled by his counterparts, Daume apparently not even present at a vote on whether or not to carry on. Instead it was decided to put back events 24 hours with the closing ceremony taking place on a Monday rather than a Sunday and becoming a more sombre ceremony than the original one planned.

It was also decided to stage a memorial service inside the Olympic Stadium just hours after the murder of the Israeli athletes. More than 80,000 people gathered with athletes taking their place on the field and the Israeli team poignantly leaving 11 empty chairs. In fairness to the IOC its decision to resume competition was endorsed by the head of the Israeli Olympic delegation, Shmuel Lalkin, bringing a huge ovation from the crowd. Lalkin declared he wanted to see athletes back in action 'in the spirit of world sportsmanship'. He added, 'With deep shock, we sorrow over the barbarous attack by terrorists against our sportsmen who were murdered.' After reading out the names of the murdered Israelis, he described them as 'brave and true comrades in sport who died in the prime of their lives'. It was, as Lalkin went on to say, 'a monstrous crime' standing 'without precedent in the history of the Olympic Games'.

The Israeli ambassador to West Germany, Eliashiv Ben Horin, also declared, 'Murderers have chosen precisely the arena of the Olympic Games as the place for their senseless crime. They have broken and profaned the symbol and expression of the friendship of the nations and the peoples.'

The West German president, Gustav Heinemann, expressed his condolences to the families of the murdered Israelis. Mr Heinemann also did raise the issue of whether or not the atrocity could have been prevented, offering the view that the question could never be fully answered. Then, it was the turn of Avery Brundage, the IOC president, to address the athletes, their coaches, the officials, the crowd and the watching millions on television.

At first his speech was warmly welcomed as he condemned the terrorists and gave sympathy for the mourning Israelis. Yet his declaration of 'the Games must go on', regardless of the terror visited on the Olympic movement, left a sour taste. It did so for a couple of reasons. Firstly, it seemed obscene to many observers to stage a joyous celebration of sport as Israeli families prepared to bury their dead. There was also his baffling insistence on comparing the tragedy with the threat of an African boycott over his decision to invite Rhodesia; a pariah country under 'white minority' rule.

Brundage declared, 'Every civilised person recoiled in horror at the barbarous criminal intrusion of terrorists into the peaceful Olympic precincts. We mourn our Israeli friends, victims of this brutal assault. Sadly, the greater and more important the Olympic Games become, the more they are open to commercial, political and now criminal pressure. The Games of the 20th Olympiad have been subjected to two savage attacks. We lost the Rhodesian battle against naked political blackmail. We have only the strength of a great ideal. I am sure the public will agree that we cannot allow a handful of terrorists to destroy this nucleus of international cooperation and goodwill we have in the Olympic movement.'

Brundage then uttered his immoral phrase to thunderous applause in the stadium, 'The Games must go on and we must continue our efforts to keep them clear, pure and honest and try to extend sportsmanship of the athletic field to other areas.'

One American journalist present at the service inside the Olympic Stadium, Jack Ellis, wrote, 'Brundage's statement that "the Games must go on" lifted away much of the heavy gloom which has permeated Munich since early Tuesday.' His colleague, Red Smith, was less generous and instead scathing and angry, 'This time surely, some thought they would cover the sandbox and put the blocks aside. But, no. "The Games must go on," said Avery Brundage, and 80,000 listeners burst into applause. The occasion was yesterday's memorial service for 11 members of Israel's Olympic delegation murdered by Palestinian terrorists. It was more like a pep rally.'

Until Brundage's declaration that 'the Games must go on' the gathering inside the Olympic Stadium had been suitably sombre and dignified in the wake of an appalling tragedy. From *New Yorker* magazine, E.J. Khan described the closing moments of the ceremony and took a sideswipe at some of his media colleagues for their appalling and disrespectful behaviour. Khan wrote, 'The memorial ceremony ended at 11.26pm and people began to leave, to the strains of Beethoven's "Egmont Overture". The Israeli contingent stayed put after almost all the other athletes had gone; then its members rose, turned around, and, for a moment, faced their half-staffed flag. At 11.42pm they filed out of the stadium for the last time. Some of the young Israeli women were in tears, and German security men were trying to shield them from photographers. One of the thwarted cameramen called one of the Germans a fascist. To a photographer, there is no such thing as a moment of private grief.'

Aside from the mourning of those killed because of their nationality and religion by politically motivated terrorists, there were other disturbing overtones. National flags, naturally, were flown at half-mast. Yet at the end of the ceremony the 80,000 crowd had hardly time to leave the stadium before officials from Arab nations moved into the arena and insisted their flags were raised again in a shocking act of disrespect. Arab athletes had also failed to turn up for the memorial service, nor did the Soviet team. As for athletes and officials from several sub-Saharan African countries, they walked out on the conclusion of Brundage's speech, feeling angered and shocked by his crass reference to Rhodesia and comparing its exclusion from the Munich Olympics with the murder of the Israelis. Brundage later offered an apology for any 'misinterpretation' of his remarks, a rare act of contrition from the stubborn godfather of the Olympic movement in the mid-20th century. He insisted, 'There was not the slightest intention of linking the Rhodesia question, which was purely a matter of sport, with an act of terrorism universally condemned.'

As his critics point out, it was odd that an articulate man had alluded to terrorism and the Rhodesia question in the same sentence in the first place. As for Brundage's typical criticism of commercialism in his speech at the memorial service, this seems odd from an arch-capitalist happy to be chauffer-driven around Munich in BMW cars, the same company advertising its vehicles on the back of Olympic tickets.

It also seemed odd but predictable for Brundage to insist, yet again, of politics having no place in sport. Berlin 1936 and his own actions in helping the Nazis stage those Games 36 years before the tragedy in Munich destroyed this particular myth. Sadly men of evil, politically motivated and using violence to further their cause without compunction, were more than happy to exploit the biggest stage of all, the Olympic Games. Today, relatives of the 11 Israeli Olympians murdered in Munich are still fighting for a formal recognition of the appalling atrocity at future Games. Guri Weinberg, son of Moshe Weinberg, one of the first Israelis to be murdered, articulated his anger at the treatment of the bereaved Israeli families by the International Olympic Committee. Weinberg ranted, 'The torture inflicted by "Black September" on the 11 Israeli athletes and their families took 48 hours. Your torture of the families and the memories of those esteemed athletes has lasted 40 years. I am not satisfied with a moment of silence in every Opening Ceremony of the Summer Games. Now I want all of you to lose your jobs and be replaced by real Olympians who care about the athletes and believe in the Olympic charter.'

Alluding to Brundage's alleged Nazi sympathies on the one hand and citing the refusal of the IOC to invite Palestinian athletes to the 1972 Games as a provocation on the other, Weinberg goes further. He claims, 'The IOC wasn't turning us down because of their "resistance to politics". Rather, it was due to the specific politics the IOC apparently still embraces. Based on its history of Nazi support, greed and the blood on their own hands for inciting the PLO, they would never support Israeli athletes.'

He believed the theory that Black September targeted Munich partly because of the refusal to invite a Palestinian team, a snub making it all the more negligent for the organisers to fail to provide adequate security for his father and the rest of the Israeli team.

Ankie Spitzer, widow of the fencing coach Andre Spitzer, has campaigned for recognition and remembrance at the Olympic opening ceremony ever since the Montreal Games of 1976. Every time she has been turned down by the IOC with the latest snub coming on the 40th anniversary of the tragedy at London 2012. Despite her anger, she remains dignified, determined to carry on with the fight. She told *The Guardian* in 2012, 'Just do it once, and I'll be gone. I just want to hear it. If they had granted a minute's silence, they would have got rid of us by now. But every four years we come back. We are a pain in the neck for them.'

Mrs Spitzer recalled the initial snub at Montreal, 'We asked for a minute's silence, or some commemoration, because it was natural in our eyes. But they told us very clearly, "There are 21 Arab delegations that will leave if we say something about the Israeli athletes." So I said, "Let them leave if they can't understand what the Olympics are all about – a connection between people through sport."'

In summary she appears to believe that the IOC, by declaring itself an apolitical organisation, is being hypocritical. By allegedly indulging the Arab nations it is being deeply political, doing so at the expense of Israel and the country's athletes murdered by the PLO in Munich. And she mocks the IOC's official stance, 'The IOC says it's not in the protocol of the opening ceremony to have a commemoration. Well, my husband coming home in a coffin was not in the protocol either. This was the blackest page in Olympic history. These 11 athletes were part of the Olympic family, they were not accidental tourists. They should be remembered as part of the Olympic framework.'

In rejecting the call for a moment of remembrance at the previous summer Olympics, the then IOC president Jacques Rogge fell back on the excuse of 'protocol', the very concept slated by Mrs Spitzer in her criticism of his organisation. Insisting the IOC would pay tribute to the Israeli athletes on the 40th anniversary of their murder in Germany, he stated, 'We feel that the opening ceremony is an atmosphere that is not fit to remember such a tragic incident.'

In fairness a service of remembrance was held on 5 September 2012 at the airfield in Fürstenfeldbruck. Rogge insisted it was the appropriate place for such a ceremony by declaring, 'We feel that we are able to give a very strong homage and remembrance for the athletes within the sphere of the national Olympic committee. We feel that we are going to do exactly the same at the exact place of the killings at the military airport near Munich on 5 September, the exact date.'

In trying to placate his critics, notably from Israel, the United States and Germany, he also insisted the IOC would penalise athletes refusing at London 2012 to compete against Israelis. In doing so he recognised the Olympic movement is inextricably linked with global politics and prone to manipulation by national powers, some with dubious agendas. At Munich on 5 September 1972, the Olympic movement became forever linked to tragedy and politically motivated terror. Perhaps a failure to recognise this dark truth is the real reason for the IOC's refusal to remember murdered athletes and coaches at future Olympics.

Even with a series of boycotts at post-Munich Olympics, the IOC still appears to be in denial over its role on the global political stage. Given in contrast to Munich, Olympiads now take place under the protection of sub-machine guns, anti-aircraft missile batteries and warships; the failure to recognise the sacrifice of those Israelis and a catastrophic security failure is for many a source of shame.

11

The Miracle On Ice

AS the Olympic movement tried and failed to come to terms with the Munich massacre, its very future came into doubt during the 1970s and 80s. Here was an organisation riven by allegations of corruption, fuelled by largesse and pomposity, ludicrously peddling the myth of sport being above politics, and divorced from a world afflicted by turmoil and terror with two great superpowers so ideologically opposed they threatened nuclear Armageddon. Perhaps it was better for the United States of America and the Soviet Union to settle their differences through the guise of sport. Where might be the best place to do so? Well, of course, the Olympics would do just nicely.

Tanks from the Red Army rolled into Afghanistan as the USA and the Soviet Union prepared to stage the 1980 winter and summer Games respectively; the Kremlin presumably calculating there would be no backlash from the West, not even the prospect of sporting sanctions. If so, Leonid Brezhnev and the rest of the Moscow politburo calculated wrongly. The invasion was duly condemned by the capitalist West as a naked act of aggression by an imperialist communist superpower, and ironically those same Western nations would find themselves bogged down in Afghan territory some decades later.

The call was made for the Russians to withdraw immediately but there was absolutely no chance of it being met. They were

Jesse Owens at the 1936 Berlin Olympics (copyright: Getty Images)

England's football team give the Nazi salute, Berlin, May 1938 (copyright: Getty Images)

Tommie Smith and John Carlos give their black power salute, Mexico, October 1968 (copyright: Getty Images)

Nelson Mandela presents the Rugby World Cup to South African captain Francois Pienaar (copyright: Jean Pierre Muller/Getty Images)

World Cup Final, 1954, Berne, Switzerland. West German captain Fritz Walter and coach Sepp Herberger are carried aloft after their victory over Hungary (copyright: Popperfoto/Getty Images)

Hungarian water polo player, Ervin Zador, emerges from the pool, Melbourne, November 1956 (copyright: Getty Images)

c~ DOE (Mr MONRO)

10 DOWNING STREET

THE PRIME MINISTER   22 January 1980

Dear Sir Denis,

  As you will know from my statement in the House of Commons
on 17 January, the Government is deeply concerned at the prospect
of the Olympic Games taking place in the Soviet Union so soon
after it has committed aggression against an independent country
by invading Afghanistan. The invasion represented a completely
new development in the history of post-war Soviet expansion.
The Soviet Union acted, on the most transparent of pretexts, to
establish a military hold on a sovereign country, in violation of
all the principles governing relations between states and peoples.
I am sure that all members of your Association will have shared
the concern of the Government at the Soviet action.

  The international community has condemned the Soviet move
on 15 January in a Resolution calling for the withdrawal of the
invaders, for which 104 states voted, an overwhelming majority
of the United Nations membership.

  In an ideal world, I would share entirely the philosophy
of the Olympic movement that sport should be divorced from
politics. Sadly, however, this is no longer a realistic view.
For the Soviet Union the Olympic Games are a major political
event which will be used to boost Soviet prestige in the world.
It would be wrong for those people and countries which deplore
aggression to co-operate in giving the Soviet Union the success
it is seeking. Indeed, to do so could give the appearance of
condoning what has happened in Afghanistan and could make the
Soviet Union believe that aggression can be committed without cost.

          / We therefore

*British Prime Minister Margaret Thatcher's letter to British Olympic
Association chairman Sir Denis Follows calling for the International Olympic
Committee to move the 1980 Games from Moscow (UK National Archive)*

We therefore ask that the British Olympic Association
should approach the International Olympic Committee urgently and
propose that the Summer Games be moved from the Soviet Union.
We believe that, with co-operation between like-minded countries,
it should be possible to hold the Games in one or, if necessary,
more than one other place. The Government are prepared to play
a full part in supporting arrangements in this country for those
parts of the Games that might be held here.

I should like to emphasise the high regard in which I hold
the British sportsmen and women who have worked so hard to reach
Olympic standards. I hope that it will be possible for them to
participate and receive the awards they deserve this summer.
The Olympic ideal is a noble one and the Games should demonstrate
the free spirit of the individual in the achievement of excellence.
The Soviet action in Afghanistan, however, stands in complete antithesis
to the Olympic ideal. It is a challenge to us all to ensure that the
Games can take place without appearing to condone Soviet military
aggression.

Yours sincerely

Margaret Thatcher

Sir Denis Follows, C.B.E.

10 DOWNING STREET

Original on:
SPORT : Olympics : Jan 80

THE PRIME MINISTER

22 January 1980

PRIME MINISTER'S
PERSONAL MESSAGE
SERIAL No. T16/80

Dear Mr President.

Thank you for your letter of 20 January about the participation of the United States in the Olympic Games.

As you will know from the discussions which have taken place between Cy Vance and Nicko Henderson, I had been thinking very much along the same lines as yourself. I now enclose a copy of a letter I have sent to the Chairman of our National Olympic Association.

A preliminary survey by my officials suggests that we have suitable facilities in this country for a number of the 21 sports in the Summer Games. We would not however be able to accommodate the major events, in particular athletics.

Yours sincerely,

Margaret Thatcher

The President of the United States of America.

British Prime Minister Margaret Thatcher's reply to US President Jimmy Carter after his call for a possible boycott of the 1980 Moscow Olympics (copyright: UK National Archive)

Palestinian terrorist on the balcony of the Israeli Olympic team apartments, Munich, September 1972 (copyright: Getty Images)

Tipperary Gaelic football team photograph 1920 (copyright: GAA museum)

Harold Larwood bowling to Australia's Bill Woodfull in the fourth Test of the 1932/33 Ashes series (copyright: Getty Images)

The Three Presidents: Brazil's Diana Rouseff, FIFA's Sepp Blatter and Russia's Vladimir Putin at the Brazil 2014 World Cup (copyright: Getty Images/ Alexander Hassenstein)

in Afghanistan to prop up a pro-Soviet puppet government under threat from Islamic rebels and in no hurry to leave. The United States and its NATO allies were impotent in the face of Soviet aggression. The only weapons would be diplomatic and economic, not military. For the politicians, the softest of targets, sport, eventually proved irresistible. An Olympic Games to be staged in the Russian capital Moscow was ripe for exploitation by floundering American leaders, a chance for them to embarrass and annoy the communist politburo sitting in the Kremlin. First though, the Americans had their own winter Olympics to stage in Lake Placid, New York state. Remarkably those Games rather than the summer equivalent would prove more fruitful for political exploitation by US politicians. It happened by accident; or a quirk of the vagaries of sporting endeavour.

On 20 January 1980, US president Jimmy Carter issued his ultimatum to his Soviet counterpart Leonid Brezhnev. 'Unless the Soviets withdraw their troops within a month from Afghanistan,' the United States would boycott the Moscow Olympics. Remarkably, Carter managed to secure the support of the United States Olympic Committee, an organisation taking notice of opinion polls showing 55 per cent support for a boycott from the American public. American athletes in contrast were, naturally, very much against a boycott. Despite the American threat to the staging of the Moscow Games, Soviet athletes travelled to the United States for the winter Olympics, no doubt in the full knowledge there was absolutely no chance of the Kremlin complying with Carter's demand.

The month-long deadline set by Carter conveniently gave both parties some diplomatic breathing space during the winter Olympics. Nevertheless, as athletes gathered in Lake Placid, Cold War tension was at its highest and back almost to the levels of the Cuban missile crisis of the 1960s. This time, though, the 'face-off' would not be in the mid-Atlantic with crews of warships on the brink of igniting a nuclear war. This time it would be on an ice rink.

But for Cold War concerns an ice hockey match between the United States and the Soviet Union, which was not even a final, would never have been feted as the greatest moment in American 20th-century sports history. Forget Jesse Owens in

Berlin, Muhammad Ali's exploits, Mark Spitz winning seven golds, or Babe Ruth becoming a legendary figure beyond his own sport of baseball, surveys at the close of the last century showed the most memorable moment for American sports fans was a 4-3 victory for a bunch of college kids from the USA over the Soviet Union. It was a sporting upset to inspire a nation though it was hardly on the radar of sports fans on the rest of the planet.

The Soviet Union ice hockey team was termed the 'Red Machine', a nickname the Russians revelled in. Many of its players were nominally members of the Red Army but they saw little military service. They were in reality hardened professional athletes in supposedly an amateur sport. On a fateful night in Lake Placid in a game not even shown live on US television they were beaten by American amateurs, a team of students still in college. Commentator Al Michaels cried as the game came to a close, 'Do you believe in miracles?' Then he screeched in disbelief, 'Yes!' A nation celebrated. An American legend was born. Ultimately, sport was being played as a trump card for politics, especially for the American public, people from a country with little traditional grasp of the importance of national team sports.

Going into the Games, the Soviet Union were firm favourites to win ice hockey gold. Their players were superstars back home. They had struck gold at the previous four Olympics and their domination of Olympic ice hockey had only been interrupted by a victory for the USA in 1960, again a win against the odds but one without the political significance of Lake Placid. The Soviets' aura of invincibility was built up prior to the Games by taking on and beating professional teams from the National Hockey League during the 1970s.

A rare defeat only came in a game with a Canadian professional national team, drawn from NHL players not eligible to compete in the Olympics because of the IOC's amateur rules. The Canadians, who viewed ice hockey as their national sport, were appalled by the Soviets' blatant breach of those 'amateur' protocols of the time by employing players in the military and allowing them to train full-time. Sweden had also boycotted previous Olympic ice hockey tournaments in 1972 and 1976 as a result in one of the few boycotts ever made purely on sporting grounds. Just to further dampen expectations among optimistic American supporters, their prospective US Olympians had met the Soviets in a warm-up game for the 1980 Olympics at Madison Square Garden in New York City. The Soviets thrashed the Americans 10-3. Even the most generous accounts in the American media described the defeat in Madison Square Garden as a 'whipping'. For ice hockey pundits, an American victory over the United States in a competitive Olympic game would be a 'miracle'. Of 34 encounters between the Soviet and American Olympic ice hockey teams, the USA had won one – their gold medal from 1960.

Yet for all the negative omens, American coach Herb Brooks was a supreme optimist. He was also a meticulous planner, which was not necessarily a common characteristic among coaches of sports teams in the late 1970s and early 80s. For 18 months prior to the Games, Brooks moulded his team, scouting several hundred players and putting them through their skating paces in trials, and unusually for the time carrying out psychological tests. Those who made the cut for his squad gathered to go into a training camp four months before the Games and also toured Europe and North America in a series of exhibition fixtures. As the American defence man Ken Morrow observed, Brooks was a revolutionary and visionary coach, key to the success of the American Olympic ice hockey team in 1980.

Morrow, who went on to win four Stanley Cup titles to add to his Olympic gold, recalled, 'He was the right guy at the right time to coach that team. I don't think we would have won with anyone else. To me he goes down with Vince Lombardi and John Wooden and all the great coaches from other sports. He was innovative, 20–30 years ahead of his time. Everything he did could have backfired but he knew it was the way you had to play to beat those teams.'

Goaltender Jim Craig had similar recollections, 'Even now I'm amazed at the vision he had, from the time he began putting the team together. And how he finally convinced us all that we didn't need to be in awe of [the Soviets], that not only could we play with them, we could beat them. And that's exactly what we did.'

Along with the traits described by Morrow, Brooks shared a familiar characteristic with all team coaches and managers of the period. He instilled 'fear' into his players as a strict disciplinarian demanding the highest levels of fitness. Another of his players, Mike Ramsey, said he 'messed' with their minds 'at every opportunity'. Tactically Brooks, of course, was astute, recognising his players' limitations as they prepared to take on hardened and experienced quasi-professionals from Iron Curtain countries. It was feared they were unable to match the Soviets, in particular, for skill, with confirmation coming in the crushing defeat at Madison Square Garden. Therefore, Brooks emphasised the need for speed and power to counter the higher skill levels of the Americans' opponents. An example cited by the players of Brooks's zealous work ethic was his reaction to a defeat to Norway in an exhibition game a couple of months before the Olympics.

Brooks ordered them as punishment for the defeat to carry out a series of what they nicknamed 'Herbies'; an exhausting series of drills. Even after staff at the sports arena had switched off the lights the players carried on skating with Brooks barking orders from the side. It is portrayed in a Hollywood movie inspired by the 'Miracle on Ice'. Morrow insists, unlike in the film, the players did not throw up. The next day they beat Norway 8-0.

In their opening game of the Olympic tournament the Americans secured an encouraging 2-2 draw with Sweden, who were one of the teams tipped to win a medal. Hopes rose further after a shock 7-3 victory over Czechoslovakia, the team seen as most likely to upset the Soviets. For the first time the American media was aware of the possibility of a bunch of college kids enjoying Olympic glory. A win over an Eastern Bloc country guaranteed front-page coverage. Until then the Americans were dismissed as 'no-hopers'. Further victories over Norway, Romania and West Germany put them through to the 'medal round' with the Soviet Union lying in wait after winning all their preliminary games. For the Red Machine it had surprisingly been a bit of a struggle to notch up a 100 per cent record. Canada and Finland took the lead against them before finally succumbing to defeat.

Those faltering performances gave Brooks some hope with his challenge being to ensure his players believed in their chances of causing an upset despite being thumped in Madison Square Garden just a few weeks earlier. One of those players, Jack O'Callahan, recalled Brooks's psychological tricks, 'He was just trying to help us relax. He sensed from our first game against them that perhaps we had a little too much respect for them to the point where it had affected our mental preparation. Most of us, and for that matter, the entire world hockey community, viewed the Russia team as the greatest ever and the Russian players as the greatest players on the planet. Herb tried to break down the myth that nobody could beat them. He tried to humanise them.'

Crucially, in the build-up, Brooks ignored the political overtones already being hyped up by the US media, concentrating instead on the sport. Phil Verchota, one of the American forwards, recalled, 'I don't think that any political tensions found their way into the locker room. Actually, I think the US players had the feeling of being second-class citizens when it came to hockey. We needed to prove ourselves in the arena. So, for me, we were playing for pride at a game we loved. I don't recall being politically motivated at all.'

Frankly, nobody at the time gave the Americans a prayer, even Verchota admitting that player for player the USSR were the superior team. Naturally, the Soviets were overwhelming favourites for a game American television decided not to cover live. The ABC network must have thought their compatriots had no chance of winning so decided to sniff out medal possibilities for American viewers to enjoy elsewhere. It turned out to be a mistake and one of broadcasting's all-time scheduling howlers.

For all the emphasis on pace and power, the man standing in front of the tiny goal in his pads and a face mask needed to be in peak form for any chance of an upset. Fortunately Jim Craig rose to the occasion, keeping the score down with a series of saves as the Soviets took a 2-1 lead with the USA goal coming from Buzz Schneider. As the clock ticked down towards the end of the first period, the only surprise was the inability of the Soviets to add to their lead thanks to the heroics of Craig. Yet just with seconds remaining a mistake from an unlikely source led to an equaliser.

Vladislav Tretiak was widely recognised as the world's best net minder and perhaps the greatest of all time. He easily saved a shot and then shoved the puck away. Unfortunately for him, his defenders lost concentration, allowing Mark Johnson to pounce and equalise. USA captain Michael Eruzione remembered, 'I think the period's over. And out of the corner of my eye I see Mark going flying behind me. I remember thinking, "Where the hell is he going?" Well, he was going in to score a goal that really did change the whole night.'

Officials debated whether or not his shot had beaten the buzzer for the end of play and the Soviets walked off. They were called back for a token face-off once it was decided to allow the score. There was one absentee, Tretiak. Instead, Vladimir Myshkin went in goal. Most of the 10,000 crowd and indeed the American squad thought it was just a temporary measure.

Yet to everyone's surprise it was a permanent substitution. It appeared as though the Americans had succeeded in knocking the world's best net minder out of the game. Eruzione said it gave his side a morale-boosting lift, 'The place went crazy, just exploded. We were crazy and pumped up ourselves skating off the ice. Then we come out for the second period and find out they'd benched Tretiak.' Years later, Tretiak's team-mates, some of whom went on to play in North America's professional NHL, described their coach Viktor Tikhonov as being 'crazy'. Tretiak recalled the moment in his autobiography, 'I don't think I should have been replaced in that game. I had made so many mistakes already, I was confident my play would only improve. Myshkin is an excellent goalie, but he wasn't prepared for the struggle, he wasn't "tuned in" to the Americans.' Tikhonov later mysteriously recalled he made the substitution under pressure from Soviet officials attending the game. He did not elaborate.

Frankly, the substitution seemed something of an irrelevance in the next 20-minute period of play with virtually all of the action being played out around the American goal. Craig foiled a wave of attacks while his opposite number Myshkin only hadz just a couple of shots to save. Yet for all their domination, the Soviets went into the third and final period with just a slender 3-2 lead, Alexander Maltsey escaping to break Craig's resistance. As a result the odds were stacked against the Americans despite them technically being still in the game at just a goal down. However, the older Soviet team, for all their professional training, were beginning to tire against a younger and more athletic outfit drilled by Herb Brooks. Johnson once again fired in an equaliser, taking advantage of another defensive mistake. Eruzione sent the arena into delirium by firing in what turned out to be the winner with ten minutes to play. It was then a rearguard action to thwart the Soviets with Craig to the fore. He said, 'What I was mostly thinking was let's not give up a cheap goal and screw up one of the great sports stories of all time.'

They held on to cue wild celebrations in the Lake Placid arena and across the American nation, Al Michaels prompting the party with his cry, 'Do you believe in miracles? Yes!' A sporting legend had been born. For academic cynics dismissive of the role of sport in Cold War geo-politics its importance was merely the stuff of fairytales. To them it was just a simple matter of USA 4 USSR 3 in the final round robin stage of an ice hockey tournament. Yet thanks to a fawning media, a president running for re-election and facing unpopularity among the American sports fraternity over the threat to boycott the 1980 Moscow Olympics, it became much, much more.

Curiously enough, for all the wild celebrations, the gold medal had yet to be won. Results could still conspire against the Americans and gift the main prize to the Russians. The USA needed to beat Finland in their final game and if they lost, they would have to hope the Soviet Union would also slip up in their final game against Sweden. The Americans' match against Finland was played in the morning giving them the chance to secure the gold before the Soviets could take to the ice. Eruizone claims that Brooks issued a psychological threat. The coach told them, before going out, that they would 'take it to their graves' if they lost the game. Morrow remembers Brooks's reaction the day after they had beaten the Soviet Union. He said, 'We came in for practice Saturday feeling pretty good about ourselves. We had just pulled off this monumental upset. The guys were signing some sticks for people and stuff. Herb came in and he just flipped out. He put the hammer down real quick. We had one of the hardest practices of the year that day. He skated our butts off; so much for the "Miracle [on Ice]". We were in the best condition of our lives. He made sure of it.' At one stage it looked as though Brooks's dark scenario might occur. Finland were 2-1 up but the Americans fought back to skate out 4-2 winners for gold and a place in sporting posterity.

They became instant all-American heroes by securing an unlikely place in the annals of sporting political history. As far as the more rabid political observers were concerned, they had beaten the Soviets' Red Machine, striking a blow for capitalism and Western democratic values. As ecstatic fans poured out of the arena to celebrate the Americans' shock victory over the Soviet Union, president Jimmy Carter was on the phone to coach Herb Brooks. The USA had yet to beat Finland and secure gold. Carter told Brooks the victory 'made the American people very proud' and 'reflected American basic ideals'.

Once Finland were beaten and the gold medals awarded, Carter was back on the phone to Brooks to congratulate him. This time even Brooks alluded to the politics of the moment, something he scrupulously tried to avoid during the course of the tournament. He apparently told Carter, 'I didn't know if we were going to do it. It was a great win for everybody in sport and the American people in general. From the things we had to overcome, to the different beliefs, ways of life. It just proves our life is the proper way to continue.' It was an odd comment, faintly ridiculous and contradicting his earlier views on the political overtones from a game of ice hockey played between the USA and the USSR. Brooks had declared, 'If we have to win a medal to prove our way of life is superior, we are in big trouble.' His compatriots were keener to latch on to his later view, expressed in the euphoria of an exchange of calls with Carter as they celebrated a victory over the 'evil communist empire'.

For Carter, presiding over a failing economy, a hostage crisis in Iran and threatening a summer Olympic boycott of the forthcoming Moscow Games, political capital was to be made. He didn't hesitate, inviting the team to the White House along with other American winter Olympians. The ice hockey players, though, were the 'guests of honour' to be feted by their president. Carter grandly proclaimed at the reception, 'For me, as president of the United States of America, this is one of the proudest moments that I've ever experienced. The US hockey team, their victory was one of the most breathtaking upsets not only in Olympic history but in the entire history of sport.'

Carter was struggling to stay in office, facing a fight for even his own Democratic Party's nomination for the 1980 US election from senator Ted Kennedy. There would then be the more significant challenge of California governor Ronald Reagan. From the *Washington Post*, Haynes Johnson observed, 'Jimmy Carter certainly was a political beneficiary of that victory. Millions of Americans heard him congratulating the American hockey team coach, Herb Brooks. If Carter made the most of the occasion, why shouldn't he? What president would have done less?'

Carter made countless references to the USA ice hockey team on the campaign trail. His rivals did the same, Kennedy even inviting players to election rallies. Jack O'Callahan felt particularly irked by the political rhetoric and the desire to exploit his sporting achievement by people intent on wrecking the next Olympic gathering in Moscow. O'Callahan said, 'All that political stuff that people wrote about, trying to make us into the young, all-American boys going against the Russians, that was garbage. None of that dawned on us until we got to Washington after the Olympics and were totally swarmed by reporters at the White House. I knew something definitely strange was going on by the way we were mobbed and questioned. Why, they were asking us questions about politics and stuff like we were senators instead of just kids. That's when I knew things had gotten completely out of hand.'

Unfortunately for Carter, it did not work and he went on to lose the presidency to Ronald Reagan. Out of office and duly writing his memoirs, the fabled 'Miracle on Ice' barely merited a mention. Suddenly one of the 'greatest moments' he had ever experienced was almost forgotten. Carter merely reflected forlornly, 'It was one of the high spots of my year when the young Americans won a very emotional moment… I was hoping this victory and the gold medal were an omen of better days ahead. But that was not to be.'

There is little doubt of a boost to national morale from the USA's ice hockey victory over the Soviet Union, and the subsequent securing of a gold medal. It probably helped that the people of the United States, unlike other countries, rarely come together in celebration of national team sport. Club franchises dominate more popular North American team sports such as baseball and the NFL. Yet the Cold War rhetoric still employed to celebrate the win made this more than just a nice tonic for the American people. It was a media portrayal of a victory of good over evil, remarkably over the top even by the standards of media hyperbole; a classic example of political exploitation of sport from those perhaps with little regard for athletic disciplines.

Carter's insistence on going ahead with his threat to impose a boycott with the support of other American political leaders of the Moscow Olympics serves to illustrate his cynical manipulation of sport. The Soviet Union's Red Machine was going home from the United States beaten and bowed. The Soviet Union's Red Army, for the moment, had no intention of doing the same from Afghanistan. Perhaps the stage was set for moments of American glory in the Soviet capital, Moscow. Sadly for aspiring athletes training for the Moscow Games, the American political establishment and a compliant US Olympic association had other ideas.

12

Cold War Boycotts

JUST a few weeks after welcoming successful American winter Olympians to the White House, Jimmy Carter invited along their summer counterparts, this time for what amounted to the athletes as a funereal wake rather than a celebration. President Carter was determined to go ahead with his Olympic boycott, even counting on US Congress to support a ban on American media outlets travelling to Moscow to cover the Olympic Games. He had the reluctant backing of the United States Olympic Committee (USOC) but not the support of the athletes, whose dreams of Olympic glory were in tatters.

Carter did enjoy support from political leaders of some Western nations, notably the British prime minister Margaret Thatcher. Yet she was one of the few of Carter's allies to support a boycott of Moscow and even eventually failed to stop her own athletes from going along. Unlike the USOC, the British Olympic Association was firmly opposed to an Olympic boycott and supported the views of the president of the IOC, Lord Killanin, an Anglo-Irish aristocrat. Carter had tried and failed to lobby him to support a boycott of a Moscow Olympics, stripping the Soviets of the Games and moving them elsewhere. Killanin was having none of it.

Carter outlined his boycott plans in a letter dated 20 January 1980 to the president of the USOC, Robert J. Kane, just before the opening of the Lake Placid winter Games. Unless the Soviet

Union withdrew its troops from Afghanistan within a month, the United States would urge the IOC to cancel the Moscow summer Games or transfer them to another country.

In attempting to justify this blatant political interference in a sports event, Carter wrote in his letter to Kane, 'I want to reaffirm my own personal commitment to the principles and purposes of the Olympic movement. I believe in the desirability of keeping government policy out of the Olympics but deeper issues are at stake. In the Soviet Union international sports competition is itself an aspect of Soviet government policy, as is the decision to invade Afghanistan. The head of the Moscow Olympic organising committee is a high Soviet government official. The Soviet government attaches enormous political importance to the holding of the 1980 Olympic Games in Moscow, and if the Olympics are not held in Moscow because of Soviet military aggression in Afghanistan, this powerful signal of world outrage cannot be hidden from the Soviet people, and will reverberate around the globe. Perhaps it will deter future aggression.'

He added, 'I urge the USOC to propose that the Games either be transferred to another site such as Montreal or to multiple sites, or be cancelled for this year. If the International Olympic Committee rejects such a USOC proposal, I urge the USOC and the Olympic Committees of other like-minded nations not to participate in the Moscow Games.'

Having sent his missive to the US Olympic Committee, Carter appeared on the long-running political TV programme *Meet the Press* to explain the ultimatum he was sending to the Soviet leadership and his proposal for an Olympic boycott if the men from the Kremlin, as expected, ignored his demands. He insisted, 'Regardless of what other nations might do, I would not favour the sending of an American Olympic team to Moscow while the Soviet invasion troops are in Afghanistan.'

Just to hammer home the point, his secretary of state Cyrus Vance took dignitaries by surprise at an IOC reception ahead of Lake Placid. Vance told his audience, 'Let me make my government's position clear. We will oppose the participation of an American team in any Olympic Games in the capital of an invading nation.' His speech was apparently met with silence from those present, the American organisers of the Lake Placid winter Olympics embarrassed by the brazen politicking of an American government minister holding the post of US chief diplomat. It was clear that the idea of a boycott, let alone transferring the summer Games from Moscow to another country, was gaining little traction in many of the world's capitals with the vociferous exception of the UK government in London. Most countries, especially in Europe, were supporting the IOC and Lord Killanin, who dismissed Carter's call to move the games as 'legally and technically impossible'.

Carter's vigour in supporting the idea of an Olympic boycott as punishment for the Soviets invading Afghanistan took the Kremlin by surprise. Some members of the politburo even went as far as questioning his sanity. Anatoly Dobrynin, the Soviet ambassador to Washington, commented, 'I had never encountered anything like the intensity and scale of this one. What particularly caught my attention was the president's personal obsession with Afghanistan.'

According to declassified CIA documents, concerns were raised by the spy agency's director, Admiral Stansfield Turner. He warned that the Olympic boycott would be ineffective and 'backfire'. Admiral Turner concluded, 'The Soviets would also be able to play the role of an aggrieved party before a partially sympathetic international audience and to utilise international disagreements over the boycott to exacerbate tensions between the US and non-boycotting (or reluctantly boycotting) states, probably including some close US allies.'

Members of Congress, though, felt differently. Jimmy Carter was struggling to stay in office, ultimately losing the election to Ronald Reagan. Yet in his State of the Union speech to Congress the boycott call found traction. The loudest applause came after reiterating plans to punish the Russians by refusing to send American athletes to the Moscow Olympics. For this particular policy, one using athletes as pawns in a political game, he enjoyed cross-party support. He also enjoyed public support, something lacking in his handling of the economy and international affairs. Carter eyed a rare chance to raise his status among the American public in his handling of world events. According to opinion polls, 55 per cent of Americans backed his Olympic boycott policy. His overall popularity figure was well below that figure by the spring of 1980.

Although neither the president nor Congress could legally stop their athletes from travelling to the Soviet capital, short of confiscating passports or enacting legislation subject to legal challenges in the US Supreme Court, Congress gathered to vote on the matter. In a non-binding vote of the House of Representatives, 386 were in favour of pulling out of the Moscow Olympics with 12 against. The Senate voted in favour by a similar margin, 88 to four. Yet for all its diplomatic lobbying the Americans were failing to persuade the international community of the merits of their case. Indeed, in the case of the IOC, they were leaving its president Lord Killanin positively irritated. British prime minister Margaret Thatcher was having a similar effect on him in her fruitless pursuit of a UK boycott.

Carter dispatched one his White House advisors, Lloyd Cutler, to meet Lord Killanin in Ireland, a diplomatic move doomed to backfire thanks to the emissary's apparent arrogance. Recalling the meeting, Lord Killanin later moaned, 'I was, as it turned out, to get a great shock. I discovered that Cutler had not flown in from Washington to discuss, but rather instruct.' Carter and his advisers had miscalculated. Killanin was never going to be coerced into calling off or moving the Moscow Games believing, quite correctly, Carter was merely 'scrambling for his political life' and together with Thatcher cynically trying to exploit the Olympic movement. Furthermore, he believed the future of the Olympic movement was at stake. Indeed, he had even previously advocated taking national politics out of the Games altogether by banning the flying of flags and playing of anthems at the Olympics, a proposal rejected by his IOC colleagues. On taking office after the Munich Games he observed, 'We have the big shots, America and Russia, trying to prove their way of life is better because of the number of medals they win. It proves nothing of the sort.'

Lord Killanin fought to keep politics out of sport but thanks to the antics of the likes of Carter he failed. The IOC leader made it clear he would only contemplate stripping the Soviet Union of the 1980 Olympics if the Kremlin prevented Israeli or Chinese athletes from travelling to Moscow. In the event, they did not turn up anyway, joining the American boycott. As for responding to the Soviet invasion of Afghanistan, Lord Killanin firmly believed it was not sufficient grounds to comply with Carter and Thatcher's demand for the Games to be moved or called off. It was, in his words, 'Moscow or nothing'. He declared, 'That does not mean that I or the International Olympic Committee are condoning the political action taken by the host country, but if we started to make political judgments, it would be the end of the Games.' Moscow was keeping the 1980 Olympic Games regardless of American wishes.

Lord Killanin's stance meant that Carter was left with little choice but to drum up international support for a boycott with Thatcher as his chief cheerleader. On 17 January 1980, the British cabinet met to endorse an Olympic boycott policy along with other sanctions against the Soviet Union. Thatcher believed it would be a 'gesture' that would 'hurt the Soviet government the most'. Her foreign secretary, Lord Carrington, was an enthusiastic supporter, declaring, 'Few things would hurt Soviet prestige more than the absence of a number of Western countries from the Olympic Games.'

There was just one snag. The British Olympic Association was determined not to match its American counterpart and comply with the demands of its government. Additionally, there appeared annoyance at the BOA of the strong-arm tactics being employed by the Thatcher government including cuts to athletes' funding and refusal to grant public sector workers such as civil servants and armed forces personnel additional leave to attend the Games. It seemed hypocritical given the softer stance from the Conservative government on the issue of the Lions rugby tour to South Africa in the summer of 1980. In the case of the Lions, Thatcher merely 'advised' them not to go rather than call off the tour. Yet in the case of Great Britain's Olympians Thatcher openly questioned the patriotism of young men and women taking pride in representing their country. She wrote to the chairman of the BOA, Sir Denis Follows, asserting, 'British athletes have the same rights and the same responsibilities towards freedom and its maintenance as every citizen of the United Kingdom.' She even went as far as accusing them of potentially condoning an 'international crime'.

As a debate and vote in the British Parliament loomed over an Olympic boycott, the former world 10,000 metre record holder David Bedford sent a petition to Downing Street on behalf of the International Athletes Club, signed by 78 UK athletes and asserting their right to compete in Moscow free of political interference. They did, though, suggest boycotting the opening and closing ceremonies and staging podium protests at medal ceremonies. The athletes added, 'We are not prepared, however, to preside over the destruction of the Olympic movement, and consider that in the end, the Government's responsibility to solve the Afghan crisis is through normal diplomatic means.'

Thatcher, though recognising the hard work of British athletes, sent an intemperate reply, once again citing the politicisation of sport by the Soviet Union as justification for the West using athletes as Cold War diplomatic weapons. She told David Bedford, 'I firmly believe it would be wrong for sportsmen and sportswomen to participate in the Olympic Games in present circumstances. I am convinced that non-participation in the Olympic Games in Moscow remains one of the most effective ways of bringing home to the Soviet people that the action of their leaders in invading Afghanistan is unacceptable.' In a cover note to this exchange of correspondence from her civil servants, they highlighted the failure of any of the potential British medallists in track and field athletics to sign the petition; for the Whitehall mandarins an indication the athletes' resolve may buckle. They were wrong.

To intensify the campaign, Thatcher tried to canvass support among those potential medal winners and their families, most notably Sebastian Coe, a future Conservative MP and peer and a man also with the ultimately successful aim of winning Olympic gold in Moscow. She dispatched Douglas Hurd, later to become the British foreign secretary but then a junior minister, to meet Coe's father and coach, Peter. The man who later became Lord Sebastian Coe recalled the meeting as he organised the London 2012 Olympics, 'I remember very clearly when my dad was asked to go and see Douglas Hurd. In the nicest possible way they were essentially saying to my father, "Can you not keep your troublesome son quiet?" My gut instinct was that there was an intellectual dishonesty about what we were trying to achieve.

History proved us right of course, because four years later when we went to LA for the 1984 Olympics the Russians were still in Afghanistan, and the boycott had no impact.'

Douglas Hurd's own note of the meeting recalled a feeling of 'bitterness' on the part of Peter Coe, who felt the calls for a boycott and the subsequent debate in favour or against was doing damage to the image of sport in Britain. Hurd was unsympathetic, lamenting that the will of Parliament was being ignored by Olympic athletes.

Yet unlike the united voice of the US Congress in almost unanimously demanding a boycott, the British Parliament was split over the issue along party political lines, voting by a disappointing majority for the Thatcher government of two to one on a motion with no legal authority. Prior to the vote the British Olympic Association had written an open letter to all MPs asserting its right to send competitors to Moscow. It noted, 'The democratic desire of British competitors to be present at the Olympics this summer does not condone Russian action in Afghanistan any more than does the presence of the British Ambassador in Moscow.' The British Labour Party had decided to back the BOA and oppose a boycott. British Liberal Democrat MPs did support a boycott but only on the specific grounds of objecting to the Soviet Union's humans rights record, something they had highlighted long before the invasion of Afghanistan. Menzies Campbell, a former Olympian and by then a Liberal MP, reasoned, 'I'm afraid British athletes must face up to the disappointing fact that human rights have to come before the chance of winning medals.' His party council backed a boycott but made it clear the primary reason was to oppose the Soviet Union's treatment of dissidents, noting support for a boycott from the Russian nuclear physicist Andrei Sakharov, perhaps at the time the leading campaigner against the communist regime's abuse of human rights.

Yet for all the lobbying and pressure on British Olympians there was disquiet even among some UK government ministers. Sports minister Hector Munro contacted Hurd to tell him in a letter that most athletes 'believe they are being singled out by the politicians as a means of attacking the Soviet Union whilst those same politicians permit the business of trade and commerce to continue as usual'. Even the Conservative-supporting press, which backed Margaret Thatcher's call for an Olympic boycott, expressed misgivings over the political tactics being employed with once again hypocrisy being the central charge levelled. Once special leave was denied to civil servants and members of the armed forces, the *Daily Mail* thundered that it was was 'intolerable that this government, of all governments – a government that abhors Communist serfdom – should now seek to make British athletes jump to the Tories' bidding by what is no more or less than a crack of the totalitarian whip'. Regardless of whether or not the Conservative government was attempting to crack the 'totalitarian whip', it was never going to work. The Parliamentary vote at Westminster was non-binding on the athletes. The BOA could not be forced to pull British athletes out of the Moscow Games.

Over in Washington, US secretary of state Cyrus Vance felt that 'the starch seems to be slowly going out of our boycott effort'. He noted the failure in particular of the UK and Australia to persuade their Olympic associations to decline invitations to compete in Moscow. As a sign of growing desperation and exasperation, Lloyd Cutler, the White House official who had tried and failed to force IOC president Lord Killanin to call off the Moscow Games, moaned of the 'serious danger' of losing the British. His view of the BOA chairman Sir Denis Follows was less than diplomatic, indeed downright rude. He dismissed him as 'a living Colonel Blimp', citing his only international experience as serving as president of the British Airline Pilots' Association. Presumably Cutler was unaware the target of his personal attacks also served as secretary of the Football Association as it organised the World Cup in England. Cutler ranted, 'He [Sir Denis] is a pure Olympian who puts aside all responsibilities as a citizen of the West in favour of sports as the last hope for world peace. His views of Mrs Thatcher and the president are visibly apoplectic, although wholly confined to how much harm they have done to sports.' On the latter point most athletes probably agreed with Sir Denis.

On 21 March 1980, Jimmy Carter gathered American Olympians at the White House to tell them that they would not be going to Moscow. Four days later, the British Olympic

Association announced it would be sending British athletes to Moscow. Thatcher, thanks perhaps in part to all the criticism from normally sympathetic right-wing British newspapers, was unable to pull off the same autocratic trick as Carter. There would be no gathering of disappointed British athletes in Downing Street to be told their tickets to Moscow were cancelled and passports revoked. They were not only going to the Soviet capital to try to fulfil their Olympic dreams but they also deeply resented the political pressure on them to boycott. In announcing the BOA's decision to defy the will of its own government, Sir Denis Follows complained of being sent a 'rather heavy letter' by Thatcher. She, though, kept up the pressure right up to the point it was time for athletes to board the plane to Moscow. She warned, 'Attendance in Moscow can only serve to frustrate the interests of Britain.' Sir Denis countered with a familiar mantra for sportsmen and women rejecting political boycotts. It was simply, 'We believe sport should be a bridge, and not a destroyer.'

British sprinter Allan Wells, who won gold in the 100 metres in Moscow, reflected, 'Thank God we had the BOA. I never would have been involved if not for them.' His chances of winning were arguably enhanced by the absence of his American sprint rivals. They were not so lucky. Unlike the BOA, the USOC bowed to pressure from the White House, cowed also by the threat of legal sanctions. Their winter sports counterparts, not least the ice hockey team, had been invited to the White House and greeted as heroes. In contrast, the athletes dreaming of Olympic glory in Moscow were gathered at the White House like a group of naughty schoolchildren to be told they must not go to Moscow. It was their 'patriotic duty' to boycott the Games. Not one of them stood or applauded as their president entered the room to address them. They sat in sombre silence. It was seen as a humiliating snub, though some observers believe the athletes were unaware of the formal protocol of standing to greet the US president as he enters the room.

ABC News called it a 'grim moment' for Carter. He claimed to be sympathetic, sharing their disappointment. He told them, 'I understand how you feel.' However, he went on to say, 'What we are doing is preserving the principles and the quality of the Olympics, not destroying it.' It was a view challenged and contradicted by the BOA chief Sir Denis Follows. Reluctantly though, the USOC complied.

Of course drumming up widespread support from other countries, especially in Europe, was proving a problem for Carter. He had the support of his ally Margaret Thatcher. But she was impotent, embarrassingly politically powerless, in her attempts to stop British athletes from competing in Moscow. West Germany agreed not to take part, the original idea for an international sports boycott coming from the country's ambassador to NATO, Rolf Pauls. Other NATO allies, including France, competed at the 1980 Olympics. Even Puerto Rico, an American protectorate, sent athletes.

American attempts to dissuade countries from competing bordered on the comical. At one point, Muhammad Ali was recruited to embark on a diplomatic mission to Africa to drum up support. It turned out to be a disaster, the legendary boxer snubbed by African leaders. The Tanzanian president, Julius Narre, took umbrage at being sent by Carter 'a mere athlete' to meet him. At the subsequent news conference Ali became tetchy as he was being grilled by the media over his support for the boycott. One journalist described him as a 'puppet' of the White House. Ali angrily retorted, 'Nobody made me come here and I'm nobody's Uncle Tom.'

His mission was a failure; most sub-Saharan African countries eventually competing in Moscow including Narre's Tanzania. For Carter it was yet another political embarrassment during a year in which he was campaigning to stay in power. The American public were never going to blame Ali, a revered sporting figure, for the disaster. The *Washington Post* observed, 'The whole fiasco was not all Ali's fault. Much of the blunder can be traced to the White House.'

Carter had no choice but to acknowledge the growing lack of support from other nations in his address to the gloomy gathering of US athletes at the White House. He told them, 'I can't say at this moment what other nations will not go to the summer Olympics in Moscow. Ours will not go. I say that not with any equivocation; the decision has been made. It's not a pleasant time for me. You occupy a special place in American life.'

His heartfelt appeal, coming from a man who was fighting for his political life, was met with dignity but no doubt bitter disappointment. It was a choice for some of between backing their president or backing the Russians. William Simon, the US treasury secretary under Richard Nixon and a member of the USOC, summed it up in these terms, 'We aren't defying a man; we are defying the office, the highest elected office in our land.' It seemed a hollow victory for Carter, effectively bullying a reluctant Olympic committee into backing his Moscow boycott and failing to garner uniform support in the international committee. In his autobiography, he later lamented, 'I knew the decision was controversial, but I had no idea at the time how difficult it would be for me to implement it or to convince other nations to join us. We had a struggle all the way; the outcome was always in doubt. Most Olympic committees were wholly independent bodies, whose members deeply resented any government involvement in their decisions.'

The United States pulled out of the Moscow Games, the lead country in a boycott by more than 60 nations. Canada joined its neighbours in refusing to send athletes to Moscow. China, for all its political differences with the United States, did the same, as did mostly Muslim countries in support for their co-religionists, the Afghan people. Yet more than 80 nations did compete, the communist nations under Soviet influence joined by western European nations including Great Britain despite the objection of Margaret Thatcher. The British Foreign Office limply concluded in declassified papers that it was 'a pity most British athletes failed to follow government advice and boycott the Games'.

In sporting terms those Games were a qualified success. More than 70 Olympic records were broken and more than 30 world records broken, though it needs to be noted that some of those were set by East German swimmers who were later revealed to be pumped up by drugs. For the British team defying their prime minister, Daley Thompson won gold in the decathlon, something he almost certainly would have done even if all his closest rivals had turned up. It was also the Games when the rivalry of world record-breaking middle-distance runners Sebastian Coe and Steve Ovett came to a head. Ovett won gold in the 800 metres, Coe avenging him by snatching gold in the 1,500 metres. It was also the Games of an infamous gesture from the gold medal-winning Polish pole vaulter Władysław Kozakiewicz to the Russian crowd. They were firmly behind their own favourite, Konstantin Volkov, and heckled Kozakiewicz every time he jumped. After his gold medal-winning and world record-breaking vault, Kozakiewicz made a less-than-sporting gesture to his tormentors in the crowd. He raised his right arm in an L shape to the crowd with a clenched fist, a gesture interpreted in polite circles as 'up yours'. Yet even this act of sporting defiance from an athlete to a hostile crowd became politicised. In Poland, a country about to be flung into anti-Soviet turmoil with the 'Solidarity' trade union strikes led by Lech Walesa, his gesture became known as 'gest Kozakiewicz'. It enraged the Soviets. The Kremlin's ambassador to Poland even demanded Kozakiewicz be stripped of the gold medal for an 'insult to the Soviet people'. Kozakiewicz kept his gold medal.

As for the male gold medal-winning 1,500 metres runner, Sebastian Coe later described Margaret Thatcher's attempts to persuade British athletes to join the American boycott as 'mean and petty and stupid', a view of the 'Iron Lady' normally articulated by Labour politicians rather than Conservative MPs and peers. He felt sport was being used as a political and diplomatic 'weapon', something he found 'both craven and self-defeating'. Ignoring Thatcher's boycott call also helped in Coe's view to maintain Britain's standing in the international sporting community, something that was vital in eventually securing the London 2012 Olympics. He told *The Guardian*, 'In hindsight it was a good decision to go for all sorts of reasons. I don't think I would have been able to stand up in Singapore in front of the International Olympic Committee and say what I said with credibility if I had boycotted in 1980. I was able to say that Britain had sent a team to every winter and summer Games. Had I not gone in 1980 it would certainly have been seized upon and exploited by rival cities.'

Coe was able to celebrate winning gold in Moscow. One other future member of the International Olympic Committee had her dreams of winning a medal, possibly gold, wiped out. Anita DeFrantz, an American rower, reflected on the futility of it all. Her president had ordered the boycott for his own political ends, yet ended up being booted out of office. The Russians failed to pull out of Afghanistan for at least another decade, once communist rule in the old Soviet Union was coming to an end. In the weeks leading up to Moscow, DeFrantz tried and failed to file a lawsuit to clear the way for American athletes to compete in Moscow, receiving hate mail for her pains. Just like Lord Coe, she dismissed the boycott as pointless, 'The sad thing is it had no result. In June, we're negotiating for the sale of wheat with the Soviet Union. June 1980. It just broke my heart.'

Not only did the Americans fail to go to Moscow for the 1980 Games, but the Russians failed to travel to Los Angeles four years later. It was an act of petty revenge but inevitable in the Cold War atmosphere of the time. Politicians, both in the East and in the West, claimed their hollow victories in using sport as their diplomatic weapon of choice. Bizarrely, ahead of the Los Angeles Games the Kremlin and the White House accused each other of acting 'politically' in their manipulation of the world's greatest multi-event sporting celebration. Both of course were right but the hypocritical cynicism of the American and Soviet leadership plunged new depths. Committing troops and risking nuclear Armageddon to settle their differences was unthinkable. Using athletes was quite something else. As it sought to justify the Los Angeles boycott, the Kremlin even went as far as inviting derision on the part of the White House by claiming it was concerned for the 'security' of Soviet athletes at the Games. There had been no such concerns four years earlier at the Lake Placid Winter Olympics of 1980.

The Kremlin statement declaring a boycott claimed, 'It is known from the very first days of preparations for the present Olympics the American administration has sought to set course at using the Games for its political aims. Chauvinistic sentiments and anti-Soviet hysteria are being whipped up in this country.' In such an atmosphere, the Soviet leadership cooked up a scenario of mass anti-communist demonstrations on the streets of Los Angeles, putting athletes at risk. It reasoned in a missive sent to the IOC in May 1984, 'On the eve of the elections, the US administration is trying to use the Olympic Games to further its own selfish political aims. In the USA a broad campaign has been developed against the USSR's participation in the Olympics. Various reactionary political, émigré, and religious groups are uniting on an anti-Olympic platform. In particular a "Ban the Soviets" coalition has been created with the support of the official services of the USA. Athletes and officials of the USSR and other socialist countries have become the targets of open threats of physical violence and provocative acts.'

Such fears were dismissed by the Americans as ridiculous. US State Department spokesman John Hughes dismissed the Soviet concerns, saying the Americans had 'gone the extra mile' to ensure the security of athletes. Given the Olympic movement had also under Lord Killanin relaxed its insistence on only 'amateur' athletes taking part, the quasi-professionals of the Eastern Bloc were no longer at an advantage. Indeed, the risk to the Soviet leadership of athletes defecting to the West, especially from eastern European satellite states, was higher than the danger of their health and safety being put in peril by Americans on the march in anti-communist demonstrations.

However, there was no doubt that Soviet athletes would have travelled to Los Angeles in a potentially poisonous atmosphere given the Cold War climate of the time. US president Ronald Reagan openly referred to the Soviet Union as the 'evil empire'. In September 1983, the Californian Legislature called for the banning of Soviet athletes in response to the shooting down of a Korean passenger jet off the Russian coast, killing the 269 passengers and crew on board. It later reversed the decision and insisted that all foreign athletes would be welcome at the Games. Yet a damaging message went out to the world that the Kremlin was able to exploit. As far as the United States was concerned the Soviet Union was not welcome at the Olympics. It was a message causing consternation in the offices of the Los Angeles organising committee.

Committee members were optimistic that the Soviets would resist the temptation to take revenge for Jimmy Carter's Moscow boycott by imposing their own of Los Angeles. Los Angeles Olympic Organising Committee (LAOOC) chief executive Peter Ueberroth explained, 'There were times in the four-year period between the Carter boycott of the Soviets and the Soviet boycott here when they were definitely coming to our Games.

They would not have paid money to us, entered into contracts. That's not their style to do that as a ruse, to pay seven figures to us and rent apartments and do things, if they weren't intent on coming.'

Indeed, Ueberroth had been encouraged by a meeting with the head of the Soviets' National Olympic Committee, Marat Gamov. On arriving in Los Angeles for those talks with the LAOOC, Gramov insisted the Soviets had every intention of attending the summer Games. Unfortunately for Ueberroth and his colleagues, Gramov would soon have a new boss. A change in the Soviet leadership meant the Kremlin would adopt a more hawkish attitude towards the West to match the rhetoric of Ronald Reagan. Konstantin Chernenko took over from Yuri Andropov after he died in February 1984. Chernenko had been a loyal acolyte of Leonid Brezhnev, the man slighted by Jimmy Carter with his boycott of Moscow. He had no hesitation in exacting revenge by stopping Soviet athletes from travelling to Los Angeles and demanding that Eastern Bloc countries did the same. Just to add salt to American wounds, Gramov cheekily informed the world's media they were not carrying out a 'boycott' because the word did not exist in the Russian vocabulary.

The White House, of course, without a hint of irony, simply dismissed the Soviet boycott as a 'blatant political act'. Ronald Reagan cited the Olympic spirit in these words, 'It ought to be remembered by all the Games more than 2,000 years ago started as a means of bringing peace between the Greek city-states. And in those days, even if a war was going on, they called off the war in order to hold the Games. I wish we were still as civilised.'

Curiously, four years earlier, he had backed his predecessor Jimmy Carter's boycott of Moscow. Reagan dismissed the absent Soviets as 'losers'. Yet again, just as in 1980, it was the athletes rather than the politicians who missed out. Anita DeFrantz commented, 'The Soviet boycott was an enormous disappointment because it meant that the athletes were taking a beating again. It was just like the US boycott of the 1980 Olympic Games, the athletes were the only ones to be penalised.'

Ueberroth philosophically summed up his disappointment with a withering attack on politicians manipulating the Olympic movement. He commented, 'History has proven that the use and abuse of athletes for political purposes only hurts young individuals rather than achieving any political gain. Sports organisations and events should not be involved in disputes between governments.'

Just like Moscow 1980, LA 1984 was a qualified sporting success, helped by the return of China to the Olympic fold. A record 140 teams took part with only 17 countries boycotting the action. Sebastian Coe secured another gold medal in the 1,500 metres. His British team-mate Daley Thompson also added LA gold to Moscow gold. For the first time women competed in the marathon, Joan Benoit winning for the United States. As for another women's distance event, the 3,000 metres, there were echoes of Moscow and the antics of Polish pole vaulter Władysław Kozakiewicz with controversy and a political sub-plot. South African athlete Zola Budd had been selected for Great Britain, much to the dismay of anti-apartheid campaigners, her British passport fast-tracked by the Thatcher government. It all ended in tears, those of American sweetheart Mary Decker. Budd tripped her up halfway through the race, infuriating the crowd and leaving a tearful Decker down and out in the infield. Budd limped home out of the medals to later ruefully wish she had never taken part in the first place.

These Games were also, thanks to the leadership of Ueber-roth, an astonishing commercial success, generating a $232.5m surplus. Unlike Montreal in 1976 and later Games at Barcelona and Athens, which were financial disasters leaving host cities heavily in debt, Los Angeles made the most of existing facilities. Ueberroth also marketed the Games to whip up public support, meaning sports fans and the plain curious went to the Games despite the boycott by Eastern Bloc nations. Indeed, these were the last Games to be hit by a mass boycott.

Politics failed to rear its ugly head at the Olympics until it briefly threatened to derail the winter Games at Sochi in 2014. Russian president Vladimir Putin was accused by critics of using the Games for political propaganda as his tanks were rolling into Ukraine. Even so, threats of a boycott turned out to be idle ones. Frankly, just as three decades earlier, it would have been pointless with only athletes, as Ronald Reagan infamously put it, turning out to be the 'losers'. Despite the political games played out by the Cold War superpowers of the United States and Soviet Union in 1980 and 1984, the Olympic movement survived, although the danger remains of it being exploited by unscrupulous politicians.

13

Zola Budd: The Barefoot Runner

QUITE a few terms referring to race, nationality or creed are quite rightly no longer considered politically correct. Yet one lingers in the thesaurus of sports politics. It is 'plastic', an otherwise innocuous word to describe an everyday product which becomes pejorative when placed in front of the words 'Paddy' to describe someone of Irish descent or 'Brit' to describe someone of British descent.

This word was bandied about without compunction by Britain's tabloid newspapers in the build-up to the London 2012 Olympics, columnists indignantly angered by the practice of British passports being handed out to athletes born outside of the UK with strong medal prospects. In the case of the *Daily Mail*, this was deeply ironic. It was largely responsible for signing up for Great Britain the South African barefoot runner Zola Budd to compete in the Los Angeles Olympics of 1984. As a teenager, despite South Africa being banned from international competition, she soon came to the attention of the athletics world thanks to some astonishing performances. She ran to school barefoot with her father even claiming she outpaced the ostriches he kept on his farm. Her heroes and heroines were not the pop stars or film stars of the day but athletes, notably the

British middle distance runners, Steve Ovett and Sebastian Coe, and a certain American athlete, Mary Decker. Their posters were above her bed.

Domestically nobody came close to the gifted young athlete, the highlight of her fledgling career being unofficially breaking the world 5,000 metres record. Her dream was the same as any other young athlete, to compete in the Olympics, perhaps win a gold medal. Yet this was not possible for a sportsman or woman from apartheid South Africa. However a loophole was open to her, a legitimate claim to run for a country other than South Africa, spotted by the veteran British sportswriter Ian Wooldridge and his colleague John Bryant, a keen amateur athlete. Bryant had followed Budd's achievements and wrote, 'If the results were to be believed, there was a teenage girl, running without shoes, at altitude, up against domestic opposition, who was threatening to break world records.'

Bryant and Wooldridge also noted that Budd's paternal grandfather, George Budd, was British-born, allowing the athlete to potentially claim UK citizenship. They alerted their editor at the *Daily Mail*, Sir David English. He seized on an editorial and commercial opportunity too good to be missed and sold it as boosting Great Britain's hopes of medal chances at the Olympics though also circumventing the South African sporting boycott. In a column some 20 years later, Wooldridge recalled the moment he alerted Sir David to Budd's potential, '"Brilliant," cried David English, our editor of the time. "Because of the British family connection she shall run for us... I can pick up this phone and get her a British passport in two days." He did. Within a week Zola was in Britain but the large sum of money involved did not bring her happiness.' Although Sir David was ultimately successful in bringing Budd to Great Britain, it was perhaps not the smooth process he envisaged. As Wooldridge also pointedly lamented, the vast sums of money involved to attract Budd and her family came at an emotional price.

Several American universities also tried to woo Budd, offering sports scholarships and potentially the prospect of US citizenship, fast-tracked in time to compete at Los Angeles. She opted with the help of the *Daily Mail* to apply for UK citizenship. A decision in her favour left the British authorities open to the accusation of trying to circumvent the South African Olympic boycott. Some of prime minister Margaret Thatcher's Conservative MPs openly supported South Africa's apartheid government. Her opponents naturally treated a talented South African's application for citizenship, one supported by a newspaper favourable to her Tory government, with suspicion. Budd had a legitimate claim to British citizenship yet the prospect of a white South African woman running for Britain drew widespread opposition from the anti-apartheid movement. Protestations from Budd's supporters claiming she herself was somehow a 'victim' of apartheid, fell on deaf ears.

Those assisting Budd and her family no doubt anticipated opposition from the anti-apartheid movement in the UK. What probably took the newspaper and its editor by surprise was opposition to the application from some government ministers. Essentially it was a clash between a Thatcher loyalist of the time, the home secretary Leon Brittan, responsible for the department controlling immigration to the UK, and foreign secretary Geoffrey Howe. Brittan supported the *Daily Mail*. Howe, from official documents since released by the British government, appeared to have deep reservations warning against issuing such a passport with what he called 'unseemly' haste. Those documents record a meeting between Sir David and the British sports minister Neil MacFarlane, in which the editor outlined his plans for Budd. Sir David had, according to the documents, 'explained that the newspaper hoped to be able to run a good story on how the government had reacted to enable Zola Budd to come to Britain and "go for gold". He thought that such action would be welcomed by the public and the *Daily Mail* was willing to acknowledge efforts made by ministers to cut through red tape. If ministers failed to do this they could be criticised as he was convinced that Miss Budd's medal-winning potential would otherwise be lost for Britain.'

Apparently, Budd was promised £40,000 in cash from the newspaper, a rent-free home in the UK and a job for her father. After the meeting, MacFarlane contacted Leon Brittan to tell him, 'David English left me in no doubt last night that he is prepared to use all his contacts to secure entry for Zola Budd and we can anticipate a *Daily Mail* crusade.'

Brittan's Home Office was willing to oblige. The Foreign Office was not so sure. Sir Malcolm Rifkind was a junior foreign minister at the time. He expressed his misgivings to his boss Geoffrey Howe. Rifkind wrote, 'This problem gives considerable scope for embarrassment to HMG [Her Majesty's Government] and it will be particularly important to show that we are not singling out the Budd family for any special treatment.' Howe acknowledged the concerns, informing Brittan of his misgivings at affording Budd and her family 'special treatment', and accusing his cabinet colleague of taking decisions 'under pressure from the *Daily Mail*'. He described the whole 'question of sport and South Africa' as a 'political minefield'. Brittan took no notice.

Budd did have a justifiable claim to British citizenship on the basis of her grandfather being born in Britain. The 'special treatment' concerning Geoffrey Howe just seemed to be the haste in which the passport had been issued under pressure from a newspaper supporting his Conservative party and how it would be viewed by the international community. Budd and her family had not shown any interest in taking out British citizenship until the intervention of the *Daily Mail*. As the Home Office weighed up its decision, editor Sir David English's newspaper had flown the Budd family to the UK and hid them away from media rivals in 'safe houses'.

In the event, the granting of citizenship turned out to be a formality despite the reservations of Foreign Office ministers, diplomats in Whitehall and Britain's embassy in South Africa. Brittan dryly observed in a counter note to Howe, 'It would be very difficult to defend a delay which led to her being unable to attempt to qualify for the United Kingdom for this Olympics.' Budd was granted her British citizenship within ten days of her application being sent to the Home Office. A spokesman confirmed to the media the decision was taken personally by Leon Brittan, adding, 'She has been granted registration as a British citizen under the immigration rules. We understand that she is an exceptionally talented athlete who needs to participate in competitive running as soon as possible.' The *Daily Mail* duly acknowledged in its front page coverage how the Home Office had 'cut the red tape'. Budd promised to run her 'heart out for Britain'.

Budd, of course, duly qualified for the Olympics, oblivious of the protests by anti-apartheid campaigners angered by her being allowed to circumvent the ban on South African athletes in international competition. She later admitted she had no idea of the fuss she would cause by going to Great Britain, unaware of the plight of Nelson Mandela, 'ignorant about politics'. One American commentator from *Sports Illustrated* said she looked like a 'frightened fawn'. Frightened or not, her qualifying runs were impressive, smashing the world 2,000 metres record. David Coleman, the BBC's athletics commentator, ranted after the race, 'The message will now be flashed around the world, Zola Budd is no myth.' Given the hype over her wondrous athletic talent and the furore over her arrival in Britain from anti-apartheid activists, nobody was ever under the impression she was a mythical figure.

The Olympic stage was set for a dramatic head to head contest with her childhood heroine Mary Decker. Budd, in fairness, was still not much more than a child despite her impressive athletic exploits. She also, as a student of her sport, recognised that Decker was not the only threat to securing an Olympic gold medal. Romania, a communist, Eastern Bloc nation, defied the Kremlin and sent a team to Los Angeles. One of its star competitors was the world cross-country champion Maricica Puică, a real threat to pre-race favourites Decker and Budd. As it turned out the clash between Decker and Budd would turn out to be one of the most dramatic contests in Olympic history. Sadly, it also turned out to be one between Budd's bare feet and Decker's spikes.

They bumped into each other on the bend going into the home straight at the 1,700-metre mark with no discernible problem. Unfortunately, they clashed again just a few strides later with Decker strewn across the infield, crumpled in a heap and in a flood of tears. She was out of the race but Budd carried on only to be met with a wave of abuse from a hostile American home crowd. She was public enemy number one in the world of sport, not because she came from a rich white family living in apartheid South Africa, but because she had ended the hopes of an All-American heroine to fulfil her dream of winning an Olympic gold. Budd persevered but once she turned into the home straight with just two laps to go Decker was still on the turf next to the track weeping and wailing. Budd slowed, rapidly falling out of contention.

Puică took control of the race, eventually winning gold. The Romanian's nearest challenger was Budd's team-mate Wendy Sly, who won silver for Great Britain. Budd jogged home in seventh place, still being booed by the partisan American crowd and was duly disqualified. Angered by her treatment at the hands of the judges, the British team appealed. Basically, it was not Budd's fault. She had been clipped by Decker's spikes and on reviewing the tape the judges had little choice but to agree and reinstate Budd. Yet the damage to Budd's sporting reputation, already a political and media pawn, was irreparable. Budd's attempts to apologise to Decker were rebuffed by the American. She simply told the South African athlete, 'Don't bother!'

After retiring from athletics, Budd ruefully looked back on the Los Angeles Olympics and concluded that she was 'too young'. She told the *Daily Mirror*, 'I never expected to win the gold. Decker was always the favourite. I thought I'd come away with a silver or bronze medal but that was it. After we tripped, I slowed down. I couldn't bear the sound of booing from the crowd.'

It was a sporting controversy to be debated for years to come with disgruntled Americans, some making death threats, failing to excuse Budd for her role in the demise of Decker. The political controversy failed to go away either. Budd was due to compete in the 1986 Commonwealth Games in Edinburgh, wearing an England vest rather than running for Great Britain. This time African nations were having none of it. It was their chance to make a political statement with Budd once again a political pawn. African athletes had not only competed against her in Los Angeles but also at the World Cross Country Championships in 1985 and 1986 when Budd won gold. If Budd competed on British soil though, they would boycott a multi-event competition already in deep financial trouble.

Under this pressure, the British athletics establishment caved in. Budd was dropped from the England team despite arguably being the world's best female middle-distance runner at the time. This time the supportive British media would not be able to intervene in her favour and by 1988 she appeared to be out of international athletics altogether. After appearing at but not competing in a road race in South Africa, the IAAF, the world governing body for athletics, informed the British Athletics Board of its decision to ban Budd from competition.

A disconsolate Budd returned to South Africa, taking time to write her autobiography. Budd tried to answer her critics, especially those angered by her apparent failure to condemn apartheid in South Africa. Budd wrote, 'My attitude is that, as a sportswoman, I should have the right to pursue my chosen discipline in peace. The Bible says men are born equal before God. I can't reconcile segregation along racial lines with the words of the Bible. As a Christian, I find apartheid intolerable.'

Those noble sentiments were not enough to see her wear a British athletics vest again in international competition. She was only reinstated by the IAAF once Nelson Mandela came out of jail and South Africa's apartheid regime was dismantled. On returning to international competition, Budd decided to compete for the land of her birth, going to the Barcelona Olympics as a South African athlete in 1992. She failed, though, to offer a meaningful challenge for the medals in the women's 3,000 metres.

Even as a veteran athlete, still keen on running and winning races, Budd is dogged by controversy. In June 2014, she was stripped of an over-40s title in South Africa's Comrades Marathon held in Durban for allegedly failing to wear the correct tag displaying her age category. As far as Budd was concerned it summed up her career. She told reporters, 'I won it fair and square. My whole athletics career has been plagued by politics and interference from administrators who are selective and do not apply the rules consistently. It feels like they are targeting me specifically.'

The British government, her 'minders' from the *Daily Mail* and boycotting African nations did not single out Budd for quite the 'special treatment' alluded to by the former UK foreign secretary Geoffrey Howe. She was just another athlete being used by government ministers and vested interest groups to play their own political games.

Indeed, once British tabloid newspapers began using the pejorative term 'plastic Brit' to describe the American-born

Team GB athlete Tiffany Porter, Budd called for politics to be taken out of sport. Her idea was similar to one unsuccessfully proposed by Lord Killanin, the IOC president in the 1970s. She concluded, 'The rules should be changed. Running is a professional sport now. Citizenship shouldn't come into it. I think the best 50 runners in the world should be allowed to take part, regardless of where they were born.'

As a child, running was fun for Zola Budd, just like for many young athletes. As an adult athlete, she suffered heartbreak at times, not least at the Los Angeles Olympics. Remarkably she is still in love with the sport of athletics, despite a career dogged in both political and sporting controversy. Given her travails over the years, Budd's call for nationalism to be taken out of sport might well have some validity.

14

Jackie Robinson: Breaking Baseball's Colour Barrier

SOUTH Africa's government formally imposed apartheid in sport. In the case of the United States, it simply and shockingly tolerated segregation in professional team sport. There were no statutes banning Major League Baseball clubs from employing African American players. The clubs just went ahead with a racist selection policy anyway. No black player was allowed to play for the fabled New York Yankees, the Boston Red Sox or the Chicago Cubs or for that matter the Chicago White Sox. Instead they plied their trade in what were termed 'Negro Leagues'. For Latinos, those with 'lighter' coloured skin were given MLB contracts. Black Latinos signed 'Negro League' contracts. American society tolerated, even embraced, sporting segregation. It did so until a visionary franchise owner and an articulate athlete and civil rights advocate came along. Their names were Branch Rickey, general manager of the Brooklyn Dodgers, and Jackie Robinson, now an American sporting and political icon.

Rickey had sound commercial reasons for breaking down the racial barriers in his sport. He simply wanted the best players available. He also though was more aware of the ethical argument for racial integration. In 1956, still being forced to justify the inclusion of black players in Major League Baseball sides, Rickey cited the political failings of his nation. He commented, 'Of course the Emancipation Proclamation by Lincoln made the southern Negro slave free but it never did make the white man morally free. He remained a slave to his inheritances. And some are, even today.'

Back in the mid-1950s, it was more than 'some' Americans believing in racial segregation as the travails of Jackie Robinson and the civil rights struggles of the sixties was about to show. Baseball, America's pastime, was just one small part of a racially segregated society. Just months after losing the Civil War, American southern states began to work to subtly reverse the result of a military defeat through legislation, enacting laws giving African Americans an inferior status and leaving them subject to segregation and dehumanisation. The US Congress passed a Civil Rights Act in 1875 to try to stop southern states from adopting these 'Black Codes' or as they infamously became known 'Jim Crow Laws', Jim Crow being a late 19th-century pejorative term for an African American. Early attempts to abolish these 'Jim Crow Laws' were thrown out by the Supreme Court in 1883. Yet by 1891 the US Supreme Court had legalised discrimination under the perverse and racist doctrine of black people being considered 'separate but equal'.

Its ruling remained effectively unchallenged until first the case of Brown v The Board of Education in 1954 leading to the 'separate but equal' decision being overturned. Then, president Lyndon B. Johnson successfully put a Civil Rights Act through the American Congress in 1964 and a Voting Rights Act in 1966. Racism was rife not just in late 19th-century but mid-20th-century America. It was a struggle for basic human decency. Rickey needed to display a degree of bravery in standing up to his racist critics. He also needed a black player with similar qualities and more, someone who was not necessarily the best baseball player but was an articulate man of courage and integrity. In Jackie Robinson, Rickey firmly believed he had his man. Rickey, though, did not act alone. His mentors were a couple of sports journalists, Wendell Smith of the *Pittsburgh Courier* and Sam

Lacey of the *Washington Tribune* and *Baltimore Afro-American* newspapers. Their role was vital in ending racial segregation in baseball and it would later to be recognised with a place in the sport's Hall of Fame.

Smith and Lacey long campaigned for racial integration in their columns but their reasonable pleas to Major League franchise owners were ignored. They had tried and failed to persuade rivals the Boston Red Sox and the Boston Braves to sign up a black player, arranging trials for Sam Jethroe, Marvin Williams and Jackie Robinson. There was probably no genuine interest from those franchises in offering any of them a contract. Their trials came about thanks to political pressure with members of the city council making it clear they would not vote to allow matches to be held on a Sunday in Boston unless the Red Sox and Braves agreed to the try-outs.

Undeterred by the Red Sox and the Braves only making a token gesture, Smith and Lacy turned to the more sympathetic ears of Branch Rickey. They decided that the best man to recommend to the Dodgers' general manager was Jackie Robinson. Lacey recalled discussing the decision with his colleague, 'We agreed Jackie wasn't the best player at the time, but was the most suitable player. He had played against white competition, was a college guy. So we went with Jackie. Wendell approached Branch Rickey first and got a promise from Branch to think about it.' He did more than just think about it and Robinson was offered a Brooklyn Dodgers contract. There was just one condition. It was taken for granted by all concerned he would be subjected to racial abuse. Rickey stipulated Robinson must turn the other cheek in the face of abuse and not answer back. Extraordinarily, Robinson agreed.

Jack Roosevelt Robinson was born in Cairo, Georgia, in 1919, the year of baseball's notorious Chicago Black Sox betting scandal. His mother Mallie raised Jack and his four siblings on her own, and they were apparently the only black family in the block. Sport played a central part in his early life. His older brother Matthew excelled in athletics, representing the USA at the Berlin Olympics in 1936 and winning a silver medal in coming second to Jesse Owens in the 200 metres. Jackie also displayed athletic prowess, not just for track and field, but all team sports. His aptitude for American football, basketball and baseball, won him a scholarship to the University College of Los Angeles (UCLA). Unfortunately, he was forced to drop out for financial reasons and signed up with the United States at war to join the American army in 1942, rising through the ranks to become a second lieutenant.

It was in the army that Robinson made his first civil rights stand, a demand to be treated with dignity. At Fort Hood in Texas he was given a court martial for refusing to obey an order to give up his seat and move to the back of a bus; the US army at the time being formally segregated. However, the charge against him was thrown out and Robinson was given an honourable discharge with the order deemed a breach of army regulations. For Robinson, this was an early precursor of what was to come in his professional sports career as he was brought to the attention of Branch Rickey.

Rickey, born in 1881, was old enough to remember black players turning out for the major professional baseball teams in the late 19th century. Moses Fleetwood Walker signed as a catcher for Toledo in a league then known as the American Association. Their rivals in the southern states were unimpressed with some fans sending him death threats. It was not just fans opposed to black players in the major professional leagues as the same applied to white players. In 1887, a white player at Syracuse of the International League refused to pose in a team photograph because of the presence of a black team-mate. It was the cue for International League owners to act and embrace the 'Jim Crow Laws' and segregate baseball.

Black players already signed up for International League teams were allowed to carry on playing but nobody else would be offered a contract. Professional American baseball willingly embraced sporting apartheid. Even in the college system, Rickey witnessed first-hand shocking degrees of racism as coach to the Ohio Wesleyan team. On a trip to Notre Dame College, Rickey recalled one of his black players, Charles Thomas, being denied a hotel room in South Bend. Thomas, according to Rickey, broke down in tears and rubbed his skin, sobbing, 'Damned skin… If only I could rub it off.' As he justified his decision to work towards breaking down baseball's racial barriers, Rickey remarked, 'Whatever mark that incident left on the black boy, it was no more indelible than the impressions made on me. For 40 years I've had recurrent visions of him wiping off his skin.'

Of course his decision to sign a black player in Jackie Robinson for the Brooklyn Dodgers would eventually go down in not just sporting but political history as a moral crusade with America's national pastime slowly but surely rejecting segregation. Yet for Rickey there was also the straightforward business imperative. Rejecting talented black players because of the colour of their skin made little economic sense, especially for the Dodgers, a franchise mired in debt. As cynics might observe, they might also, in the context of 1940s and 50s America, be cheap labour. Rickey wryly commented, 'The greatest untapped reservoir of raw material in the history of the game is the black race.'

He went on to assert, '[They] will make us winners for years to come. And for that I will happily bear being called a bleeding heart and a do-gooder and all that humanitarian rot.' Whether or not it was for humanitarian or commercial reasons, Rickey signed Jackie Robinson as the first black Major League Baseball player since the end of the 19th century. Robinson's record in the army of standing up for his civil and human rights was arguably as much a factor in the signing as his athletic ability. As a second baseman for the Kansas Monarchs in the 'Negro Leagues', Robinson proved he had the ability but just as importantly for Rickey, Smith and Lacey he had the temperament.

At first Robinson went to one of the Dodgers' minor league affiliates, the Montreal Royals, boasting impressive figures of a 0.349 batting average and taking 40 stolen bases. Sending him north of the border to a French-speaking city in Canada was perhaps a shrewd move. Robinson, in wearing the baseball uniform of an all-white team, would not attract quite the same attention in a country not bedevilled by the levels of racism and formal segregation practised by its neighbour. Robinson's Canadian venture paved the way for him to move back to the supposedly politically liberal and enlightened city of New York to play for the Brooklyn Dodgers. Robinson made his debut at Ebbets Field on 15 April 1947. Robert Lipsyte and Pete Levine declared, 'It was the most eagerly anticipated debut in the annals of the national pastime. It represented both the dream and the fear of equal opportunity, and it would change forever the complexion of the game and the attitudes of Americans.'

In the *Pittsburgh Courier*, Robinson's mentor Wendell Smith wrote, 'No player in history has worked harder to become a big leaguer.' He went on with a dramatic flourish, 'If Robinson fails to make the grade, it will be many years before a Negro makes the grade. This is IT!' Plenty of people in baseball wanted him to fail. Not everybody shared Branch Rickey's cosmopolitan dream. Robinson faced resistance from players and fans not only of rival clubs, especially in the American south, but even from within his own club.

Any resistance to Robinson's presence in the Dodgers' line-up from his own team-mates was firmly dealt with by the coach, Leo Durocher. If those players objected to turning out with Robinson then they had better find another club. Crucial support also came from the club captain, Pee Wee Reese. In one game, Robinson was suffering a torrent of abuse from spectators simply because of the colour of his skin. Reese simply responded by walking over to Robinson and putting his arm around him, a symbolic act of defiance and support.

It was in games against the Philadelphia Phillies that Robinson endured the most vile of abuse, not least from the franchise's notoriously racist manager, Ben Chapman. During his playing and managerial career, Chapman, a man from Alabama, became infamous for his anti-Semitic barracking of Jewish players. He also made no apology for hurling abuse at players of Italian origin, notably the New York Yankees' Hall of Famer Joe DiMaggio. Chapman explained in a newspaper interview long after his retirement, 'It was all part of the game back then. You said anything you had to say to get an edge. Believe me, being a southerner, I took a lot of abuse myself when I first played in New York. If you couldn't take it, it was a case of if you can't stand the heat, get out of the kitchen.' Back in 1947, he was keen to inform journalists his team would 'ride' Robinson during the Phillies' visit to Brooklyn. The extent to which they did so shocked even members of baseball's establishment, some of whom had been reluctant to embrace Rickey's 'great experiment' in ending the sport's racial segregation.

Robinson suffered a barrage of abuse from the Phillies' players. One of them told him 'to go back to the cotton fields'. Another allegedly yelled out from the bench, 'When are you going back to the jungle, black boy?' Robinson, heeding Rickey's advice, ignored the taunts though he later recalled, 'I wanted to grab those white sons of bitches and smash their teeth in with my despised black fist.' For their part, the baseball commissioner A.B. 'Happy' Chandler and Ford Frick, the National League president, warned Chapman about his future behaviour, telling him to cut out the racial abuse. Chapman had become an embarrassment to Major League Baseball. As far as the Phillies hierarchy was concerned the way to stop their manager and players from abusing Robinson was to try to stop the Dodgers' second baseman from travelling to Philadelphia for the return series in May 1947. The historic city of Philadelphia is home to the United States' Liberty Bell, the venue for the signing of the Declaration of Independence. In the 1940s it was also home to racists intent on dehumanising people with black skin. Just to make the point, Phillies general manager Herb Pennock told Rickey not to bring Robinson because the city was 'not just ready for that sort of thing'. Pennock was right.

The Benjamin Franklin Hotel informed the Dodgers it would not offer a room to Robinson. Sadly this was a regular occurrence for Robinson and the Dodgers on away trips, especially in segregated southern states. On this occasion the racist snub came in one of the more supposedly liberal northern states, Pennsylvania. Dodgers officials eventually found a hotel. The Phillies and the Dodgers played a four-game series, thankfully without incident. Even Chapman realised he and his players had gone too far in their baiting of Robinson back in Brooklyn. Either that or they did not want to upset the bosses of Major League Baseball who were left embarrassed by the Phillies' more than dubious antics.

It was not just the Phillies who forced the MLB president to intervene on behalf of Robinson and the Dodgers in his inaugural season. The St Louis Cardinals threatened to boycott the Dodgers simply because they had the 'audacity' to field a black player. President Ford Frick told the Cardinals that if any player refused to take to the field against the Dodgers he would be suspended. Frick tersely warned all franchises and players, 'I don't care if it wrecks the league for five years.' Instead of boycotting the game or indulging alone in verbal abuse, two Cardinals players, Enos Slaughter and Joe Garagiola, resorted to violence, maliciously spiking Robinson as he slid in on base. No disciplinary action was taken against them. Slaughter later dismissed allegations his behaviour was racially motivated, claiming, 'There's been a hell of a lot of stuff written on that because I was a Southern boy. It's just a lot of baloney.'

For all the abuse, snide acts of violence on the field of play and death threats against him and his family, Robinson set about sealing his reputation as one of the greats of baseball, not just as a civil rights pioneer. As the Dodgers won the National League title he hit 12 home runs and led the league in the number of bases stolen. Thanks to Robinson's presence in the Dodgers' team, another milestone in the cause of desegregating baseball was reached with a black player taking part in the World Series for the first time in the sport's history. Sadly for Robinson, the Dodgers lost the series 4-3 to the New York Yankees. He was named 1947's Rookie of the Year and two years later took the accolade of the National League's Most Valuable Player. His aggressive style of play won over sceptical critics and his career blossomed despite still being subjected to racial abuse. Even though Rickey warned him not to respond to the insults, Robinson began to become a vocal advocate of civil rights, accusing the New York Yankees in 1952 of being a racist club for failing to hire black players, five years after he had first appeared on a Major League Baseball diamond. His vocal advocacy of civil rights though was not enough to avoid him being brought into conflict with those in the African American community, who feared he was being manipulated by the white establishment.

After being summoned before the House of Representatives' Un-American Activities Committee (HUAC) to give testimony against singer Paul Robeson, he felt he had no choice but to appear. He delivered powerful political testimony with Rickey's co-operation. Robeson was being investigated because of his advocacy of socialism in his quest for civil rights, the desegregation of baseball being one of the Hollywood star's cause celebres. His comments allegedly asserting that black

Americans would never fight against the Soviet Union brought him to the attention of the committee in its witch-hunt against alleged communist sympathisers with Robeson, in the members' eyes, being one of them. In fairness it was not just committee members with a dubious record in race relations who were quick to castigate Robeson for his outspoken comments at the World Congress of Partisans in Paris. Robeson stated, 'It is unthinkable that "American Negroes" would go to war on behalf of those who have oppressed us for generations against the Soviet Union which in one generation has raised our people for full human dignity.'

Not only was Robeson condemned by the 'white' press for his incendiary comments but leading black civil rights leaders of the time also had their say. The Washington politicians, including a few racist bigots, eyed their prey in Robeson. They called for Robinson, by then the most prominent black person in American life, as a 'friendly' witness to rebut Robeson's claims.

Robinson, who in his autobiography regretted testifying before the committee, told members, 'I don't pretend to be any expert on communism or any other kind of a politicalism.' He added that he was 'an expert at being a coloured American' and reminded members he was one of only seven African American Major League Baseball players out of a total of 400. As far as communist conspiracies were concerned Robinson offered this view, 'The white public should start toward real understanding by appreciating that every single Negro who is worth his salt is going to resent any kind of slurs and discrimination because of his race, and he is going to use every bit of intelligence such as he has to stop it. This has got absolutely nothing to do with what Communists may or may not be trying to do.

'And one other thing the American public ought to understand, if we are to make progress in this matter: The fact that it is a Communist who denounces injustice in the courts, police brutality, and lynching when it happens doesn't change the truth of his charges. Just because Communists kick up a big fuss over racial discrimination when it suits their purposes, a lot of people try to pretend that the whole issue is a creation of Communist imagination. But they are not fooling anyone with this kind of pretence, and talk about "Communists stirring up Negroes to protest" only makes present misunderstanding worse than ever. Negroes were stirred up long before there was a Communist Party, and they'll stay stirred up long after the party has disappeared – unless Jim Crow has disappeared by then as well.'

Robinson made it clear to the Congress committee members that he wanted 'Jim Crow' wiped out from American sport altogether, not just baseball. He concluded his testimony with the following comments on being an American patriot, 'That doesn't mean that we're going to stop fighting race discrimination in this country until we've got it licked. It means that we're going to fight all the harder because our stake in the future is so big. We can fight our fight without the Communists and we don't want their help.'

For the most part Robinson's testimony was received positively, though some black newspapers accused him of being naïve for going before the committee and testifying, if not directly, ostensibly against Paul Robeson. One writer in Pittsburgh went as far as calling him an establishment 'stooge'. Those journals opposed to Robinson ostensibly giving testimony against Robeson had a couple of complaints. Firstly they objected to him humouring men they considered racist. This committee, set up to investigate un-American activities, failed to investigate the Klu Klux Klan. It had absolutely no inclination to do so. As one black media commentator of the day put it, 'How come your committee can investigate everything from Reds [Communists] to Second Basemen and can't investigate the Klu Klux Klan?' The clear suspicion on their part was the Klan was not being investigated because some members of the committee were known racists, including Martin Dies (Texas) and John Rankin (Mississippi). Secondly, there was the simple reason of Paul Robeson being one of their own, a black sports and showbiz star beyond reproach.

Robinson, as the highest-profile black sports star of his generation, did receive a sympathetic appraisal from other sections of the American black media. Yet even then with the positive coverage of Robinson's testimony, the difference in emphasis in the reporting of his appearance in mainstream journals and black newspapers was telling. Black media outlets concentrated on Robinson's advocacy of civil rights before the committee while establishment writers focused on any criticism of Paul Robeson. From the *Chicago Tribune* newspaper came the banner headline 'Robeson silly, Jackie Robinson tells red quiz'. The *Philadelphia Inquirer* offered 'Dodger star raps Robeson'. The *Washington Post* praised Robinson and accused Robeson of peddling 'insulting libels'. It was all about the Cold War fear of 'Reds under the beds'.

For black community newspapers, the enemies within American society were those maintaining racial division, so their emphasis was on Robinson's testimony promoting civil and human rights. The *Philadelphia Afro-American* headlined 'Lynchers our chief enemy Jackie tells "Red" probers', dismissing the hearings as a witch-hunt. For all the support in some sections of the African American community, his reputation at the time suffered damage in others for appearing on Capitol Hill to testify against Robeson.

It was only temporary damage. His place in American history was assured for his exploits on the baseball diamond and advocacy of civil rights. Indeed he offered his own regrets about going before HUAC in his autobiography, 'I have grown wiser and closer to painful truths about America's destructiveness. And I do have increased respect for Paul Robeson who over a span of that 20 years, sacrificed himself, his career, and the wealth and comfort he once enjoyed because, I believe, he was sincerely trying to help his people.'

Fortunately, Robinson was able to put the political controversy behind him to concentrate on sport. His 'revenge' over the New York Yankees came in 1955 as the Dodgers finally beat the most successful team in baseball history to win the World Series. Up until then, there had been a succession of glorious failures in the Dodgers' quest for a title, losing out to the New York Giants in National League campaigns or eventually to the Yankees in the World Series. Up until then Robinson and his Dodgers had lost in four World Series attempts against the Yankees. This time around they won 4-3, though Robinson was left out of the side for the clinching seventh game.

A year later Robinson was part of another National League pennant-winning Dodgers team but his career was coming to an end and he was traded to the New York Giants at the end of the season. He never played for them, instead retiring from the sport with his legacy etched into the history books. Even then there was the whiff of controversy with some baseball writers upset by his failure to tip them off about his plans to end his playing career. They also questioned his assertion he planned to retire before being traded by the Dodgers to the Giants rather than after the deal. They claimed the opposite was the case and he had done the Dodgers a disservice.

But perhaps they were just miffed at Robinson's decision to give the news of his retirement to *Look* magazine. In an article entitled 'Why I'm quitting baseball' Robinson reflected on his spat with Robeson, 'I don't regret any part of the last ten years. There's no reason why I should. Because of baseball I met a man like Branch Rickey and was given the opportunity to break the major-league colour line. Because of baseball, I was able to speak on behalf of Negro-Americans before the House of Un-American Activities Committee and rebuke Paul Robeson for saying most of us Negroes would not fight for our country in a war against Russia.'

The rapprochement with Robeson would come later although Robinson, a politically conservative supporter of future Republican president Richard Nixon, never shared the singer's liberal views on US foreign policy. As for his reasons for quitting and taking up the offer of a job with a restaurant chain, Robinson explained, 'Baseball has been awfully good to me. My memories are all good… I'm quitting baseball for good and there shouldn't be any mystery about my reasons. I am 38 years old with a family to support. I've got to think of the future and our security… After you've reached your peak there's no sentiment in baseball. You start slipping and pretty soon they're moving you around like a used car. You have no control over what happens to you. I didn't want that.'

Robinson's formal place in sporting history was sealed by his induction into baseball's Hall of Fame in 1962. For the remainder of his life he kept up the campaign for greater integration in sport and society in general, an advocate for baseball and other sporting disciplines bringing people together rather than setting them apart. In looking back on his life and sporting career he was quoted as saying, 'A life is not important except in the impact it has on other lives.' He might well have found, as he mentioned to the members of Congress he met in the 1940s, that it wasn't 'exactly pleasant to get involved in a political dispute'. Frankly those politicians were not interested in reforming a racially divided society. In breaking baseball's colour barrier he became an iconic figure in something far more important than a mere 'political dispute'; the fight for basic human decency.

15

Fight of the Century: Joe Louis v Max Schmeling

ONE was hailed an American hero, the other Adolf Hitler's 'pet'. Their meeting in a boxing ring was billed as the 'Fight of the Century' and a clash between the flag-bearer for freedom and democracy in one corner and the embodiment of the Nazi doctrine of Aryan supremacy in the other. At least that's how historians, academics and contemporary journalists liked to portray the rematch of Joe Louis, the 'Brown Bomber', and the German former world champion Max Schmeling in June 1938 with the world on the brink of war. Yet the political context of this fight appears far murkier than this simplistic analysis suggests; a curious consensus between Nazi propagandists and writers in the free press of a democratic American nation.

There's no hard evidence that Schmeling was a Nazi. Yet he did inadvertently serve as a totem for Hitler and Goebbels. As for the United States being the 'land of the free', American society deemed Joe Louis as a black man able to box professionally but not to forge an alternative lucrative career in Major League Baseball or the National Football League. No blacks needed to apply for the elite clubs of those sports. Indeed, in certain southern states, bouts between black and white fighters were illegal. Louis was representing 'Jim Crow' America, a segregated country bitterly divided along racial lines. But the impending fight in the summer of 1938 managed to unite black and white Americans in support of the cotton picker's son from Alabama. Schmeling was more than just an opponent for the United States' greatest boxer of his era. He was the enemy.

Louis and Schmeling first met in the ring at Yankee Stadium in the Bronx borough of New York City on 19 June 1936. Louis was expected to win. He expected to win. Bookies were offering generous odds of 10/1 for Schmeling to win. Yet Schmeling went into the ring feeling optimistic, the former world champion claiming he had spotted a 'weakness', a tendency on Louis's part to hold his left hand too low.

The first three rounds of the fight were uneventful and then in the fourth Schmeling struck. He countered with his right then followed up with another right to send Louis crashing to the canvas. Louis never recovered with Schmeling being dominant for the rest of the fight, eventually knocking out his opponent in the 12th round. For Louis, it was the first and quite possibly the most painful defeat of his career, a battering. He recalled, 'I had taken such a terrible beating that I just couldn't go up.'

It later emerged from the American's own admission he had not prepared for the fight properly. There was the distraction of his tangled personal life at the time, splitting up with his mistress, the Norwegian film star and Olympic ice skating gold medallist Sonja Henie, but still cheating on his wife with a string of other women. More importantly, Louis simply didn't train properly. Instead he headed off to the golf course. He later explained, 'Instead of boxing six rounds, I'd box three. Punch the bag one round instead of two. I had this idea that I was going to do a lot of hard work for nothing. I thought that I could name the round that I would knock Schmeling out.' He was wrong. He had underestimated Schmeling. It was a complacent mistake he was not likely to repeat.

On his return to Germany, Schmeling was feted by an ecstatic Nazi regime, flying back across the Atlantic aboard the Hindenburg airship as a guest of honour. As he boarded the vessel Schmeling apparently told German reporters, 'At this moment I have to tell Germany, I have to report to the Fuehrer in particular, that the thoughts of all my countrymen were with me in this fight; that the Fuehrer and his faithful people were thinking of me. This thought gave me the strength to succeed in this fight. It gave me the courage and the endurance to win this victory for Germany's colours.' It was just a couple of months before the Berlin Olympics and as far as Hitler, Goebbels and their cronies were concerned they had already enjoyed a sporting propaganda victory. A Nazi magazine, *Das Schwarze Korps*, commented, 'Schmeling's victory was not only sport. It was a question of prestige for our race.'

Goebbels resorted, of course, to overtly racist terms to write in his diary, 'In round 12, Schmeling knocked out the Negro; fantastic, a dramatic, thrilling fight. Schmeling fought for Germany and won. The white man prevailed over the black, and the white man was German.' The Nazi propaganda chief immediately commissioned a film of the fight to be shown in German cinemas as part of the build-up to the forthcoming 1936 Olympics entitled *Max Schmeling's Sieg – Ein Deutscher* or in English, *Max Schmeling's Victory – a German Victory*. More than three million Germans went to the cinema to watch the film and were left in no doubt about what it meant to a delighted Nazi regime.

Despite this shock defeat, the boxing career of Joe Louis continued to flourish uninterrupted. Just a year after losing to Schmeling, Louis took on the world heavyweight champion James J. Braddock in Chicago, knocking him out in the eighth round. Braddock had been scheduled to fight Schmeling but the bout was cancelled. American promoters possibly reasoned that Braddock was vulnerable to Schmeling. They did not want to take the risk of the world title making its way back across the Atlantic to Germany for another Nazi propaganda victory. As far as Louis was concerned though, he could not be considered the true champion of the world until he avenged his 1936 defeat to the German boxer. Louis bluntly told reporters covering his victory over Braddock, 'I don't want nobody to call me champ until I beat Schmeling.' There would have to be a rematch. Louis demanded the fight and it was duly arranged for 22 June 1938, the two men meeting once again in Yankee Stadium.

As Schmeling arrived in New York he was met with a tide of hostility, with his hotel being picketed by protestors chanting 'Nazi, Nazi'. His pleas of it just being 'another fight' and of him being a 'fighter, not a politician' were ignored by the US media. It hardly helped that he sipped tea with Adolf Hitler just before leaving Germany for New York. Schmeling later explained in his autobiography, 'Hitler invited me for lunch. I went – I had to go.' It didn't help either that there was allegedly a Nazi propagandist in his entourage spewing out poison for the American media to spread. He told them it was impossible for a black man to beat Schmeling and the prize money from the fight would be used to build German tanks, already being mobilised for the Nazis' annexation of Czechoslovakia and Austria. There were also claims in US newspapers of Hitler sending bouquets of flowers bedecked with swastika ribbons.

The novelist Richard Wright dubbed Schmeling 'Hitler's pet' and added for good measure he 'looked like a soft piece of molasses candy left out in the sun'. Just to add to the political fever gripping a sports event, or 'just another fight' as Schmeling protested, president Franklin D Roosevelt invited Louis to the White House for a pep talk. The *New York Times* reported that Roosevelt told him, 'Joe, we need muscles like yours to beat Germany.' In the event, the United States would not even enter the war against Germany when it broke out in Europe just over a year later. It seemed easier in the 1930s for the USA to focus on a boxing match. Lewis ruefully recalled in his autobiography, 'I knew I had to get Schmeling good. I had my own personal reasons [after his bruising defeat to the German in 1936] and the whole damned country was depending on me.'

More than 70,000 fight fans packed into Yankee Stadium. Tens of millions more were listening on the radio on both sides of the Atlantic. As Schmeling entered the ring, he was pelted with missiles by a crowd already worked up into a frenzy. The action in the ring did not last long as from the opening bell Louis pounced, putting Schmeling immediately on the defensive and pinning him against the ropes. At one point the German fighter had to hang on to the ropes to steady himself. Louis responded by unleashing a barrage of punches to the head, then following up with a body shot which appeared to stun Schmeling. It was later claimed the body shot was an illegal punch to the kidneys.

As Schmeling grimly used the ropes as a prop, a Louis right body shot left his knees buckling, forcing referee Arthur Donovan to intervene. He gave Schmeling a short count but allowed the fight to continue. It did not last much longer. Another barrage of Louis punches sent Schmeling crashing to the canvas. He somehow got to his feet as the referee gave him another count. Once again the fight resumed but Schmeling crumpled to the canvas thanks to another vicious combination of punches from Louis. The German's corner, led by his Jewish-American manager Joe Jacobs, had seen enough and threw in the towel. The fight lasted just 124 seconds and Schmeling threw just two punches. He had not just been defeated, he had been humiliated. This time there would be no hero's reception from the Nazis on his return to Germany. His career as a boxer was effectively over with the war in which Louis and Schmeling would both serve looming.

American boxing journalists and historians delivered their political verdict on the fight as being a knockout blow delivered by the might of a free and democratic United States against the tyranny of Nazi Germany. New York boxing writer Heywood Broun gave his patriotic and arguably jingoistic assessment, 'One hundred years from now, some historian may theorise, in a footnote at least, that the decline of Nazi prestige began with a left hook delivered by a former unskilled automobile worker who had never studied the policies of Neville Chamberlain and had no opinion whatsoever in regard to the situation in Czechoslovakia.'

As far as boxing historian William Dettloff was concerned, 'The vertebrae that were cracked in Schmeling's spine and that kept him in the hospital afterward represented a warning to the rest of the world of America's might and its will. On that night, Joe Louis was America, whether or not he saw it that way or saw himself as the icon he was. All that mattered was the way America saw him. It's how history sees him.' Yet all this rhetoric ignores the reality of Schmeling never being a Nazi, though admittedly something of a reluctant propaganda puppet of

Hitler, and Louis as an African American in 'Jim Crow America'. He lived in a society with blatant officially endorsed racism and segregation. Louis in such a context was never truly a 'free' man.

As much as he was left devastated by the defeat at the time, Schmeling later saw it as some sort of blessed relief. He reflected in his autobiography, 'Every defeat has its good side. A victory over Joe Louis would perhaps have made me the toast of the Third Reich.' It was a theme he returned to in an interview in 1975, 'Looking back, I'm almost happy I lost that fight. Just imagine if I would have come back to Germany with a victory. I had nothing to do with the Nazis, but they would have given me a medal. After the war I might have been considered a war criminal.'

After serving in a parachute regiment of the German army during the Second World War, Schmeling came to the attention of British military investigators looking into war crimes. The former champion was cleared of any wrongdoing. For American writers and until his defeat to Louis in 1938, and for Hitler and Goebbels also, Schmeling was the embodiment of Nazism. Yet he never joined the Nazis, he kept his Jewish manager Joe Jacobs despite pressure to dump him, and it later emerged that he helped to save two Jewish brothers from the concentration camps. On the night of 9 November 1938 Nazi thugs raided Jewish homes, businesses and synagogues on Kristallnacht, ransacking and destroying them. Schmeling hid Henri and Werner Lewin in his Berlin apartment until he was able to find a way to make sure they were given a safe passage to the United States.

Henri Lewin gave his account in an interview for the *Jewish Bulletin of Northern California*. Reflecting on the stubborn insistence of Schmeling's critics labelling him a Nazi, Henri said, 'He risked his life for us; our lives weren't worth a penny. I said, "If this is a Nazi, he's a good Nazi, but I want you to know one thing: I wouldn't be sitting here today if it wasn't for this Nazi." For risking his own life by saving the two boys, Schmeling was honoured by the International Raoul Wallenberg Foundation, a campaign group set up to honour those who helped Holocaust survivors. In its obituary of the German boxer it reflected, 'Memory is unkind to many, but to Max Schmeling more than most.' He turned down the chance to be honoured publicly by the Foundation and instead his medal and certificate recognising his work was popped in the post.

Louis was more than aware of the political significance. In his own autobiography he wrote, 'To me and Schmeling, it was just best man wins, but we both knew what was at stake. To the world, Schmeling's defeat foretold of things to come for Nazi Germany.' Just a couple of years after the infamous Berlin Olympics, yet again a couple of athletes had become unwitting political pawns. The debate among sports historians is of just how much Schmeling, the boxer who dined with Adolf Hitler, was an unwitting pawn or was willing to be promoted as the very symbol of Aryan supremacy. His actions in saving Jewish brothers from Nazi thugs suggest the former rather than the latter.

Once Louis's boxing career was finished the American nation did little to help this pugilist, a man once deemed by a fawning American media as a fighter for the virtues of freedom and democracy. He became destitute needing handouts from his German friend, one Max Schmeling. Ironically for all the opprobrium heaped upon him before and after their rematch in Yankee Stadium, Schmeling earned a fortune in the post-war years as a businessman backed by the very symbol of American capitalism, Coca-Cola. The money allowed him to pay for Louis's funeral. The two were enemies in the boxing ring but that's where the enmity ended. For those with different agendas, political rather than sporting, it was quite a different story in the summer of 1938 as Europe fell under the Nazi jackboot and the world resigned itself to the prospect of war.

16

A Gaelic Game and the Garrison Game

FANS gathering at any great sporting occasion go along with a sense of anticipation, perhaps among the more nervous among them apprehension. Many quite often savour the tension. I stood in the bowels of the upper tier of Croke Park in Dublin on 21 February 2007 in such an atmosphere, yet the focus was not on the game of rugby about to unfold on the pitch.

Quite ludicrously it was on the playing of an anthem. England's rugby union team was lining up to play Ireland in the home of Gaelic sport, the hallowed ground of Irish nationalism and the struggle for independence from British rule. Croke Park had been the scene of a massacre of civilians by British Crown Forces in 1920. Almost 70 years later around 80,000 people, the vast majority Irish, stood to attention for the playing of England's anthem, 'God Save the Queen'. For fervent nationalists and republicans, the rendition of an anthem praising the Queen of England amounted to a gross insult to those who died at the hands of men in the service of her grandfather. It was something not to be countenanced. As far as they were concerned, even the playing of rugby in Croke Park, a British imperial sport in their opinion, amounted to a crime against the Irish state.

For days before the game British and Irish newspapers speculated about the reception the crowd would give to the English team and the playing of 'God Save the Queen'. Forget what might happen during the course of the game. What will the crowd do? Will they boo? Will they refuse to stand for 'God Save the Queen' in an act of disrespect? Will many of the Irish supporters refuse to enter the stadium until the last strains of the British anthem had been played by the combined bands of the Republic of Ireland's police service, An Garda Siochana, and the Irish army?

In the event the crowd stood in dignified silence, politely applauded then belted out the two anthems for an all-Ireland rugby team, players drawn from the Republic of Ireland and British-ruled Northern Ireland. Sport and politics mixed. They did not clash. When it came to Anglo-Irish political tensions, the Irish public demonstrated to the watching world they had moved on. Times had changed. This was modern Ireland, a confident vibrant nation running its own affairs, and its rugby team was about to thump England in a bone-crunching exhibition of sport.

For the benefit of the English players, the Rugby Football Union had taken the precaution of asking a member of staff to give them a lesson in politics. It might seem an extraordinary step yet it was deemed prudent to ask the RFU's National Academy manager Conor O'Shea, a former Irish international, to inform young Englishmen, unaware of the travails of the Irish struggle for independence, of the context of a game being played in the home of Gaelic sport. To a minority of followers of the Gaelic Athletic Association (GAA), rugby along with association football, cricket and hockey are dismissed as 'garrison sports', athletic endeavours brought to Ireland by British imperial rulers backed by members of Her Majesty's armed forces in keeping the Irish people under subjugation. Playing such sports in Croke Park amounted to sacrilege in their view.

It proved deeply controversial for the GAA to open its doors to these 'garrison sports' while the Irish Rugby Football Union redeveloped its own ground at Lansdowne Road in Dublin. Even as rugby fans strode into Croke Park, pockets of Republican activists, mostly from Sinn Fein, stood outside to vent their feelings. One teenager stood in the green and white hooped shirt of the Glaswegian soccer team, Celtic, with a banner reading 'No Foreign Sports'. The irony of such an incongruous and frankly deeply ignorant act was not lost on those in favour of welcoming both rugby and soccer to Croke Park. It demonstrated an astonishing lack of political sophistication.

Gaelic sport and the GAA, for all its protestations to the contrary, had always being inextricably linked to politics in the guise of Irish Nationalism and also linked to religion in the guise of the Roman Catholic Church. Croke Park itself had been named after a Catholic archbishop, Thomas Croke, the founding patron of the Gaelic Athletic Association. In his acceptance letter after being invited by GAA founders to take up the post, Archbishop Croke summed up the organisation's aims as being to promote Irish native sport and eradicate the playing of pastimes from Great Britain. He wrote:

> To Mr Michael Cusack, Honorary Secretary of the Gaelic Athletic Association. The Palace, Thurles, 18 December 1884.
>
> My dear Sir — I beg to acknowledge the receipt of your communication inviting me to become a patron of the 'Gaelic Athletic Association', of which you are, it appears, the honourable secretary, I accede to your request with the utmost pleasure. One of the most painful, let me assure you, and, at the same time, one of the most frequently recurring reflections that, as an Irishman, I am compelled to make in connection with the present aspect of things in this country, is derived from the ugly and irritating fact that we are daily importing from England not only her manufactured goods, which we cannot help doing, since she has practically strangled our own manufacturing appliances, but, together with her fashions, her accent, her vicious literature, her music, her dances, and her manifold mannerisms, her games also and her pastimes, to the utter discredit of our own grand national sports, and to the sore humiliation, as I believe, of every genuine son and daughter of the old land.

In fairness, the Archbishop of Cashel, in his highly political and at times xenophobic rant, did describe sports such as cricket and lawn tennis as 'excellent in their own way'. There were also genuine fears from Croke and the other founding fathers of the GAA of the growing popularity of cricket threatening to consign the sport of hurling to the annals of ancient history. His references to sport and healthy pastimes, however, were not the most striking aspects of this letter. It was its brazenly political nature from a senior Catholic churchman. At one point he even refers to his fears of the 'bloody' red of England being put above the 'green' of Ireland. His letter to Michael Cusack served as a manifesto for politically motivated followers of Gaelic sport for more than a century, right to the point of Ireland and England playing rugby at Croke Park in the early 21st century. As far as the more extreme zealots were concerned, any sport thought up by the public schoolboys of Victorian England was the work of the devil; pastimes to avoid at all costs even in more enlightened and friendlier times. Various 'bans' and sanctions were imposed to protect the integrity of Gaelic sport. Members of the British armed forced were banned from participating. GAA members were banned from attending 'foreign' sports, specifically English sports such as cricket, rugby and football. GAA grounds were also banned under the organisation's Rule 42 from staging rugby and association football.

This block was temporarily lifted to allow the Irish national rugby and football teams to play at Croke Park. For the sports to be played on the site of a massacre, almost a sporting and political shrine for Irish Republicans, only added to their sense of pain and expressions of shame.

In the decades after the GAA's foundation, hurling and its own code of football across Ireland grew in popularity with the GAA immersing itself in the life of the nation. Despite suspicions to the contrary from British rulers of Ireland, Michael Cusack consistently denied that it was as much a political body as a sporting organisation. It hardly helped in the campaign to present the GAA as an apolitical organisation for it to split among political lines in its early years threatening the very existence of the sports it was trying to promote. Archbishop Croke was forced to intervene to bring the warring political factions together, those promoting peaceful or 'constitutional' nationalism and those advocating 'advanced' nationalism or to put it bluntly, violence. Croke succeeded but a pattern was set with the GAA unable and indeed unwilling to distance itself from the wider struggle for Irish independence; a stance culminating in the tragedy of 'Bloody Sunday' on 21 November 1920, an event with a significant impact on the prosecution of the Irish war of independence and eventual partition of Ireland.

Publically, the British government of David Lloyd George insisted that the 1920s rebellion in Ireland was being brought under control. Lloyd George referred to the IRA as a 'small murder gang' and just a fortnight before the fateful events on Bloody Sunday he boasted, 'We have murder by the throat.' The reality was different. Britain was losing control of its troublesome neighbour. Crucially the British military's High Command based at Dublin Castle was in a mess, its intelligence services severely compromised by the IRA's own spy network under the command of Michael Collins. To counter his activities the British put a bounty on his head of £20,000 for his capture, dead or alive. The tactic failed and he was never betrayed. Given a series of IRA successes, the British government decided to call up its most experienced intelligence officers, men based at the time in Cairo, to deal with Collins and his followers. After some close shaves, coming close to capture, Collins decided to act against these men, the so-called Cairo Gang. He ordered their assassination on the night of Saturday 19 November. What turned out to be a ruthless operation was largely carried out in the early hours of the following morning.

Historians to this day dispute the effectiveness of Collins's operation against the Cairo Gang; a blood-letting spree with the danger of turning Irish public opinion against the IRA out of revulsion for their activities. The eventual cack-handed and bloody British backlash in response to Collins's activities ensured the opposite. Collins had a list of 35 'targets'. In the event once his men had gone about their work 14 members of the British armed forces and alleged informers were dead, shot and killed in supposedly safe houses and hotels. It is now believed that at least two or those victims may have had nothing to with British intelligence. One was an army veteran who just happened to be visiting Dublin to buy horses for a polo club and opted to stay at the Gresham Hotel on O'Connell Street.

The manager, James Doyle, later revealed that he discussed the death of Captain McCormack with Michael Collins. Doyle, who got to know Collins reasonably well as he stayed often at his hotel during the period of negotiations for a peace treaty between Britain and Ireland, stated in his evidence to the Irish Bureau of Military History, 'McCormack had been staying here since September and had made purchases of race horses. He had booked his passage back to Egypt for December by the Holt Line. Although he had been a veterinary surgeon in the British Army there would appear to have been grave doubt to his being associated with British intelligence. While he was here I never saw him receiving any guests. He slept well into the afternoon and only got up early when a race meeting was on. When I found him in his room "Irish Field" was lying beside him. I mentioned to Collins after the truce that there was grave doubt as to Captain McCormack being a British agent. He said that he would make inquiries into the matter, but after this the matter was never referred to again.'

Another of Doyle's guests at the Gresham, Alan Wilde, was also shot dead in his room. Yet he was later dismissed by former IRA men as something of an 'oddball civilian' who was not a threat to IRA operations. Collins, for all the bloodshed with the likes of Doyle as his 'eyes and ears' suggesting he had targeted the wrong men, may also have been disappointed not all the agents he believed to belong to the Cairo Gang had been found.

Christopher 'Todd' Andrews, later to become the chairman of the Irish transport company CIE, was a member of Collins's assassination squad. He recalled both the ruthless nature of events of Bloody Sunday and some of the bungling of his comrades. His mission was to kill British army officer Captain William Noble at his lodgings in Ranelagh. Andrews admitted to feeling a sense of unease, recalling, 'Killing a man in cold blood was alien to our ideas of how a war should be conducted.' Once it turned out there was only a half-naked woman in Noble's bedroom when he burst in, Andrews revealed later years he did not know whether to feel 'glad or sorry' that the British army man was not there. Andrews also criticised some of his colleagues, accusing them of being no better than the British 'Black and Tans' they so despised. As for the success of the operation, he summed it up in these words, 'The fact is that the majority of the IRA raids were abortive. The men sought were not in their digs or in several cases, the men looking for them bungled their jobs.'

Nevertheless 14 men were dead and dying on the morning of Sunday 20 November 1920 and the British establishment based at Dublin Castle was in full panic. Retaliation seemed inevitable. It came at Croke Park, less than 24 hours after Michael Collins's men began setting about their gruesome task.

Given Collins was intent on carrying out the attacks on British army intelligence officers on the night of Saturday 20 November it might have been prudent for the IRA to tip off their friends at the GAA. Then again, given members of the GAA were also volunteers for the IRA, they might not have needed tipping off and just postponed the planned game of Gaelic Football at Croke Park in advance of Collins's operation. There was always going to be the danger of the British targeting the game in revenge for the IRA assassination spree. However, to have called off the game might have compromised Collins's mission; a warning to the British something was afoot.

Once the attacks had been carried out and word went around Dublin of the activities of Collins's men, GAA president Jim Nowlan met with fellow committee men Luke O'Toole, Dan McCarthy and the Leinster GAA secretary John Shouldice, who were all prominent Sinn Fein sympathisers with strong links to the IRA. Nowlan had been jailed by the British shortly after the Easter Rising of 1916, despite there having been no evidence that he actually took part. They considered calling off the match between Tipperary and Dublin after being urged to do so by three members of the IRA, Sean Russell, Tom Kilcoyne and Harry Colley. They warned through their intelligence contacts that a raid on Croke Park was imminent.

Colley gave his account of their attempts to call off the match in an interview about his time in the IRA with the Irish Bureau of Military History in September 1957, almost four decades after the tragic events of Bloody Sunday. He said that at the time he felt 'downhearted' as the game went ahead, the

GAA officials stubbornly ignoring their pleas to call it off. Colley, in his evidence, referred to Sean Russell doing most of the talking as the senior IRA officer, 'He [Russell] appealed to those officials to close the gates and stop any more people from entering Croke Park. He pointed out what an appalling thing it would be if the enemy opened fire with machine guns on that crowd. The two officials [John Shouldice and Luke O'Toole] pointed out the difficulty of getting the crowd out now, that they would probably demand their money back, and that if an announcement was publicly made it might lead to panic and death in another form.'

One problem the GAA had for the game was that there were no stewards. Russell's IRA battalion was supposed to be providing the stewards for the game but they were withdrawn because of the fear of British reprisals following the attacks on the Cairo Gang. They didn't turn up but thousands of everyday Dubliners were flocking to the ground oblivious of any impending danger. O'Toole, in particular, did not want to induce panic with so many people already present in the ground.

Shouldice gave another reason for pressing ahead with the game in his own interview for the Irish Bureau of Military History in 1952. It was perhaps complacency, discounting a violent British reprisal.

Shouldice, who organised the match to raise money for the families of Irish Republican prisoners being held in British jails, recalled, 'About an hour before the game started, officers from the Dublin Brigade came to the grounds and advised us not to proceed with the match as they had reason to know that a raid would take place on the grounds. I consulted with GAA officials present. They considered that if we called it off the GAA would appear to be identified with what had happened the previous night.

'Raids anyway were common but we never anticipated such a bloody raid. Though anxious about its outcome we decided to carry on.' Despite the IRA warning of the possibility of British troops firing on the crowd, GAA officials decided to ignore Russell, Colley and Kilcoyne and go ahead with the game anyway. Surely, Shouldice, O'Toole and their colleagues must have reasoned, the British would not target an occasion with thousands of civilians just going along to watch an exhibition of sport? If such a calculation was made, it was wrong.

Officially the throw-in for the game to start was due to take place at 2.45pm. It was delayed as GAA officials argued with the IRA contingent over the wisdom of going ahead with the match. At 3.15pm, the Gaelic football match between Dublin and Tipperary finally got under way. Colley remembered being at the St James' Avenue entrance along with Russell and Kilcoyne trying to close the turnstile and stop more people from going into Croke Park, much to the crowd's displeasure. 'A big crowd had now collected in St James' Avenue and were getting very impatient as the match was due to start. The next thing we heard was the match starting and immediately the man on the turnstile came back, swearing at us, and proceeded to let the crowd in. As we could do nothing further, we withdrew,' he recalled. Colley and his IRA colleagues were nowhere in sight once the British army units, the 'Black and Tans' and police officers from the RIC arrived. Members of Dublin's Metropolitan Police were already at the ground in their capacity to ensure public order; something they were doing without the assistance of stewards provided courtesy of the IRA.

Less than a quarter of an hour after the game started, a military aircraft flew over the ground and dropped a red flare, a prelude to the raid by British Crown forces. They entered the ground at an end backing on to a canal and firing began immediately, though who fired first remains to this day a matter of dispute. However, the raid ended with 14 people dead or fatally wounded, including a young woman and two children. Scores of others were injured, some from gunshot wounds, others crushed in the panic to escape from the ground.

Shouldice gave a chilling eye-witness account of the blood-letting and mayhem. He recalled, 'We had not long to wait for the game was not in progress more than 15 minutes when lorries of the raiders swooped down on the grounds and without any warning burst their way to the railings surrounding the playing pitch, opening fire on the people on the far side and on the players. Fortunately they were scattered and only one of them, young Hogan of Tipperary, was shot dead – the other players threw themselves flat and managed to crawl off the pitch and mingle with the crowd who were flying in panic behind the banks or tumbling over the wall into the waste ground on the Ballybough side. It was amongst the spectators on this side that the greatest havoc occurred.' Shouldice described those who died as being 'murdered in cold blood'.

In his account he made no reference to whether or not members of the crowd fired first, just the British troops bursting into the ground, opening fire, and the resulting blind panic. An armoured car blocked the St James' Avenue entrance to Croke Park just minutes after the IRA had tried in vain to stop spectators from going into the ground. It fired a total of 50 rounds, doing so according to the troops inside, as warning shots to the crowd. At the opposite Railway End, hundreds of spectators and some of the players managed to escape from Croke Park through the gardens of houses backing on to the ground. The rest were forced to stay inside at gunpoint, forced to raise their hands in the air, the ground gradually surrounded by British forces. At a bridge over the canal on Jones Road, a British army lorry was parked up, a perfect vantage point for viewing the Croke Park arena, its machine gun trained on those trapped inside. Gradually the crowd was allowed to disperse; at least those fit enough to leave without the assistance of an ambulance crew, but only after everyone had been searched.

Again Shouldice takes up the story, 'The bulk of those present remained inside the grounds – they had to do so – as the whole place was surrounded by the Crown Forces and a wholesale searching began. I had my little office under the old stand but vacated it when the shooting started and mingled with the crowds, with armed forces all round. They were perched up on the old stand, on the railway walls and any position overlooking us. Rifles and machine guns were trained on us, the commands rang out, "Put up your hands and keep them up." The searching went on for an hour or more.' Just a few people were arrested, Shouldice among them. He remembered being interviewed by a senior army officer, a veteran of the Great War with ribbon honours on his tunic. The officer appeared disgusted at the behaviour of his British colleagues, allowing Shouldice and a ragbag of other suspects to go, declaring there had been enough bloodshed for the day.

Ostensibly, the British forces were sent to Croke Park to search for suspects but instead went on a killing spree. They claimed the IRA fired on them first; pointing out also a gang of young men had tried to flee as soon as they arrived. It seems, though, from eye-witness accounts these were terrified ticket sellers rather than IRA men.

Yes, IRA men were present at the ground but this can hardly justify the slaughter of innocent civilians. Aside from the delegation trying to call the game off, three of Collins's henchmen, fresh from assassinating members of the British intelligence service that morning – Tom Keogh, Dan McDonell and Joe Dolan – were at the match. They left the ground undetected, though Keogh was wounded and treated in the nearby home of Harry Colley's mother. The raid on Croke Park was not the end of the bloodshed on Bloody Sunday. Later in the evening the RIC arrested two prominent IRA men, Dick McKee and Peadar Clancy. Both of them had taken part in Collins's operation to 'liquidate' the British intelligence-gathering efforts in Dublin. They were taken to Dublin Castle, interrogated, tortured and then killed without there being any attempt to stage a trial by the forces of law and order in Ireland at the time, the British Crown. A friend of theirs, Conor Clune, was also arrested and also executed. He was not though a member of the IRA and certainly had nothing to do with Collins's operation the night before. By midnight on Bloody Sunday, 30 people had been killed and one of the Croke Park victims, Thomas Hogan, died days later in hospital.

Exactly what happened at Croke Park on Bloody Sunday in terms of who fired first and when is difficult to assess with any certainty. Just one official account is available to recall the events. Naturally, that is the British military inquiry which remained classified for more than eight decades. It was held in secret and most of the witnesses from the British military and the police were not named. Even though the inquiry doubled up as an inquest on the deaths of 14 spectators and a player, Michael Hogan, their families were not allowed legal representation. A couple of lawyers, brothers Michael and James Comyn, did turn up to represent the family of Jane Boyle, the 26-year-old woman who died in Croke Park. She had gone to the match with her fiancé but in the stampede to escape the gunfire fell and was trampled underfoot. The Comyn brothers did not stay long at her inquest, Michael telling the presiding panel they would not take part because it was being 'held behind closed doors'. They made their critical point and left.

The evidence and the findings of the inquiry are now held at the UK National Archive at Kew and accuse the IRA of firing first; unknown civilians in the crowd with guns attacking British patrols going about what the inquiry deemed was their lawful business. Even so, the British senior army officers sitting in judgement on their own men and supporting officers from the Royal Irish Constabulary conceded that the response by opening fire and killing 14 unarmed civilians, including two children, was unauthorised and excessive.

Readers familiar with the findings of the inquiry into the events of Bloody Sunday in the city of Derry in January 1972 might find a chilling echo. The version of events put forward by the British establishment in November 1920 was contradicted at the time by those present. Spectators at the game, including Luke O'Toole, gave evidence to the inquiry. O'Toole spoke in his capacity as manager of Croke Park. None of the spectators corroborated the version from British troops and RIC police officers of members of the crowd firing first, nor crucially did members of the Dublin Metropolitan Police on duty at the match back up the British army and RIC version of events. Three DMP officers gave evidence to the inquiry and they all failed to back up the stories of the RIC and the British military, who were adamant they were fired upon once they arrived at Croke Park. Here is the statement of one of the RIC officers, 'On 21 November I was in the first car of the convoy detailed to go to Croke Park. Immediately we came to the canal bridge on the rise overlooking the park I observed several men rushing back from the top of the bridge towards the entrance gate of the park. I observed three of them turning backward as they ran and discharging revolvers in our direction. Almost immediately the firing appeared to be taken up by members of the crowd inside the enclosure. At this time the members of our party were jumping out of the cars. Most of them rushed down the incline towards the entrance gate.'

However, his claims are contradicted by a member of the DMP with a totally different recollection of events, 'On Sunday 21st, I was on duty outside the main entrance to Croke Park in Jones's Road. At about 3.25pm, I saw six or seven large lorries accompanied by two armoured cars, one in front and one behind, pass along the Clonliffe Road from Drumcondra towards Ballybough. Immediately after a small armoured car came across Jones's Road from Fitzroy Avenue and pulled up at the entrance of the main gate. Immediately after that, three small Crossley lorries pulled up in Jones's Road. There were about ten or twelve men dressed in RIC uniforms in each. When they got out of the cars they started firing in the air which I thought was blank ammunition, and almost immediately firing started all round the ground.'

For the civilian police service, the DMP, to fail to back up the militarised RIC's version of events is surprising and can only lead to the suspicion that tales of the IRA firing first were nonsense. However, the inquiry team concluded otherwise, blaming the IRA. As far as Gaelic football fans and Irish nationalists are concerned to this day, British regular army units, the auxiliaries, along with members of the RIC, fired first. It was to them a clear act of revenge for the IRA killing members of the Cairo Gang in the hours prior to the game.

In some respects the dispute is of little consequence given the wider historical and political context of a sporting event in which 13 innocent spectators and a player were killed by British Crown forces. Collins's ruthless operation the previous night may have been met with widespread revulsion even among moderate Irish Nationalists; a military victory but politically a propaganda defeat for the IRA. Instead, the slaughter in Croke Park meant the opposite. The British government of David Lloyd George and Britain's forces, not the IRA, were subjected to domestic and international opprobrium. Contemporary British newspapers reported the shootings in Croke Park as a clear 'reprisal' and the tragic events of that November showed the Irish problem was not being 'contained'. The Irish War of Independence dragged on for several more months before a truce was called and the eventual partition of Ireland with 26 'southern' counties forming an independent 'Free State' and six counties in the north-east,

'Northern Ireland', remaining in the United Kingdom. It was in the immediate aftermath of Bloody Sunday 1920 that the Archbishop of Perth in Australia, Patrick Clune, began acting as an intermediary between Sinn Fein and the British government, eventually helping to negotiate a peace settlement. Events in Croke Park on Bloody Sunday helped to concentrate minds. Croke Park was no longer just a sports stadium. It was an Irish nationalist shrine; a place of martyrdom.

It was in this cathedral of Irish sport and politics that the English rugby team lined up for the playing of 'God Save the Queen', a source of deep regret to those opposed to them even setting foot inside the stadium. It was a sign for others the Irish nation had moved on from the bloody events of nearly a century earlier. Croke Park had changed to an ultra-modern stadium complete with corporate refinery. Ireland and its relationship with England had changed for the better. The nephew of murdered Tipperary player Michael Hogan, who was named after him, told the BBC he was 'not keen' on the playing of 'God Save the Queen' in Croke Park. Mr Hogan also reflected in an interview with the *Daily Mirror* newspaper, 'I will feel a tinge of sadness when I watch the game – it will get to me. But I just hope it's a good game. That's what matters. I'm not anti-English at all. I hope everybody has an enjoyable time. We will welcome the English team and supporters. We've to respect their anthem like they will respect ours – we have to do that. I hope we beat England, but I also hope their supporters have an enjoyable day and there's no violence. A lot has changed since Michael was killed and everything has moved on. But there are some small-minded people. They will protest about anything.'

Those protestors were in a minority. The anthems were respected, the crowd standing in dignified silence for the playing of 'God Save the Queen'. Mick Hogan junior's wish of victory for Ireland was granted. Perhaps the entire occasion proved too much for the English players unwittingly finding themselves at the centre of political attention. They were hammered 43-13, a record number of points conceded by an English rugby team in the history of the sport's home nations championship.

One rugby commentator wryly observed that the GAA would be more than keen to invite the England rugby team back. The organisation did invite Queen Elizabeth to Croke Park in 2011, during a first state visit to Ireland by a British monarch since independence. Such an invitation to the site of a massacre by Crown forces and respect shown to the British head of state by the GAA was once unthinkable. After all, the GAA had once shown a remarkable lack of respect to the first head of state of the Republic of Ireland, an extraordinary tale of political interference by the governing body of a sport bordering on comedy rather than tragedy.

17

The Strange Tale of the GAA and President Hyde

IN the annals of sport clashing with politics, the tale of the Gaelic Athletic Association throwing the president of Ireland, Douglas Hyde, out of the organisation and stripping him of his status as a patron ranks as among the strangest of all. Hyde, the Republic of Ireland's first president, was a Gaelic scholar, a firm supporter of Gaelic sport, and from 1902 a patron of the GAA in recognition for his role in helping to establish the sports body as a firm part of Irish life in the late 19th century. Unlike most of his peers in the Gaelic movement, he was also Protestant.

Cynical historians believe Eamon de Valera, the prime minister or Taoiseach of the Irish Free State, nominated Hyde as its first president for the very reason he was Protestant; a sign to the world the soon to be Republic of Ireland was not a nation in the grip of the Roman Catholic Church and seen by critics as a satellite state of the Vatican.

Given that it was thought most Protestants voted against the implementation of de Valera's constitution for the fledgling Irish Republic, nationalist historian Tim Pat Coogan dismissed Hyde's unopposed nomination as a 'spot of tokenism'. If so, there were unintended consequences when it came to dealings between the Irish political establishment of the day and the GAA. Hyde was determined to be a president for all Irishmen and women, regardless of their faith, political leanings or for that matter sporting preferences. It was a stance to bring him and the very office of the Irish head of state into conflict with the Gaelic Athletic Association because of its infamous Rule 27; the ban on 'foreign games', specifically cricket, hockey, rugby and soccer.

This block, a punitive measure to stop GAA members from playing or even attending the so-called 'garrison sports' being popularised by the British, had a chequered history even before the appointment of Hyde. Originally designed to ensure the uninterrupted promotion of hurling and the Gaelic code of football, it was lifted by the GAA in 1897 only to be reinstated in 1901; a decision influenced by members of the Irish Republican Brotherhood (IRB), a forerunner to the IRA. In 1911 there was a falling out between GAA headquarters and its London county branch, members in the English capital wanting approval for being exempt.

To try to enforce it in England was frankly unsustainable and counter-productive. The GAA hierarchy gave such arguments short shrift and a year later sacked members of its London County board for 'playing foreign games' and appointed more compliant committee members to run the GAA in the English capital.

Even the lord mayor of the Irish capital was not safe from the wrath of the GAA in contravening Rule 27. In 1913, Dublin's lord mayor, Lorcan Sherlock, decided to take up an invite to become honorary president of soccer's Leinster Football Association, which would later morph into the Football Association of Ireland (FAI) after the partition of Ireland. As a result of his appointment, Mr Sherlock's invite to attend the All-Ireland GAA finals failed to arrive in the post. The GAA decided to snub him for being in breach of its precious Rule 27. This behaviour paled into insignificance two decades later when Hyde decided to take up an invite from the FAI to attend an international football match between Ireland and Poland. It brought the GAA into direct, bitter and embarrassing conflict with the Irish state.

Hyde had been feted by the GAA as a patron and leading advocate of the Gaelic movement. He had helped to bring warring factions in the fledgling GAA together, men divided over their brand of Irish nationalism, constitutional or violent. Hyde and others ensured that the GAA would survive any political splits and went as far as leading fundraising missions to the United States to guarantee its financial viability. On inviting him to open the newly-built Cusack Stand at Croke Park in August 1938, GAA general secretary Pádraig Ó Caoimh wrote, 'We know that you always did your best for the Gaelicisation of Ireland, and we greatly desire that, as patron of the Gaelic Athletic Association, you should be with us in order to participate in the joy we all feel at the erection of this stand.'

A few weeks later, the Irish president was present at the All-Ireland football final between Kerry and Galway. All seemed well. Ó Caoimh knew the GAA owed Hyde a great debt of gratitude. Yet once Hyde took his seat in Dalymount Park on 13 November 1938 for an international football match, leading members of the GAA, including Ó Caoimh, decided to repay him by insulting the high office he held. They were able to do nothing about the attendance of the prime minister Eamon de Valera or his minister for post and telegraphs, Oscar Traynor, who were both leading members of the IRA in the fight for independence from Britain. Neither of these men were members of the GAA. Indeed, Traynor had played soccer for Belfast Celtic and de Valera's sporting preference was rugby. Hyde, a GAA patron, was about to be shown the metaphorical red card.

The game itself went well for Hyde and his countrymen on the pitch. Ireland had been thrashed 6-0 by Poland some months earlier so the omens were not good. However, this time on home soil the Irish won 3-2. At the post-match dinner, the Polish consul-general Mr W. T. Dobrzynski declared it a great 'honour' for the country's president and prime minister to both be present at the match. As an act of international diplomacy with the threat of war looming over Europe, Hyde's decision to attend seemed vindicated, despite indications he might have had reservations, aware of provoking the ire of his 'friends' from the GAA.

Hyde's personal secretary, Michael McDunphy, explained the president's reasons for attending. It was, of course, simply impractical to accept the GAA's invitations to attend matches while snubbing the Irish Rugby Football Union (IRFU) and the FAI during his seven years in office. The more important factor was the popularity of football, particularly among the working-class people of Dublin. Cormac Moore, in his excellent exposé of this peculiar episode in Irish sport and politics, *The GAA v Douglas Hyde*, cites McDunphy in claiming the president felt soccer was a sport popular among 'a very large section of the Irish people, a big number of whom are and have been earnest workers in the National Movement'. This view would have irked the men at the GAA, McDunphy went further, believing Hyde did not want 'to ally himself with the narrow parochial outlook of those who regard it as an offence against nationality to play or even look at any healthy game of which they do not personally approve'. As Moore concluded, if Hyde had not attended any games of international football or rugby because of the GAA's ban on its members from attending 'foreign games', it would have amounted to a gross 'dereliction of duties'. Moore wrote, 'He could not have called himself impartial and above politics.'

As the Irish and the British media praised the attendance of Hyde and de Valera at the match and welcomed the positive result of the game, the leaders of the GAA began working up a maelstrom of indignant fury. The mood of the most ardent advocates of the ban on 'foreign games' was hardly helped by especially triumphalist reporting of the attendance of Hyde and de Valera in Dalymount Park by English newspapers. Those journals were all aware of the symbolic importance of the GAA's patron, the president of Ireland, openly flouting one of its most precious regulations. One newspaper, the *Daily Express*, went as far as to suggest the ban might be lifted. It was wrong.

County GAA boards across Ireland began mobilising in recommending action against Hyde for his sleight against them. The first moves came in Ulster, though in counties of Northern Ireland rather than the Republic of Ireland. The Patrick Pearse club in Derry proposed a motion on 4 December 1938 to remove Hyde as patron of the GAA. It also decided to have a pop at the FAI for accepting the partition of Ireland. Given the FAI in its original guise of the Leinster FA was forced to split from its Belfast-based parent body, the IFA, in acrimonious circumstances more than a decade earlier, this motion appeared just a little gratuitous. It added salt to the wounds of Dublin soccer folk in their spat with their counterparts in Belfast. At the time, the IFA and FIA both fielded Ireland teams with players representing the entire island. Furthermore, hundreds of GAA members in Northern Ireland were in the employ of the British state, including the organisation's own president Pádraig McNamee, arguably an acceptance in itself of partition.

The Derry club was widely condemned in the Irish and British media for putting forward its motion. Yet the path for conflict between the Gaelic Athletic Association and the Irish state was inextricably set. Many GAA members had reservations, not least those in Hyde's home county of Roscommon and home province of Connacht. Yet it was from Connacht that the decisive move was taken to end Douglas Hyde's tenure as patron of the GAA. The Central Council of the GAA met on 17 December 1938 after weeks of speculation in the media over how it might respond to Hyde attending a game of soccer.

The Galway County Board proposed the fateful motion. The minutes read, 'That the Central Council at its next meeting be requested to consider the position of a patron whose official duties may bring him into conflict with the fundamental rules of the association.

'The chairman said that his ruling was that such a person ceased to be a patron of the association. Some people thought that a patron should be above the rules, but that was not his view. It was no pleasure to rule as he was doing, but he saw no other course. Mr Farrell, Roscommon, dissenting from the ruling said Dr Hyde had done some good work for them in Roscommon. Chairman – He did good work in many places and in many ways. There was no further discussion.'

There would be no further meeting to discuss Hyde's future. As far as Pádraig McNamee was concerned, Hyde was in breach of Rule 27 and he was no longer patron of the GAA. Effectively, as far as McNamee bizarrely argued, Hyde had removed himself as patron by attending the match at Dalymount Park.

McNamee and general secretary Pádraig Ó Caoimh were both advocates of an Irish-Ireland, something their critics latched on to by making comparisons with Nazi Germany. For them the rules of the organisation were sacrosanct. Nobody could disobey them regardless of their status in society, not even the man holding the highest office in the land. It meant the GAA faced a storm of criticism, not just from those in England sniping from the outside but even its friends in Ireland. The most scathing criticism came from the *Irish Times*. It thundered in an editorial, 'A connection of 30 years' standing is to be broken by a display of intolerance which it would be difficult to parallel even in those countries in which party zeal passes for patriotism.

'A name which shed lustre on the GAA for the greater part of its history will do so no longer. The loss will be to the GAA. Misplaced zeal cannot go farther; the zealots, at least, might have the decency to feel ashamed. Their little victory over president Hyde will be pyrrhic, because the head of the state will continue to be the representative of all the people, and not of any clique, however large it may be.'

The *Irish Press*, a newspaper run by the de Valera family, wryly noted that the GAA meeting to punish Hyde for attending a 'foreign game' had been held in a foreign language; i.e. English. It mischievously suggested the Gaelic League ought to send its friends in the GAA a note of admonishment for this outrageous oversight.

Despite the best efforts of the GAA, which even instituted 'Vigilance Committees' to enforce the ban, it was widely flouted with players using pseudonyms on rugby or football team sheets. In de Valera's home county of Limerick, rugby managed to enjoy strong working-class support alongside the GAA, which was a mystery unless for decades the ban was being openly flouted. Not surprisingly the *Limerick Leader* newspaper took a dim view of the insult meted out to Douglas Hyde by the GAA. It declared, 'The shameful and small-minded action taken is the result, of course, of keeping the foreign games "ban", which was decided upon for a specific purpose when the circumstances were altogether different from what they are at present. In the Ireland of today this "ban" is an insult to the games it is supposed to protect, and its continuance is nothing more than a degrading manifestation of the slave mind.'

It was left to the journal of Hyde's home county of Roscommon to make the Nazi comparison in its stinging editorial, 'Hitler and Mussolini might do that sort of thing; the GAA should not try to do it. The serfs of the dictators have no choice but to obey, but the people of Ireland have fought to free themselves from serfdom. We say that the GAA has covered itself with ridicule by "banning" the president of Eire.' None of the criticism mattered. If anything it emboldened McNamee and Ó Caoimh with both stubbornly refusing to bow under external pressure. For them it became a matter of personal honour, ironic given they had dishonoured the head of state.

On Easter weekend in April 1939, the GAA held its annual congress in City Hall Dublin with the ratification of the decision to remove Hyde as patron of the organisation being the most important item on the agenda. Three county boards, Roscommon, Mayo and Kildare, put forward motions calling for Hyde's reinstatement, all of which McNamee considered to be out of order. Roscommon and Mayo withdrew their motions but Kildare insisted on a vote. It was roundly defeated. Only 11 delegates supported the motion and 120 voted against. The latter had backed McNamee's assertion the organisation must not bow to external pressure. It had an inalienable right to impose whatever rules it liked and the president of Ireland was in breach of those rights.

McNamee also took a pop in his speech to Congress at the international nature of football and rugby, dismissing it as an English Imperial conspiracy. He ranted, 'The critics tell of a wonderful thing called "internationalism"… The people who talk of internationalism really mean Anglicism. They describe English games as international. They pander deliberately or unwittingly to England's superiority complex.'

Clearly in his insular world view, McNamee had failed to notice that the sport of 'association football' was developing quite happily without the help of its founding nation, England. FIFA, the sport's world governing body, had successfully introduced its premier competition, the World Cup, without the presence of British teams. England was conspicuous by its absence, the FA in London perhaps in a blinkered world sporting view mirroring the insularity of its Irish neighbours, the GAA.

Hyde responded to his expulsion from the GAA with dignity and refused to comment on the decision. He even financially contributed to the training expenses of Gaelic footballers from his home county of Roscommon. Sadly though, the GAA's intransigent and bizarre behaviour meant Hyde was absent from Croke Park in 1943 and 1944 when his home county won back-to-back All-Ireland titles. Hyde stood down as president at the end of the Second World War in 1945, leaving his successor and the Irish government to sort out the diplomatic mess with the GAA.

Despite all the stubborn statements at the time of Hyde's removal as patron, there was a growing tacit admission it was a grave and embarrassing mistake. Sean T. O'Kelly was elected president of Ireland in June 1945 and the GAA's new president, Seamus Gardiner, tried to arrange a courtesy call to the new head of state's office. He was rebuffed. Instead, Eamon de Valera, who until that point had publicly failed to comment on the GAA's decision to remove Hyde, summoned Gardiner and Ó Caoimh to his office for effectively a polite dressing down. De Valera explained that the new president could not ignore their insulting behaviour towards his predecessor and they must accept that the head of state represented all segments of the community. The two GAA men agreed. The 'Hyde incident' had been 'unfortunate', they apparently concurred.

The GAA Central Council met on 17 August 1945 and passed a motion agreeing to invite the president of Ireland to all of its 'principal functions'. The motion also recognised the president 'cannot in any circumstances put himself in such a position as to seem, by implication or otherwise, to discriminate against any section of the community'. In other words, the GAA finally accepted it was in no position to stop Ireland's head of state from attending football, rugby or for that matter cricket and hockey matches even if he or she was a GAA member. It might have also been simpler to lift the ban on GAA members from attending 'foreign games'. Yet this bizarre form of sporting apartheid remained in place until 1971.

Though the ban no longer brought the GAA into direct conflict with the office of the president of Ireland, it did rile de Valera, a rugby fan careful not to indulge in his love of this 'foreign sport' for fear of upsetting the GAA. At least he did until dropping his guard in making a speech to a reunion dinner for pupils from his former school, Blackrock College, in April 1957. De Valera remarked, 'I have not been at a rugby match since 1913 because I do not want it being raised as a political matter and having rows kicked up about it.' He went on to extoll the virtues of rugby, at the expense of soccer and crucially Gaelic football, observing, 'There is no football game to match rugby. If all our young men played rugby not only would we beat England and Wales, but France and the whole lot of them together.'

Naturally enough reports of his comments enraged the GAA. Its mouthpiece on this occasion was the journal *The Gaelic Weekly*, asserting members of the GAA had been 'shocked and affronted' by de Valera's remarks, extolling the virtues of rugby football as opposed to Gaelic football. It went on to comment, 'Apart from its excellence as a sport, our national game should not be discredited in this manner – by innuendo or otherwise – by any Irishman, particularly by any national leader.' Thanks to the outcry, de Valera, who had at the same dinner expressed his regret at hurling being no longer played at the school, felt the need to send Padraig Ó Caoimh a personal letter clarifying his remarks. He was anxious to point out he did not mean offence but did not back down in both his support of rugby and more importantly his opposition to the GAA's infamous ban on the playing of 'foreign games'. De Valera wrote, 'My views are very simple. I am in favour of all outdoor games. I think they make for the health and vigour of our young people. They provide enjoyable recreation and brighten country life. Team games are the most valuable of all. Without damping individual initiative they teach the value of and give practice in combined effort for agreed objectives. If I had my way I would have a sports field established in every parish. The work the GAA has done and is doing in this respect, apart from what it has done to encourage a true national sport, is beyond praise. The one thing that is wrong, in my opinion, is that the GAA should continue to maintain the ban.'

De Valera warmed to his theme, 'Aptitudes for particular games and the consequent enthusiasm and likings for special games vary with the individual. Anything that tends to restrict individuals from playing games for which they feel themselves specially fitted or which they like particularly should, if possible, be avoided, and such a thing as bans taboo.' As for the merits of rugby and soccer, de Valera pointed to the international nature of those codes of football in stark contrast to Gaelic, 'The ban has this other consequence... With soccer and rugby established in the international field I think it unlikely that we can succeed in getting hurling and Gaelic football into that field, except where our own are established, as for example in some of the cities of Britain and the United States. If Ireland is to match herself in football and play with the national teams from England, Wales, Scotland and from France it must be in rugby or soccer, as at present. Many who play Gaelic football would, if this ban did not prevent them, be inclined to play rugby also. And, I have not the slightest doubt that if this were permitted our successes in the international field would be outstanding, and our prestige abroad enhanced.'

De Valera was careful to point out in his letter to Ó Caoimh he felt no 'antagonism' towards Gaelic football, having played the sport as a boy. As for hurling, de Valera found it a pity rugby players were prevented from playing what he described as the 'most manly of sports'. One key point he was anxious to make to Ó Caoimh and the GAA leadership was the views he held were purely 'personal'. They were not being expressed in his capacity as prime minister of the Republic of Ireland. Despite questioning the validity of the GAA's ban on the playing of foreign games by its members or for that matter the attendance of a football match by the country's president in 1938, de Valera and his colleagues refused to exert any political pressure to end it. Even a rather lame patriotic appeal to enhance the pool of players available to Ireland's rugby and soccer teams fell on deaf ears.

A minority of GAA clubs had their reservations over the maintenance of Rule 27 with various attempts to remove it failing during the 1960s. Yet by 1971, with the Northern Ireland Troubles under way, the mood had changed. The country was facing more important issues than an anachronistic measure to preserve an Irish sporting identity from the 19th century. The ban had been frankly a source of embarrassment to younger members. As a result in a shift of attitudes, the old guard, the GAA hierarchy, while still being staunch advocates of the ban, were about to be usurped by grassroots members of the clubs. At a GAA congress held in Galway, a motion was put forward by the Meath County Board calling for every club to hold a meeting to discuss the abolition or retention of Rule 27. As the clubs duly met, it became clear there was widespread opposition to the ban. Only two of the 32 counties, Sligo and Antrim, showed any appetite for retention. At a GAA congress held at Queen's University Belfast in April 1971, the organisation's president, Pat Fanning, put forward motions to end the ban and simultaneously proposed a new constitution fit for the late 20th century. His speech to delegates was widely praised by those on both sides of the argument. Fanning commented, 'Do we reject the past and with deletion proclaim ourselves a mere sports organisation? Do we forsake the tradition that nurtured, gave purpose to, and made of this GAA a great weapon in the cause of Ireland and Ireland's people?'

Fanning, in making these political points, was confident the answer was 'no' but he went on to tell delegates, 'Let us delete this rule but in a "ban-less" GAA let us maintain the spirit that made this association great. Let us remain a national organisation; pledge to work, as always, towards an Irish-Ireland, proud not only of our games, but of our language, our songs, our dances, our nationhood. Today, let there be no sounding of trumpets as a rule disappears; nor should there be talk of defeat. If victory there be, let it be a victory for the association. If defeat there be, let it be for those who hoped that change would give them a less nationally motivated GAA.'

Though Fanning insisted on a commitment to an 'Irish-Ireland', a concept so bitterly criticised as echoing the conduct of mainland European fascists in the row over the removal of Hyde, the political and social climate in Ireland was rapidly changing. As much as a younger generation enjoyed Gaelic sport, they were also embracing those garrison sports of football and rugby, international and English domestic games growing in popularity with a captive TV audience even in the early 1970s. Rule 27 had no part to play in a modern Ireland. It was an embarrassment and was dropped.

Even then Rule 42, a ban on rugby and football being played at GAA, remained in force and was only being temporarily lifted to allow international matches to be played in Croke Park from 2007 to 2010. The GAA's Rule 21, banning members of the British army and the Northern Ireland police from playing hurling and Gaelic football, also remained in force until being lifted in November 2001. GAA president Sean McCague declared, 'I feel the issue of the rule is now in the past. We have taken a step that means we no longer have an exclusion rule. We can move forward with confidence as we do not need exclusion rules, and I think we will be a better organisation for that.'

Not only was the GAA opening its doors to a wider membership, it was also belatedly taking Eamon de Valera's advice from the 1950s, cautiously embracing the Irish Rugby Football Union. In a gesture which would have been unthinkable to the agitators behind the plan to remove Hyde in the 1930s, the GAA backed the IRFU in its attempts to bring the Rugby World Cup to Ireland. De Valera would no doubt have approved.

As for Douglas Hyde, there was one final snub to endure from Irish and Catholic society, this time in death, coming from Ireland's notorious Roman Catholic hierarchy. Hyde, a Protestant, died on 12 July 1949 with his funeral being held in St Patrick's Cathedral. In an echo of the GAA's ban, the Roman Catholic upper echelons threatened members of the church with excommunication if they attended a Protestant service. The Irish political establishment, including de Valera and Taoiseach John Costello, stood outside the cathedral, inviting much widespread criticism. One of the few Catholics to venture inside was the bemused French ambassador. Ireland, thanks to de Valera, had become a de facto Roman Catholic state. The only government minister to attend was Noel Browne, Costello's health minister, who had long been at loggerheads with Roman Catholic bishops over his proposed reforms to Irish medical services, and quite happy to ignore their threats of excommunication. His colleagues stood in the street waiting for the end of the service.

It was one final and shameful snub to Hyde. Yet the GAA did posthumously seek to make amends for its behaviour. Once the ban on 'foreign games' was dropped in 1971, the GAA council in Hyde's home county of Roscommon took the opportunity to honour him by renaming its main stadium as Dr Douglas Hyde Park. Finally, in 1984 to mark the GAA's centenary, president Paddy Buggy placed a plaque on the former patron's grave, recognising and honouring his contribution to the organisation. It was an admission that a mistake had been made from a very different generation of sports administrators than those in the 1930s daring to face down a country's political establishment.

18

Defying Terrorist Threats: 'At Least We Turned Up'

I T is an immortal line in Anglo-Irish sport, 'We may not be any good but at least we turn up!' It was a line delivered with understated humour by an England rugby captain in an act of defiance against terrorist threats. On this occasion, in February 1973, England had travelled to Dublin for an international rugby match at the height of the Troubles in Northern Ireland. The players, some reluctantly, agreed to travel in an act of sporting solidarity with their sporting neighbours, which was something the Scottish and Welsh teams had failed to do just a year earlier.

Decades later came another act of solidarity and defiance; this time at Wembley as England's footballers welcomed France just days after deadly terror attacks in Paris by men and women purporting to be from the Middle Eastern terror group Islamic State in the Levant, or, as it's also known, Daesh. The first attacks on a horrific Friday night in Paris were at the national football stadium, the Stade de France, as the French played Germany, with terrorists unable to gain entry to the ground then blowing themselves up. By the end of the night, 130 people lay dead and scores critically injured with the victims having planned on a leisurely night out in restaurants, a concert hall and a sports stadium. It seemed inevitable that a forthcoming international friendly match between England and France at Wembley would be called off. Remarkably it went ahead in the spirit of fraternity, solidarity and defiance, becoming an inspiring moment for a sport so often blighted by overblown national rivalries.

International sport, ever since it was organised in the late 19th century, has thrown up fierce rivalries that too often inevitably mirror mutual feelings of antipathy, ending in political and diplomatic conflict and war. England versus Germany in football allows the more Neanderthal English fans to rehearse their well-worn clichéd chants about winning two World Wars and one World Cup. France versus England in rugby, 'Le Crunch', appears to drag the antagonistic rivals back a couple of centuries to the Napoleonic era. For English and French football fans any ancient animosities were put to one side at Wembley in the aftermath of the Paris terror attacks in November 2015 with no sign of the English harking back to victory at Waterloo and Agincourt some two and six centuries earlier.

Then again, when it comes to ancient rivalries, there are the Celtic nations against their so-called Saxon foe, England. The English are seen by their Welsh, Scottish and Irish neighbours simply as arrogant foes; the 'auld enemy'. For some the bile directed towards them is more than just a simple matter of banter. As fierce as the rivalry may be, it is for the most part friendly. Yet as Irish teams took to the field in the 1970s there was all along the spectre of terrorism with the Northern Ireland Troubles leading to players, fans or administrators fearing that the Provisional IRA, in its violent quest for a united Ireland, might in pursuit of its political aims try to target rugby or football, bringing bloodshed into what's 'only a game'.

Those fears led to the IRA disrupting rugby's Five Nations Championship in 1972 without even priming a bomb or firing a shot. The rugby unions of Scotland and Wales refused to send a team to Dublin to play Ireland in Lansdowne Road for fear of a terrorist attack. They did so even though Dublin and the rest of the Republic of Ireland was largely untouched by the Troubles over the border. Scottish and Welsh players had been sent threatening letters, purporting to come from the IRA. The SRU and the WRU cancelled their flights to Dublin. Ireland, who had beaten France and England away from home in the games they did get to play in the tournament, were robbed of the rare chance of a Grand Slam by winning every game in the tournament thanks to home victories over Scotland and Wales.

It left the Irish players frustrated and dismayed. In his autobiography, legendary Irish rugby player, Willie John McBride, articulated his anger. McBride noted, 'Rugby football had lived through an awful lot in Ireland over the years, yet the game had always carried on, whatever the background and however difficult it might have been.' Clearly unimpressed by the behaviour of the Scottish and Welsh rugby administrators, though absolving the players of any blame, McBride added, 'Rugby had proved itself bigger than any man of violence, for it had conspicuously refused to allow itself to be intimidated by anyone, whatever their views. It was something of which all of us involved in rugby in Ireland felt immensely proud. Imagine our feelings then, when we were let down – and I mean those words – by the administrators…those gentlemen who took the decision to abandon their matches with us that year failed Ireland, failed their own countries and failed the game of rugby football.' He even went as far as accusing them of cowardice, 'I believe they were just scared, that was the bottom line of it.' As far as McBride was concerned, a man living in the midst of the Troubles, the Irish had been let down by their 'friends'.

Twelve months later it was the turn of the 'auld enemy' with England due to travel to Dublin. The prospect of an Ireland versus England rugby match going ahead seemed remote given the Scottish and Welsh decisions to refuse to set foot on Irish soil. Yet remarkably the English did turn up and their sporting tormentors from the Irish rugby fraternity would remain eternally grateful. This time, just months after the Munich Olympics were defiled by the deadly work of terrorists, the phrase 'the game must go on' had an honourable and dignified meaning.

The decision to send the England rugby team to Dublin in February 1973 was made by the committee men at Twickenham. These were the men of the stereotypical English stiff upper lip.

As far as these gentlemen were concerned they could not be seen to be giving in to terrorism. The men themselves, of course, were not directly under threat. It was the players who were in the potential firing line. Four England players dropped out of the squad, declining the invitation to go to Dublin. One was a policeman, the lock forward Nigel Horton. Another served in the Royal Air Force, again a lock forward, Peter Larter. Scrum half Jan Webster and full-back Sam Doble also stayed at home. Naturally enough their colleagues were apprehensive and agonised over whether to travel in the weeks before the game.

Any qualms were understandable given the historic political conflict between England and Ireland, which had led to the explosion of violence in Northern Ireland in a modern conflict that would last for at least another quarter of a century. In the year the Scots and the Welsh declined to play the Irish in Lansdowne Road, more than 100 British soldiers had been killed in Northern Ireland with another 500 injured. The risks were obvious. The Irish Rugby Football Union feared the game would not go ahead, despite the bluster of its blazered counterparts at Twickenham. For Irish rugby, a sport at the time enjoying nowhere near the popularity of football and Gaelic games, the cancellation of the fixture with England would have been a severe blow. The IRFU would have taken a severe financial hit. It would also be a blow to the promotion of rugby football to young people in Ireland.

Willie John McBride recalled in an interview with the *Daily Telegraph* some years later, 'For England to cancel would have been devastating but as the date got nearer there was still no word and we began to hope.' There was relief when England's Rugby Football Union (RFU) informed the IRFU it would fulfil the fixture, regardless of the IRA death threats. The English players still needed to be persuaded.

One of them, England and British and Irish Lions winger David Duckham, sought reassurances from McBride. They had become friends on the Lions tour of New Zealand in 1971. Duckham was newly married and he and his wife Jean were apprehensive. McBride recalled, 'I knew for a certain fact that if David Duckham, the first name down on any England team sheet along with John Pullin, withdrew that would be curtains, others would follow.' As a result, McBride took the 'spur of the moment' decision to invite Duckham and his wife to spend a weekend with him and his wife, Penny, in Dublin. Duckham agreed. As McBride remembered, 'It was a deal. He also joked that he would be getting stuck into the rucks and mauls much more than usual because he didn't particularly fancy standing out on the wing in a pristine white England shirt for too long. I assured him he would be welcome at the bottom of an Ireland ruck anytime.'

The bonding weekend in the Irish capital worked. Duckham was won over. As for Pullin, he claimed he had no qualms, citing his 'ignorance' of Anglo-Irish history and the Northern Ireland Troubles as 'bliss'. He explained, 'Had I known the full story and the depths of feeling I might have thought more deeply about things but I didn't. I just wanted to captain my country against some old Irish mates and great rivals at their place.' The game went ahead on 10 February 1973 and for the first and last time in the history of sport an Irish crowd gave an English team a delirious reception.

Beforehand, it was agreed that Ireland and England would walk out together as a sign of unity, sporting camaraderie being more important than international political rivalry. Yet such was the scale of the ovation from a 50,000 capacity Lansdowne Road crowd, the England team were urged to step forward to take the applause. McBride recalled the moment with a hint of pride in his sport and Irish rugby folk, 'I for one had never heard a roar like it, on any rugby ground anywhere in the world... the warmth of the welcome and the noise was unique in my experience.'

The match, it seemed, was almost incidental and Ireland, for the record, won 18-9. England's captain, John Pullin, admitted the scoreboard flattered the English. He felt the Irish had given them a 'thumping'. Yet the Irish were not celebrating the victory, just the very fact the match took place at all. The occasion warranted the following citation in the official history of the Irish Rugby Football Union, 'For over a century the happenings on the field of international rugby have stirred men's emotions but it is doubtful if there was ever a more emotional scene than that at Lansdowne Road when the English side ran on the field.

The entire concourse to a man stood and applauded the English team for a full five minutes. It was hardly material that Ireland won a close match, 18-9, in which England missed more chances than they took.' At the post-match dinner, Pullin summed it all up succinctly with his famous quip, 'We may not be any good but at least we turn up.'

If any comment served the mantra of it not about being the winning but about taking part, that was it. Although this line has gone down in the annals of Anglo-Irish history, not just sporting history, Pullin insists it was an off-the-cuff remark. He explained, 'I never used to prepare any of my captain's speeches, in fact I found that stuff a bit of a burden, but I just said what I felt and it seemed to go down well. A big night followed as you can imagine.'

McBride remembered, 'His quip brought the house down but the whole day was an unexpected triumph, the result utterly irrelevant once the final whistle blew. From that day on we knew for certain that Irish rugby would outlive and survive the Troubles, whatever they threw at us.'

Indeed, the 1972 season was the last in which European rugby was disrupted by the threat of violence. It was not until 2007, when England turned up at the home of the GAA in Croke Park, that politics would rear its ugly head again in sport. Even then, though, an Irish victory was almost an irrelevance no matter how much it was enjoyed by Irish fans. It was a small triumph in the tortured history of Anglo-Irish relations.

Although the Provisional IRA used the threat of terrorism to disrupt sport, it never actually carried out a physical attack on a major sporting venue. On Friday 13 November 2015 for the terrorists allied to Daesh there was no such compunction on a night of carnage and horror throughout Paris. For these warped individuals the thought of people actually going out for a night to enjoy themselves was too much. They set out instead on a night of barbarity and depravity, destroying innocent lives, instilling fear into visitors and citizens of one of the world's great capitals.

The attacks began at the Stade de France in the north Parisian suburb of Saint Denis. France, due to host the European Championships in the summer of 2016, were facing world champions Germany in a prestige international friendly with the French president Francois Hollande among the VIP guests. Twenty minutes into the match a large explosion was heard outside the ground, followed minutes later by another blast. Many spectators dismissed it as a few hoodlums letting off fireworks. But as news came though on mobile phones of gun attacks across Paris the awful truth of being targeted by terrorists dawned. President Hollande was whisked away by his security staff yet the match went on with the crowd left locked inside the ground. French security officials felt it was better to carry on rather than abandoning the game and perhaps triggering panic among the crowd. It was safer for the 80,000 football fans to stay inside the ground rather than allow them to spill on to the surrounding streets with terrorists on the loose.

After all, security measures at the Stade de France appeared to have kept the terrorists out. One of them had apparently backed away from security guards after being refused entry to the ground and detonated his suicide vest. An accomplice did the same minutes later after also failing to enter the ground. A third suicide bomber blew himself up at a fast food restaurant near to the ground. If they had succeeded in entering the stadium, the carnage on this fateful night would have been far worse.

As Hollande was taken from the stadium to safety, a series of deadly gun attacks unfolded in the city centre. Men with semi-automatic rifles opened fire indiscriminately. On Rue Albert, 15 people were killed while dining at Le Petit Cambodge restaurant. Further attacks were carried out at the Café Bonne Bier and La Casa Nostra pizzeria in Rue de la Fontaine, killing five people and injuring several others. At all those locations, eye-witnesses reported that the attackers were travelling in a black Seat car. It was also sighted in an attack on La Belle Equipe bar in Rue de Charonne in the 11th district of Paris. By the time the terrorists left that bar 19 people lay dead there, with nine critically injured, having all been gunned down in a clinical, calculating and callous act of violence. It was far from the end of the carnage. The worst was yet to come, at the Bataclan concert hall.

Around 1,500 people were packed into the venue for a concert by the Californian rock band Eagles of Death Metal.

According to the chief prosecutor of Paris, Francois Molins, three attackers wearing suicide belts and carrying Kalashnikov assault weapons arrived in a black Volkswagen Polo, got out, and stormed the entrance, one of them yelling in Arabic 'God is Great'. Eighty-nine people were killed and scores were injured. As a siege at the Bataclan developed, hundreds of terrified concert-goers either fled or hid from the terrorists in alcoves, fearing they were about to die. In the early hours, elite security personnel were ordered into the concert hall by the French government to take out the terrorists. A police officer shot one of the gunmen, detonating his suicide vest. The other two blew themselves up, ending the siege. It was the worst act of violence on French soil since the end of the Second World War.

As the country began three days of national mourning, the prospect of staging a football match at Wembley between England and France seemed unthinkable. There were surely better things to do than something as trivial as play a football match. After all, one of the French players, Lassana Diarra, lost his cousin in the attacks. Another, Antoine Griezmann, was grateful that his sister managed to escape alive from the Bataclan. In such circumstances, sport did not matter. But a decision was made to go ahead with the game despite the reservations of the French players. Yet again, a sports event was being used as an opportunity to defy terrorists and as an opportunity for sporting rivals to offer a display of solidarity in the face of evil.

In the build-up, the usual mind-numbing speculation over tactics and formations was thankfully absent from mainstream media commentary. In the context of the Paris terror attacks, the symbolism of staging a game of football just days after terrorists tried to cause widespread loss of life at the Stade de France mattered most. The match as a sporting contest was almost an irrelevance. It went ahead but only with a level of security almost on a par with measures taken at the London Olympics in 2012, certainly at levels of protection unprecedented for a friendly international football match. Football Association chief executive Martin Glenn explained, 'We spoke to the French Federation on Saturday, and were in touch with the French president's office and there were two conditions to hold the game. UK authorities and government needed to make sure it was safe and the French wanted to play. They wanted to go ahead, for mainly symbolic reasons, and we were very happy to meet their concerns.'

In offering reassurances to fans turning up, Metropolitan Police deputy assistant commander Peter Terry said, 'London and Paris are sister cities. They are extremely diverse and dynamic cities. They will not be cowed by the threat of terrorism. It's extremely important we show support to the people of Paris, people we have the greatest sympathy with at this moment in time, and show people we will go about our daily business.' Glenn offered similar sentiments, again striking a defiant tone, 'This is going to have massive global significance – the first major event since Friday. It is a chance to demonstrate terrorism can't win. We can't afford to let this act of terror cow us.'

As for the French team, manager Didier Deschamps summed up the mood of his players, admitting many had been reluctant to travel to London but decided to go ahead anyway. In particular he reflected on the decisions of Diarra and Griezmann to turn up at Wembley. Deschamps said, 'We have two players who have been profoundly touched by the incidents. Antoine Griezmann was fortunate to have a feeling of relief and happiness that his sister managed to stay alive despite being at the Bataclan. As for Lassana Diarra, his life has been touched by the deep loss of a relative who he was close to. It was good he stayed with us; I have talked with him, as all of us have, and his place has been a source of reassurance for us. We have learnt the value of unity and solidarity.' Deschamps added that it was a test of 'character' for his players. England's manager Roy Hodgson said the game would not be a 'normal friendly'.

If it had have been, British prime minister David Cameron would probably not had turned up at Wembley. In response to the Paris attacks he decided to go along, joining in this act of 'solidarity and defiance'. Mr Cameron stated a few hours before the kick-off, 'The barbaric terrorist attacks have shocked the world but also united us in our unwavering resolve to defeat this evil. Tonight at Wembley, football fans will send a clear message – the terrorists will never win.' The leader of the opposition, Jeremy Corbyn, also attended, as did London mayor Boris Johnson. They left it to the Duke of Cambridge, Prince William, to lead the tributes in his capacity as president of the Football Association. Yet even as they made their way to Wembley terrorist threats once again began to dominate the airwaves.

News filtered through of the stadium in Hanover due to stage a game between Germany and the Netherlands being evacuated. A match between Belgium and Spain had already been called off due to security concerns with the chief suspect for organising the Paris terror attacks being a Brussels resident. Now the decision was taken to cancel the fixture between Germany and Holland with the authorities unable to guarantee the safety of players, officials and fans. Wembley, though, was still defiant, its steel arch rising high above the pitch resplendent in the blue, white and red colours of the French tricolour flag.

Traditional pre-match rituals were abandoned in a concerted effort to show support for the victims of the Paris terror attacks, to their families and to the people of France. English fans were encouraged to sing the French anthem 'La Marseillaise'. Many fans did so with gusto, if rather badly. Yet the quality of the singing mattered little, the gesture mattered most in this moving show of support for the French. David Cameron struggled for composure, appearing to shed a tear as his countrymen and women sang the anthem of a foreign neighbour.

Moments later, the biggest round of applause erupted. Normally, fans ignore the pre-match team photo. On this occasion the players from both sides were photographed together, many of these international rivals being club-mates in domestic competition. They mingled and linked arms, blue-shirted player alternating with white-shirted player, in a gesture deeply appreciated by the crowd of 80,000. Once the applause ebbed away the players gathered around the centre circle for an impeccably-observed minute's silence. Once it was time for the referee to blow his whistle for the kick-off, the match seemed almost an irrelevance, except for one more outpouring of emotion. Almost an hour into the game France made a substitution. Lassana Diarra came off the bench to a standing ovation, English and French fans applauding his personal act of defiance after his loss. The result of the match was of no importance though for the record England won 2-0. Yet the real winner was sport. Terrorists targeted a sports event involving the French players only days earlier, the concept of any leisure activity being an anathema to them.

Afterwards, Didier Deschamps described it as a 'very heartfelt, special, moving, grandiose moment'. He was grateful to the Football Association, the English players, coaching staff and above all the fans. He said, 'We have had a moment of communal grief and this has been good for us. There was a sporting meaning and a sporting dimension, but on a human level the match had far greater importance. We had desire and will but all things considered the human aspect was maybe more important.'

His English counterpart Roy Hodgson simply and accurately observed that it was a 'very poignant occasion'.

Unlike Dublin in 1973 there were no dry quips to sum up the occasion, just the equivalent of a French Gallic shrug and a simple statement of intent from the English captain. Wayne Rooney commented, 'The world will go on and stand against terror. We need to stand tall together in these tough times.'

Although the circumstances were quite different, the fans and players at Wembley on a November night in 2015 had done the same as the rugby fans and players some four decades earlier at Lansdowne Road in Dublin on a February afternoon in 1973. It hardly mattered if the match was any good. They had turned up.

19

Bodyline

ONE sport can define a nation. It can be at its heart and soul. In the case of England, there's nothing more quintessentially English than cricket. No other sport quite epitomises English Corinthian notions of fair play. 'It is just not cricket!' is the phrase of choice for those in polite English society for any underhand behaviour. Cricket was also the sport of Empire, a civilised sport for Britain's colonial subjects rather more preferable to the ruling classes than the more vulgar discipline of football.

Perhaps it was inevitable that a game of cricket, indeed a series of matches, served to signal the beginning of the end of the British Empire. The colonial masters from England stood accused of foul play. It was Australia versus England and as far as the Australians were concerned, they were the only ones playing cricket. The English, the 'Poms', had resorted to underhand and violent tactics. It was just not cricket. The upper crust gentlemen of Marylebone Cricket Club (MCC) at its offices at the Lord's cricket ground were outraged at such an accusation. How dare the colonial upstarts suggest such a thing of English gentlemen and players? The fall-out from the row threatened diplomatic relations between Great Britain and Australia. It was early 1933 and a new word entered the sporting lexicon, 'Bodyline'.

Controversy lingers over this series of cricket matches over 80 years later with various disputes emerging over the conduct of players and cricket administrators, even diplomats and politicians. Bodyline as a concept is almost in the realms of sporting mythology as much as history. There are many curious aspects. Bodyline is credited with being a theory of tactical bowling thought up by the England team to counter cricket's greatest ever batsman, Don Bradman. It is not quite true. The England team, led by their captain Douglas Jardine, simply adopted the 'leg theory' tactic of bowling quite commonly used in the 1920s and early 30s. The bowler delivered fast, sharp bouncing balls on the line of the batsman's leg stump with a coterie of fielders placed around him on the leg side to gobble up any catching opportunities. It helped Jardine that he was able to deploy Nottinghamshire's Harold Larwood, one of the finest fast bowlers ever to play the game of cricket. Larwood was ably supported by his county colleague Bill Voce. As a bowling tactic it was nothing new. One of Larwood's former team-mates, Fred Root, even claimed he was offered a contract in the late 1920s by the Australians to help coach leg theory bowling.

The term Bodyline was conjured up by Australian journalists to describe the tactic as their team's batsmen began returning to the pavilion, battered and bruised from the brutal deliveries they were receiving. Whether the England team 'adopted' or 'adapted' leg theory to come up with Bodyline bowling – or as the distinguished English cricket writer of the day, Neville Cardus, termed it, 'fast leg theory'– is one of many moot points. Cardus wrote, 'Our esteemed and beloved editor of *Wisden* writes of fast leg-theory as a method of play which has often been practised in the past by Australian as well as by English bowlers. For my part, I have never heard of fast leg-theory being exploited in a Test match until this present series. And by fast leg-theory I mean the sort of bowling described by reliable writers in the Australian newspapers in their accounts of the methods of Larwood and Voce.'

Another England bowler on this controversial Ashes tour, Bill Bowes, disagreed with the venerable cricket writer Cardus. In his 1958 book *Express Deliveries*, Bowes explained, 'Any ball pitched outside the off stump could be left alone. If it whipped in and hit them on the pads the batsman did not need to worry about being given out LBW, for in those days one of the rules for an LBW decision was that the ball must pitch in line from wicket to wicket. With bats held high above their heads and without any semblance of a stroke they could let the off-theory bowlers waste their energy on thin air. The only time they had any need to play the bowling was when it was coming directly on the body. So the leg glance or the push to wide of mid-on became their chief scoring shots.

'Leg-theory then was a natural development in cricket; but as bowled by Larwood with his extra pace and splendid direction it put him in a class of his own. When [Gubby] Allen, [Bill] Voce, or I "dug" a ball into the pitch it bounced rather like a tennis ball with much of the pace taken out of it. Larwood, hurling them down at express speed, secured the ricochet, which did not deprive the ball of its speed; at least not to the same extent.' To explain later, it was an obvious bowling tactic for England to hatch in combating the Australian batting line-up.

Just to complicate matters further, two key flashpoints in the Bodyline controversy – Harold Larwood felling the Australian captain Bill Woodfull, then wicketkeeper Bert Oldfield – did not actually come about as a result of Bodyline bowling. Larwood was bowling to a conventional field. In the subsequent furore this mattered little.

The other curious aspect is a common analysis of the two teams representing the old order of the British Empire, disgruntled colonists and their colonial masters. Yet both teams were riven by social division along class and even sectarian lines. England were still a team of amateur 'gentlemen' and professional players with the amateur toffs being in charge. There certainly seemed to be evidence of good relations between the amateurs in captain Jardine and his vice-captain Bob Wyatt, and the professional players. As for Gubby Allen, later to become a leading English cricket administrator, it may have been a different matter.

Unlike the captain, he refused to call the professionals by their first names, instead insisting on the snobbish practice of surnames only. Allen dismissed Larwood and Voce in letters to his parents as 'swollen headed uneducated miners'. In his assessment of Jardine, a fellow gentleman amateur, he was equally lacking in charm, calling him 'an absolute swine'.

Jardine, in his naivety, wrote to Allen's parents praising their son for his support!

In such circumstances, the English cricketers displayed remarkable team spirit. Perhaps the bitter hostility from the Australian media and crowds helped force the adoption of a siege mentality. As for the Australian cricketers, they were anything but champions of anti-Imperialism in this clash between the colonists and their colonial masters. The Aussies were simply deeply hard-nosed cricketers putting aside their own personal differences, often between those with an Irish Catholic background and those of English ancestry. They just wanted to win a series of games of Test match cricket. The England cricket team wanted to do the same of course, the brazenly open 'win at all costs' attitude of Jardine sticking in the craw of the Australian media. All of this personal intrigue though is the subplot to an explosive political and diplomatic row over a few games of cricket, with one particular encounter taking place in Adelaide.

England had lost the Ashes in a home series in 1930 thanks to the genius of the young Australian batsman Don Bradman. He was unplayable. In Tests and games against English county sides Bradman amassed a total of 2,960 runs at an astonishing average of 98.66. In his 36 innings he scored six double centuries, ten centuries and 15 half-centuries. His highest score on tour was a then world record of 334 in the third Test against England at Headingley and his average in Tests was a remarkable 139.14. The challenge for Jardine and his team, as they prepared to set sail for Australia to regain the Ashes, was therefore how to stop Bradman. Australia did have other talented players but stopping Bradman was a priority. The clue to doing so apparently came in the final Test of the 1930 series at The Oval thanks to the bowling performance of Harold Larwood.

Bradman had managed to score 232 in the final Test at The Oval, carting Larwood around the ground as much as any other bowler. Yet this seemed not to matter to either Jardine or Larwood. Both believed they had spotted a flaw in the prolific batsman's armoury. There could not be two more contrasting characters than Jardine and Larwood, both almost stereotypical representatives of English Test cricketers of the day. Larwood fulfilled the stereotype of the miner being whistled up from the pit to play cricket for England, one so cuttingly sneered at by Gubby Allen. Jardine, a man of Empire born in the Indian city of Bombay to a family of well-to-do Scottish lawyers, was privately educated at Winchester College and a businessman in the city of London. The Scotsman captaining England had also from his Imperial outlook supposedly developed almost a pathological hatred of Australians, something his family vehemently deny to this day. Yet this was the impression given to the Australian media and by the observations of some of Jardine's own mentors.

On Jardine being appointed England captain, his cricket master at Winchester College, Rockley Wilson, offered an unerringly prescient insight. Wilson commented, 'He might well win us the Ashes, but he might lose us a Dominion.' It might have been a glib prediction yet it almost turned out to be accurate. Jardine, of course as a gentleman of English cricket, saw himself as superior to the minion professionals in his team, including Larwood. As for his Australian opponents, they were an uncivilised rabble. During the Ashes tour of 1928/29, Jardine allegedly told the England wicketkeeper Stork Hendry, 'All Australians are uneducated and an unruly mob.' In his zealous determination to defeat this 'unruly mob' he invited Larwood, Bill Voce, and their Nottinghamshire County Cricket Club captain Arthur Carr to the rarefied surroundings of the Piccadilly Grill rooms. The food mattered little. There was just one main item on the menu – how to stop Bradman.

For months during the summer of 1932 Jardine wrestled with the problem of countering Bradman, captaining England in a Test series against India being of minor concern. He pored over the Australian's batting records, scoring charts, newspaper accounts of his innings, the observations of senior England colleagues and film clips. The footage he viewed in a committee room at Lord's cricket ground merely showed Bradman imperiously taking bowling attacks apart. As the reels were beginning to run out, it was only as Jardine viewed action from the final Test at The Oval that he found what he saw as a tiny chink in Bradman's armoury. In those days cricket pitches remained uncovered during breaks for rain. On this occasion showers had spiced up The Oval pitch, leading to deliveries from Larwood viciously rising off the surface. Jardine was convinced he saw Bradman flinch. Apparently the MCC members' afternoon nap was disturbed as Jardine yelled out loud, 'I've got it, he's yellow!' Bradman went on to score 232 despite Larwood's hostile bowling. It mattered little to Jardine. He noticed that Bradman consistently backed off in the face of a rearing delivery. His batting partner at the other end took a different approach, moving into the line of the ball.

As Jardine sat down for dinner with Larwood, Voce and Carr he told them of this flaw in Bradman's technique. Larwood agreed. He remembered Bradman stepping back from the livelier deliveries two years earlier at The Oval. Larwood later wrote, 'I told Jardine I thought Bradman had flinched and he said he knew that. Finally Jardine asked me if I thought I could bowl on the leg stump making the ball come up into the body all the time so that Bradman had to play his shots to leg. "Yes I think that can be done," I said. "It's better to rely on speed and accuracy than anything else when bowling to Bradman because he murders any loose stuff."'

They hatched their plot to exploit the leg theory of bowling in the comfort of a West End dining room, feeling they would rely on the unerring pace and accuracy of Larwood and Voce. As Larwood's biographer Duncan Hamilton put it, 'He [Larwood] had two things. Firstly he was incredibly accurate, he claimed never to have bowled a wide in his career, and accuracy was essential to Bodyline. Secondly he was devastatingly fast. All his contemporaries said he was the quickest they had faced. At certain times during that series he must have got close to, if not passed, the 100mph [160kph] mark. Every fast bowler who sees that old footage says, "Wow, that's quick."'

One of those contemporaries, vice-captain Bob Wyatt, wrote some years after the 1932/33 Ashes series, 'The type of bowling employed by Larwood would certainly not have been so successful if used by any other fast bowler. Having so amazingly accurate a bowler as Larwood, I think Jardine was fully justified using him as he did.' At the time of agreeing to deploy their leg theory tactic, neither Jardine nor his bowlers foresaw the subsequent furore.

At the conclusion of their meal, the plotters even agreed to give the tactic – a common one at the time – a trial in a county match at The Oval between Jardine's Surrey and his fellow diners' Nottinghamshire. None of the other players from either side appeared to be aware of the plan with Carr packing the leg side with fielders and Larwood and Voce duly offering up short-pitched deliveries on the leg stump. Surrey's batsmen were adept at hooking such deliveries to the boundary. The tactic in the context of a County Championship match in the dying days of an English summer seemed madness. Surrey batsman Alf Gover asked Larwood why he was bowling so badly. Larwood apparently simply replied, 'We're trying something out.' Nottinghamshire did the same in subsequent games against Essex and Glamorgan, even persisting with the tactic as the Welsh county batsmen hammered more than 500 runs.

To try to do the same in the Test arena appeared to be tactical madness. Yet nobody apart from Larwood, Voce, Jardine and Carr knew what they were really up to. The real competition was the battle for the Ashes between Australia and England, not a few end-of-season county games. They had hatched their plan and were going to stick to it, seeking victory at unforeseen costs.

England's cricket team, or to be pedantic the Marylebone Cricket Club touring side, arrived in Australia in November 1932 as underdogs. Jardine decided to limit use of his leg theory tactic during the early matches of the tour. It hardly helped two of his fellow amateur 'gentlemen' players were opposed to the Bodyline plan. Gubby Allen refused to bowl to a field packed with players on the leg side. The Nawab of Pataudi refused to field there, leading to Jardine's dismissive comment, 'Ah, I see his highness is a conscientious objector.' As the tactic was mainly for the benefit of England's chief tormentor Don Bradman, it also could be used sparingly because the little genius was ill and perhaps consequently out of form.

The first demonstration of fast leg theory, or Bodyline as it came to be known, took place at the Melbourne Cricket Ground in a warm-up match between MCC and an Australian XI. Jardine was not even there. He was 200 miles away on a fishing trip with cynics claiming he was afraid to play in case the tactic backfired. Instead, Bob Wyatt captained the English side. Australian spin bowler Bill O'Reilly later mocked, 'If Bradman had sailed to a century, Wyatt would have been left carrying the can.'

MCC batted first in a somnolent innings, scoring 282. On Saturday 19 November 1932, Australian captain Bill Woodfull and Leo O'Brien walked out to open their innings. Wyatt had set them an unusual field. The magazine *Australian Cricketer* gave this account, 'A fan-shaped back wicket field spread out.' The perky O'Brien, making his way to the non-striker's end, looked at the men placed on the leg side as Woodfull walked to take strike. He thought it was the slip cordon and turned to the fielders helpfully, "It's the right-hander down that end. I am the left-hander." The Englishmen smiled but did not move.' For O'Brien the fielders stayed where they were with the English only resorting to their leg theory tactic for right-handed batsmen, notably Bradman.

Carnage soon followed. Woodfull was given a portent of what was to come in Tests by being struck just below the heart from a rising ball delivered by Larwood. After Woodfull was dismissed LBW by Bill Bowes, Bradman entered the fray to the roars of a crowd of more than 54,000 in the MCG. They were dismayed to see Bradman struggle to cope with the lively pace of balls delivered by Larwood, Voce and Bowes, and he was regularly hopping out of the way to avoid being hit. Larwood took Bradman's wicket relatively cheaply, LBW for 36.

The English players, at least most of them, liked what they saw. Their controversial tactic seemed to be working. In the second innings, Bradman was out cheaply again to Larwood, chopping the ball on to his stumps for 13. Already there were discontented murmurings from the Australian camp over the aggressive tactics being employed by their opponents. In contrast the English were confident, demonstrated by this dispatch from the *London Standard*, 'Provided that Larwood retains his present demon speed, the Bradman problem has been solved. Bradman dislikes supercharged fast bowling.' Bradman reassured his fans he would be fine in the Test series. He commented, 'Don't worry; I'll be right as pie.'

In the event, Bradman was not even fit to play in the opening Test in Sydney and England won it. From start to finish, Jardine did little to endear himself to his hosts, not just because of his leg side tactics leaving Australian batsmen hopping around like rabbits. His haughty, condescending manner also infuriated the

Australian press, with whom he refused to co-operate. There would be no public relations gloss to mask the behaviour of Jardine and his England team, on and off the pitch. Jardine reasoned, 'We're here to win the Ashes, not provide stories to the newspapers.'

Bradman returned for the second Test in Melbourne, failing to score in the first innings after Bowes removed his stumps. He did score an unbeaten century in the second innings with Australia going on to to win thanks partly to England's abysmal batting. The scene was set for the third Test in the ecclesiastical city of Adelaide, an explosive game of cricket both on and off the pitch leading to one unholy row at the highest levels of government.

Wisden, cricket's bible, described the Adelaide Test – beginning ominously on Friday the 13th – as 'probably the most unpleasant Test ever played'. It concluded, 'Altogether the whole atmosphere was a disgrace to cricket.' That was in the 1933 edition. Subsequent editions in the following decades have failed to spot a match worthy of a similar dubious epithet. Tension between the sides was high even before the game. As it progressed the atmosphere became toxic with the players at each other's throats and the crowd on the brink of a riot. Given the hostility, Jardine took the step of banning spectators and the media from observing net practice, making him even more unpopular. In Michael Arnold's book *The Bodyline Hypocrisy*, Larwood told the author, 'At times it was pure bedlam. You just couldn't even try to conduct a serious practice when you're surrounded by a mob like that making rude and filthy comments every couple of minutes and obviously trying to put us off whether batting or bowling. We were very relieved Mr Jardine did keep them out the next day. It wasn't aimed only at Mr Jardine. All of us were targeted.' Jardine risked the ire of the Australian media by banning public access to training sessions. Frankly, he did not care.

During this infamous encounter, there were two key flashpoints with the game in progress on the field of play. There also came a third flashpoint in the supposed privacy of the Australian dressing room. England's tactic of 'Bodyline' bowling was blamed for the explosion of Australian fury. Yet when Larwood roared in towards the crease, ball in hand, about to deliver a fateful delivery with Woodfull facing at the other end he was bowling to a conventional field. Jardine had not adopted his leg side theory, decided against packing the leg side field. Woodfull became a victim simply of the vicious pace of a ball delivered by Larwood. It hit him just under the heart. Woodfull staggered from the blow, dropped his bat, and clutched his chest in agony. Concerned England players gathered around him with just one major exception. Jardine yelled out loud for everyone to hear, especially Bradman at the non-striker's end, 'Well done Harold.'

Just to add to what appeared to be a deliberately provocative gesture, he then changed the field and much to the disgust of an increasingly frenzied crowd, he adopted his Bodyline field. Yet the England players consistently denied that Jardine was being provocative. Jack Hobbs, in his 1934 book *The Fight for the Ashes*, asserted, 'The facts are that Harold opened the attack, as usual, with a few overs of normal bowling. Woodfull was struck by the last ball of the second over. Uproar sufficient to shatter the nerve of any bowler broke out from the crowd. So that Larwood should not get rattled, and for no reason at all, Jardine said to him, "Well bowled, Harold." When Woodfull recovered from his injury, there was an over from the other end, and then following his usual practice, Jardine switched his field to leg-theory. Facts, as you see, have a knack of changing rumours.'

Larwood himself was dismissive of Australian objections. He believed that Jardine was merely trying to encourage him and the adoption of leg theory after a few overs followed an agreed strategy. The bowler explained to writer Michael Arnold, 'What he [Jardine] was doing was simply to reassure me that it was an accident, and that I should not let it upset me or allow myself to be put off either by what had happened or the noise of the crowd, that's all. And the switch to leg theory was planned at that time anyway, because the ball was no longer swinging away. That ball just got up because of unpredictable bounce and it wasn't pitched anywhere near leg stump.'

After being clean bowled by Gubby Allen, Woodfull was back in the pavilion. It was to there the drama switched. England maintained their hostile bowling attack with Australian batsmen going back and forth, battered and bruised. In the pavilion, bruised egos as well as bodies ensured a game of cricket became ultimately a diplomatic and political crisis. It was down at first to the sporting diplomatic crassness of the tour manager, Pelham 'Plum' Warner, himself a former England captain. Knocking on the dressing room door of an angry opponent just minutes after he had left the field of play is never a good idea in any circumstances. On this occasion it was disastrous.

However well-intentioned Warner may have been he merely wafted some more metaphorical poison gas into the already toxic atmosphere. Here was a man of Empire, a typical English gentleman feeling his word was his honour and believing deeply in a sense of fair play. Privately, he felt uncomfortable with the ruthless antics and tactics of Jardine despite his captain's undoubted success on the field. Here was a chance in Warner's mind to restore a sense of decency to proceedings by checking on the health and welfare of the injured Australian captain. Sadly for him, Warner had miscalculated badly. Along with Woodfull, who was lying down waiting for a doctor to examine him, Jack Fingleton was in the dressing room. Leo O'Brien was also there although he claimed his captain was not laid out prone but standing upright in a towel. Both men did agree roughly on what followed.

At first Woodfull ignored Warner, refusing to accept the diplomatic gesture. He then turned to him with an ill-tempered spat, telling the hapless Warner, 'I don't want to see you, Mr Warner. There are two teams out there on the Oval. One is trying to play cricket and the other is not.' Just to add to the insult he went on, 'This game is too good to be spoilt. It is time some people got out of it.' Mortified by his treatment, Warner turned tail and retreated, not to the England dressing room but to the privacy of his hotel room. As an English gentleman he expected to be treated with dignity and respect, not dismissed as a serf. An angry cricketer felled by a razor-sharp delivery from one of the finest fast bowlers in cricket history was hardly going to do so. Not only was Warner upset, he was, as a man with a Victorian 19th-century view of the world order, baffled. The next morning, much to his horror, he was able to read the comments back in the Australian press.

Just what happened in the Australian dressing room once Warner had popped his head around the door is not in dispute. How the world got to hear about it, a private exchange, is in dispute thanks to the fractious nature of the Australian team with internal personal rivalry and resentment coming to the fore. Woodfull's fateful words were leaked to the press, much to Warner's outrage. Fingleton, a working journalist, was blamed for a breach of the sporting protocol of what goes on in the dressing room stays in the dressing room. In turn Fingleton blamed Bradman, a man adept in media relations and who regularly wrote his own newspaper column. Whoever was to blame, it further soured relations as England players read the comments in their newspapers on the morning of the following day's play. They were unhappy with Woodfull's dismissive treatment of their manager. Woodfull was also furious that one of his players had leaked details of his rant to the press. As for the mood of the Aussie spectators gathering in the Adelaide Oval, the newspaper accounts of Woodfull's terse verbal rebuke of the England cricket manager served as a rallying cry. It further darkened their mood. Mounted police sent along for fear of a riot must have hoped for calm, with no further incendiary incidents to inflame the passion of the crowd. Sadly, the opposite occurred.

As Larwood ran in to bowl to Australian wicketkeeper Bert Oldfield, a conventional field was once again in place rather than the detested Bodyline formation. Oldfield, known to Australian fans as the 'gentleman in gloves', was playing well against the fast bowlers. On 41 after just dispatching Larwood for four, Oldfield ducked into a vicious delivery rising off the pitch from Larwood. Apparently he had lost the flight of the ball thanks to a low sightscreen in place. The ball fractured his skull with the crack of bone heard by alarmed English fielders. He was lucky not to be killed.

The resulting uproar from a crowd already worked up into a lather of hatred, directed at the English team, was understandable. English players out on the field feared for their own safety with spectators on the brink of rioting as Oldfield was carried back to the dressing room. Larwood remembered, 'I felt as if one false move would bring the crowd down on me.'

He went on to recall turning to his team-mate Les Ames to tell him, 'If they come, you can take the leg stump for protection. I'll take the middle.' Thankfully a riot never materialised. What did materialise was the sending of a metaphorical riot act from the top brass of Australian cricket to the gentlemen members of Marylebone Cricket Club at Lord's with a telegram protesting at Jardine's tactics in an admonishment of the startled elite of England from men they considered to be colonial upstarts.

The decision to send a cable to MCC had been made the night before Oldfield needed hospital treatment. Once Woodfull sent distraught Warner packing from his dressing room he sought the help of the Australian board in trying to stop his English counterpart, Jardine, from employing the tactics of fast leg theory, or Bodyline as it had become termed by the hostile Australian media. Support for Woodfull was by no means automatically forthcoming. Some of his bosses thought he ought to stop moaning and just get on with playing cricket. They majority felt differently. Eight members of the Australian board voted yes to the sending of a cable to MCC protesting against the behaviour of the England team. Five voted against.

The wording of the telegram turned out to be more explosive than perhaps even they had envisaged. It was drafted by four men meeting Woodfull in the Adelaide dressing room; B.V. Scrymgeour, H.W. Hodgetts and R.F. Middleton of South Australia and Bill Kelly of Victoria. They wrote, 'Bodyline bowling assumed such proportions to menace best interests of the game, making protection of body by batsmen the main consideration and causing intensely bitter feelings amongst players as well as injury. In our opinion it is unsportsmanlike and unless stopped it is likely to upset friendly relations existing between Australia and England.'

It was sent at 3.12pm South Australian time, the early hours of the morning in London. As Lord's officials picked up the telegram along with their breakfast, they must have choked on their food and responded with indignant fury. How dare the Australians accuse the English of being 'unsportsmanlike'? It mattered little they had not even seen a day's play in Adelaide and had only read reports in their newspapers. This was long before the era of satellite televisions. Newsreels showing the exploits of Bradman, Larwood, Jardine et al took weeks to arrive from Australia to England. To the gentlemen of MCC, English honour in an Imperial world was at stake and they had been challenged by men of influence from a colonial dominion. Their reply matched the ill-tempered missive of the Australians. 'Friendly relations between Australia and England' were indeed at risk.

On hearing that the board had sent the message, England captain Jardine feared that MCC would not back him. He was outraged at the charge of being 'unsportsmanlike' and demanded a retraction or effectively he would ask his players to go on strike and refuse to play the two remaining Tests. He needed the backing of MCC and he was by no means certain it would be forthcoming. Gubby Allen revealed decades later to the *Sydney Morning Herald*, 'I remember Douglas Jardine saying to me, "Have you seen the cable?" And I said, "Yes I have. It's awful." He said, "That word unsportsmanlike…" I said, "Douglas, you're absolutely wrong. That's the best thing that could have happened." He said, "No, they'll let me down at Lord's." And I said, "Douglas, no one can call an Englishman unsporting and get away with it. They'll back you to the hilt." I can still see the smile that came over his face. He thought I'd perhaps hit the nail on the head.'

Allen was right. MCC's riposte on 24 January, once the Test was over and England had won, read: 'We, Marylebone Cricket Club, deplore your cable. We deprecate your opinion that there has been unsportsmanlike play. We have fullest confidence in captain, team and managers and are convinced that they would do nothing to infringe either the Laws of Cricket or the spirit of the game. We have no evidence that our confidence has been misplaced. Much as we regret accidents to Woodfull and Oldfield, we understand that in neither case was the bowler to blame. If the Australian Board of Control wishes to propose a new Law or Rule, it shall receive our careful consideration in due course. We hope the situation is not now as serious as your cable would seem to indicate, but if it is such as to jeopardise the good relations between English and Australian cricketers and you consider it desirable to cancel remainder of programme we would consent, but with great reluctance.'

A simple row over tactics was inexorably developing into a diplomatic crisis with the elite of English and Australian society at loggerheads.

The English touring team and their manager were delighted by the response of MCC with Warner describing it as 'superb'. Given that the Australian Cricket Board had already been divided over the decision to send its missive to MCC, the less hawkish members decided on a more conciliatory message. Yet even this crucially failed to withdraw the accusation of 'unsportsmanlike behaviour'. It simply asserted, 'We did not consider it necessary to cancel the remainder of the programme.' It also fired a further broadside criticising Bodyline as 'opposed to the spirit of cricket' and 'unnecessarily dangerous to the players'. For the disgruntled England team and an affronted MCC in London, this did nothing to end the impasse. Jardine, for one, demanded a full retraction of being 'unsportsmanlike' otherwise he was going home. Warner feared the tour was over and quite possibly the Australian board felt the same. It was at this point that the Bodyline crisis moved from the committee rooms of two sporting organisations to the offices of the corridors of power of government.

As a typical English gentleman of the Empire era, more than just a cricketer and sports administrator, Warner had friends in high places. On 1 February he sent a telegram to the British representative in Australia, the modern-day equivalent of an ambassador or high commissioner, expressing his concern and seeking help.

His note to Ernest Crutchley read, 'Have under consideration cancellation of all remaining matches of tour including Test owing to failure of board to withdraw stigma of word unsportsmanlike in their first cable. Beg you use your influence to get word withdrawn.' He added for good measure, 'Matter very urgent.'

It was a gamble calling on the good offices of diplomatic and political leaders but in terms of saving a fractious series of cricket it worked. Crutchley picked up the phone and contacted the Australian prime minister Joseph Lyons. Quite whether he had the authority of British ministers back in London to phone Lyons is not clear. Nevertheless, Lyons took him seriously, remarkably fearing financial sanctions from the United Kingdom if the row was not amicably resolved.

Canberra historian Dr Brian Stoddart unearthed a diary entry from Crutchley of his conversation with Lyons. It read, 'I phoned the PM at Melbourne. He said to start with, "It looks as though we were leading two armies." I told him exactly what had happened and he agreed that the cancellation of the tour would be a very grave thing for Australia especially just when feeling was so good. He promised to get hold of Dr Robertson, chairman of the Australian Board of Control, and see what could be done.' Lyons duly kept his word. He contacted Dr Robertson to issue a startling warning.

At the time, with Australia in the grip of the 1930s economic depression, he was running what might in modern parlance be termed an austerity programme. For this to work he needed favours from Great Britain; namely in the form of 'conversion loans', old debts renegotiated to allow easier repayment. Such was the scale of the row over a few games of cricket, Lyons feared these might be stopped. The economic consequences for Australia would have been disastrous. Long-term relations between Australia and Great Britain, the supposed 'mother country', would be changed irrevocably. After hearing from Lyons, the cricket board chairman contacted its secretary via cable informing him of the Australian government's intervention. He wrote, 'Prime minister interviewed me today. Stated that British representative had seen him and asked us to withdraw word objected to. If not, likelihood of England pulling right out. If we do withdraw, has no doubt [English bowling] attack will be modified. Government afraid successful conversions endangered.' Given the intervention of the country's prime minister, the Australian Board of Cricket felt it had no choice but to back down and send a retraction to MCC.

Lyons's dealings with Crutchley were not the only diplomatic and political manoeuvrings. Gubby Allen revealed that an Australian civil servant from the External Affairs Department had met England's players, presumably hoping to soothe their furrowed brows. In London meanwhile, MCC committee members had met cabinet minister Jimmy Thomas, the secretary to the dominions, to discuss the row. Quite whether the British government ended up exerting pressure on its Australian counterparts, leading to Lyons fearing financial sanctions, is unclear. It might have been just an irrational fear on his part. Then again, the British may have applied the metaphorical diplomatic thumbscrews on behalf of the England cricket team. The clue to the conundrum probably lies in an Australian government file 748/1/21 entitled 'The English Cricket Team 1932'. Unfortunately this file is missing from the archive with no explanation given. Whatever the reason, cricket bosses from Britain's Australian dominion resolved to send one final telegram in the spirit of conciliation on 8 February. It began, 'We do not regard the sportsmanship of the team as being in question.' The tour had been saved. The bad feeling and deep controversy lingered for decades.

Intriguingly the Australian prime minister felt that perhaps with the help of the most senior British government diplomat in his country, he might be able to influence the tactics adopted by Jardine. In this respect, they failed. Jardine stubbornly refused to back down, allowing Larwood and Voce to bowl to Bodyline fields. England duly won the series 4-1 and regained the Ashes. His tactics worked. Larwood went back home to a heroic welcome but never played for England again and was shunned to the point he even decided to emigrate to Australia in 1950, befriending Bert Oldfield. The former Nottinghamshire coal miner effectively was blamed for putting Anglo-Australian relationships at risk. The MCC establishment would not be seen publicly to punish one of its own for stirring up a political hornets' nest. Yet in reality it did so.

Jardine's own career would slowly and quietly fizzle out. His daughter, Fianach Lawry, in an interview with the *Daily Telegraph*, commented decades after the controversy, 'He was never angry about the furore surrounding Bodyline but, yes, there was this distinct air of sadness more than anything else in that father believed he had done what the MCC had agreed to. He felt that having said one thing, when the going got really difficult the MCC made him the fall-guy.' Just as Jardine had stubbornly refused to change his tactics in Australia despite intervention at government level, MCC ignored calls to change the laws of cricket and outlaw Bodyline. Its obduracy ended after the West Indies deployed Bodyline tactics on their tour to England in 1934. The English had been given a taste of their own medicine and the laws were duly amended by MCC. It ruled that 'any form of bowling which is obviously a direct attack by the bowler upon the batsman would be an offence against the spirit of the game'.

Sport, politics and diplomacy did not mix but suffered an uncomfortable collision in a bizarre controversy against the backdrop of a fading Empire, a young country finding its way in the world at times of deep economic depression, and frankly social snobbery. Despite winning the series, England's captain and his best bowler effectively ended up winners with their Ashes victory but losers in hopes of furthering their sporting career. It is a familiar story in any clash between sport and politics.

20

The Brazil
World Cup 2014

FOOTBALL was coming home. Thousands of cheering people were out on the streets of towns and cities throughout Brazil feeling triumphant with the World Cup returning to the spiritual home of the beautiful game of football. England may be the birthplace of the world's most popular team sport but in Brazil it matured into a bewitching spectacle for millions of besotted followers.

It was October 2007. The Brazilian economy was flourishing with the awarding of the 2014 FIFA World Cup a source of national pride and celebration. They were back on the streets in celebration two years later with the award of the 2016 Olympic Games to Rio de Janeiro. Then the worldwide economic crash came. Brazil floundered and the people returned to the streets once again as the World Cup loomed. This time there was no celebration. They were out in protest, furious at their government, suspicious of the largesse being demanded by the guardians of the beautiful game at FIFA, who were embroiled in allegations of greed and corruption.

Those FIFA officials were made welcome by Brazilian politicians, including the country's beleaguered president, but not by the people in a country mired in debt in part as a result of staging the FIFA World Cup. Just months after the tournament, which was marked by the humiliation of a 7-1 semi-final defeat for Brazil to eventual winners Germany, the nation's disgruntled electorate went to the polls. President Dilma Rousseff narrowly held on to power, the popularity of her Workers' Party diminished not just by the impact of the worldwide economic crash but also by the party's role in bringing the 2014 World Cup to Brazil and the lamentable failure to use it to boost the country's ailing infrastructure. Such a political scenario seemed unthinkable as her predecessor celebrated FIFA's awarding of the tournament seven years earlier. It also seemed unthinkable that the men running Brazilian football would be running scared of investigators from America's FBI. In the spiritual home of the beautiful game, football had turned ugly.

As Brazil bid for the 2014 World Cup, it did not seem a political or indeed financial gamble for the country's ruling classes. Football was part of the fabric of the Brazilian nation and was loved and embraced by tens of millions across the land. The then president Luiz Inacio Lula da Silva boasted, 'Soccer is more than a sport for us. It is a national passion.' There was the added benefit of being the sole bidder for the 2014 World Cup. Only South American countries were allowed by FIFA to bid for the right to stage the 2014 tournament and only Brazil bid. No other South American country was interested, perhaps wisely fearing the political fall-out from indulging the apparatchiks of FIFA with their exorbitant demands. Brazil though, buoyed by a growing economy before the worldwide economic crash of 2008, had no such qualms.

Naturally enough FIFA's controversial president Sepp Blatter was ebullient. Nobody to this day knows quite what was written in the bid document outside of the offices of FIFA, the Brazilian Football Federation and the Brazilian government of the day. For the governing body of world football there appears to be no such concept as a transparent deal. The Brazilian delegation was led by Ricardo Teixeira, head of the country's football federation. Their bid document was written by future FIFA general secretary Jerome Valcke. Blatter, who at the time was considered Valcke's friend and mentor, claimed, 'There was an extraordinary presentation by the delegation and we witnessed that this World Cup will have such a big social and cultural impact in Brazil.'

Blatter turned out to be right but certainly not for any reasons he may have envisaged at the time. The World Cup 2014 and its troubled legacy turned out to be one last hurrah for Blatter and his cronies running or more to the point apparently exploiting the world game. He may never have anticipated Teixeira resigning from his post as head of Brazilian football and the organising committee for the 2014 World Cup before even a ball had been kicked. Teixeira was fighting persistent allegations of corruption, though he denied any wrongdoing. Blatter may never have anticipated Teixeira and other Brazilian officials later coming to the attention of criminal investigators from a foreign power, namely the United States of America. Its investigators took it upon themselves to look into corruption at the heart of Blatter's organisation with the US Justice Department alleging racketeering and bribery offences. Nor did Blatter anticipate being kicked out of his own organisation amid corruption allegations he denied. As for anticipating the worldwide economic collapse as Brazil prepared for the tournament, Blatter and the other bosses of FIFA, with allegedly their seeming contempt for financial propriety, were quite possibly at the time not too bothered.

If there was any warning of troubled times ahead for Brazil it did perhaps come in FIFA's own inspection report of potential facilities for the tournament. It was guarded in its enthusiasm for the Brazilian bid, offering the following observation, 'Brazil has a rich history of hosting sporting and other international events. But the standards and demands of the World Cup will far surpass those of any other event staged in the history of Brazil in terms of magnitude and complexity. The inspection team wants FIFA experts to review the process and progress of host city selection to ensure that adequate financing is committed and secured.'

The progress was slow and deeply troubled. It helped to fuel the anger of an increasingly outraged nation as costs spiralled out of control, against a backdrop of increased austerity as the country sank further into economic recession. One notorious phrase in the FIFA World Cup handbook from its team of inspectors stuck in the craw of the critics. It referred to 'FIFA standard' stadiums and facilities. The Brazilian people wanted 'FIFA standard' schools and hospitals. Their calls grew louder as infrastructure projects promised on the award of the World Cup fell by the wayside. Instead Brazilian taxpayers' money went towards the building of the state-of-the-art stadia, some of them white elephants with no well-supported full-time professional club available to move in once the tournament was over. President Lula boasted, 'Stadiums will be completely built with private money. Not one cent of public money will be spent.' His promise was quickly broken, leaving his successor Dilma Rousseff to take the flak.

FIFA's Confederations Cup gave protesters the first opportunity to vent their fury. It is staged in the World Cup host country 12 months before the main event as a smaller dress rehearsal. The resulting violent protests as the FIFA fat cats arrived in town from a people supposedly in love with football guaranteed international media attention. It was not the kind of attention a government wanting to showcase the best its country had to offer was seeking. The spark for the protest was a rise in bus fares. Yet there were deeper reasons such as plain anger at millions of dollars being spent on a sports event with public services being woefully neglected.

Tens of thousands of protesters demonstrated outside match venues during the course of the tournament. On the night of 21 June 2013 it was estimated that more than a million took to the streets of scores of cities to make their unhappiness known. For the most part these protests were peaceful with some in the crowds wearing red noses as a symbol the people were being taken for clowns. Yet violence broke out as riot police sought to break up the demonstrations. In Sao Paulo, a teenager was killed as a car driver drove into the crowd, allegedly in frustration at being held up on his way home by the protests. In Rio de Janeiro, police fired rubber bullets at gangs of masked men trying to break into City Hall. More than 20 people were injured. There were also reports of looting though many banks and shops had already boarded up, anticipating the violence. There were similar scenes in other major cities. Football was coming home but it was not welcome back. To be more precise, its fat cat bosses were, in the opinion of a nation in love with the sport, distinctly *personae non gratae*. It was a view shared by football fans worldwide.

President Rousseff, herself a former student revolutionary, cancelled a planned trip abroad and held an emergency cabinet meeting to discuss a growing crisis. She had been booed by Brazilian fans in Brasilia at a Confederation Cup tie against Japan as she sat alongside Blatter. She tried to appease the protesters, praising their commitment to the spirit of democracy and 'voices calling for change'. Blatter, though, was classically thick-skinned and in denial over his organisation's role in unwittingly helping to ferment the unrest. He told the Brazilian newspaper *O Globo*, 'I can understand that people are unhappy. But football is here to unite people. Football is here to build bridges, to generate excitement, to bring hope. Brazil asked to host the World Cup. We didn't force it on them. It's obvious that stadiums need to be built but that isn't the only thing in a World Cup: there are highways, hotels, airports and a lot of other items that remain as a legacy.' By the time he returned to Brazil a year later many of these so-called 'items' were still missing.

Brazilian World Cup winner Romario, now a left-wing politician, outlined the problems behind the civil unrest to *The Guardian*. He had been in favour of the World Cup going to Brazil but despite once being one of the country's finest players, he swiftly changed his mind. Reflecting on the impact of the worldwide economic crash on Brazil, Romario wrote, 'Brazil has been affected by the turbulence in the world economy just like any other country. Government plans were redrafted, public investment was cut – yet the commitments signed with all-powerful FIFA stayed the same. Investment in cities hosting World Cup matches were prioritised over the people's needs. Money was channelled predominantly towards sport projects, at the expense of health, education and safety.'

He posed the question, 'Why are we organising the most expensive World Cup in history, without any of the benefits to the community we were promised?' The protesters Romario was championing were asking the same question. He went on to conclude, 'FIFA has announced that it will make a $4bn profit from Brazil's World Cup, tax-free. Its easy profit contrasts with the total lack of an effective legacy. President Dilma Rousseff repeats what former president Lula said, reassuring us that we'll "host the best World Cup of all time". I don't agree, because we have failed on what matters most: a legacy to make us proud. Only FIFA is profiting, and this is one more good reason to go to the streets and protest.'

FIFA, an organisation beset with allegations of corruption on an industrial scale, acted all along as if it was immune from economic reality. Its exacting demands had to be met regardless of the cost to the rest of Brazilian society. Blatter and his cronies were shamefully, in the opinion of their army of critics, exploiting the Brazilian people's love affair with football. It appeared to Brazilian opposition politicians that they were being aided and abetted by craven politicians remarkably and bizarrely even putting their own careers at risk.

Rousseff's popularity was at an all-time low as the World Cup kicked off in June 2014 and she faced a fight for political survival. Fortunately for her there was by and large no repeat of the outbreaks of violence during the Confederations Cup. Football was the focus with the potential success of the national team billed as a chance to build the country's self-esteem against a backdrop of economic doom and gloom. Unfortunately, a sixth World Cup triumph for Brazil, their first on home soil, failed to materialise. Firstly, their talisman Neymar was injured in a game against Colombia and ruled out of the rest of the tournament. Then without Neymar in the side his team-mates capitulated against a rampant Germany in the semi-final. They were humiliated, losing 7-1 to a team soon to be crowned world champions.

As the ball regularly hit the Brazilian net, obscene chants directed at Rousseff grew louder. It was a chance for a largely middle-class crowd paying FIFA's exorbitant ticket prices to vent their fury. Her tenure in charge of the country appeared at risk. Yet for all the controversy she managed to survive. In contrast the FIFA apparatchiks she sat alongside and wined and dined were on the run, trying to escape American justice on charges of corruption. Rousseff was leader of the People's Party. The Brazilian people forgave her and the government despite all the problems brought about by the staging of the FIFA World Cup.

Her victory over Accio Neves from the centre-right Social Democracy Party was narrow, 51.6 per cent to 48.4 per cent. Neves had the support of the business community and the wealthier districts of Brazil. Rousseff clung on to her support from the poorer districts, especially in the north of the country. Given allegations of financial irregularities, involving not just allegedly FIFA officials but individuals in the heart of Brazilian government, she responded by promising a 'rigorous fight against corruption'. She added, 'Sometimes in history, close outcomes trigger results more quickly than ample victories. It is my hope, or even better, my certainty that the clash of ideas can create room for consensus, and my first words are going to be a call for peace and unity.'

Her optimistic idealism failed to quell further unrest in the aftermath of the 2014 World Cup. A year on from Brazil being the focus of the football world and with a year to go before hosting the Olympics, protestors were back on the streets. The largesse in staging world-class sporting events was proving incongruous in a land wracked by poverty and with promised infrastructure projects still failing to materialise. Instead stadiums erected as cathedrals of sport for those at the high altar of FIFA became empty, expensive, embarrassing follies in the months following the World Cup. One became a bus station. One estimate put the operating losses for two-thirds of the stadia in the 12 months after the Brazil World Cup at £22m.

To compound matters further, allegations surfaced of irregular payments being made in the awarding of contracts to build stadia and ancillary facilities for the World Cup. In March 2015 the German engineering company Bilfinger admitted that its employees may have paid almost one million Euros in bribes to Brazilian public officials in connection with a contract for the installation of large television screens at security centres. In a statement it declared, 'Bilfinger received internal information last year indicating that there may have been violations of the Group's compliance regulations in connection with orders for the supply of monitor walls for security control centres in several large municipalities in Brazil. The company immediately launched a comprehensive investigation.' It concluded that 'suspicions have now been substantiated'.

In May 2015 the embarrassed German company hired legal teams to go before Brazilian courts to plead for leniency under a new anti-corruption law brought in to quell growing public anger over alleged financial chicanery at large in Brazilian society with impropriety in football being a mere symptom of the problem.

This stench of corruption led to millions of demonstrators taking to the streets in protest throughout the summer of 2015, Brazilian life dominated by political turmoil mid-term between a World Cup and an Olympics. Just to add to a catalogue of scandals, their anger was further fuelled by revelations that the federal police was investigating a multi-billion dollar bribery scheme with allegations money was being channelled from the state-controlled oil company, Petrobas, to Rousseff's People's Party. Given the country's deep economic problems, her time in office once again appeared in peril. These protests were not directly linked to the staging of the World Cup or indeed the forthcoming Olympics. Yet it hardly helped the beleaguered president that the men she feted from FIFA were themselves embroiled in one of the worst corruption scandals in sporting history. Ricardo Teixeira, the man responsible for helping to draw up the blueprint for the Brazil World Cup of 2014, was indicted by the FBI in December 2015, though he consistently denied any wrongdoing. His successor as the head of Brazilian football, Marco Polo del Nero, was also indicted by the Americans and he also protested his innocence.

In all, the Americans charged 41 individuals and companies during 2015 in connection with the FIFA corruption scandal. The alleged schemes involved payments of bribes from sports marketing executives seeking the media rights to various international tournaments, as well as the alleged payment and receipt of bribes in connection with the sponsorship of the Brazilian Football Confederation, CBF, by an unnamed US sportswear firm. For the past decade or so Brazil's national team has worn shirts made by Nike. The re-election of Sepp Blatter as FIFA president in 2011 also came under scrutiny from the law enforcement officials from the United States, a country seemingly smarting at its failure to secure the hosting of the 2022 World Cup. Much to the surprise of sports fans worldwide it was awarded instead to the tiny Gulf state of Qatar. The US attorney general, Loretta Lynch, in her condemnation of FIFA, observed, 'The Department of Justice is committed to ending the rampant corruption we have alleged amid the leadership of international soccer – not only because of the scale of the schemes, or the brazenness and breadth of the operation required to sustain such corruption, but also because of the affront to international principles that this behaviour represents.'

Blatter was not indicted by the Americans in 2015. Instead he faced investigation in his Swiss homeland. The Swiss attorney general began an investigation into suspicions of what was termed a 'disloyal' payment of two million Swiss francs to the boss of European football's governing body UEFA, Michel Platini. Both denied any wrongdoing, Platini, a former French national team captain and manager, insisting it was legitimate payment for work as a FIFA consultant. Yet by the end of 2015, Blatter's controversial tenure as the boss of world football was over. He vowed to 'fight on' to clear his name but FIFA's own ethics committee suspended him from football for eight years. The man strutting the global stage and promising the World Cup would bring a 'big social and cultural impact' to Brazil was being ostracised by his own supporters.

Blatter had lost his once impregnable power base. He moaned that he had been 'abandoned' by FIFA. It also in the meantime suspended and then banned from all football-related activities Jerome Valcke, the man deemed responsible for writing the Brazil 2014 World Cup bid document. Again Valcke denied any wrongdoing but his former friends at FIFA, working on its ethics committee, found him guilty of misconduct in relation to the sale of tickets, and the sale of TV and media rights plus assorted alleged abuses of expenses claims. Blatter abandoned Valcke long before FIFA acted against his general secretary as he tried to cling on to power. It was to no avail.

As Blatter railed against what he dismissed as 'false claims', his former friends and allies in Brazilian football were fighting to restore their own battered reputations, facing unwanted scrutiny from the US justice system. These men, some of them rounded up by Swiss and American officials in dawn raids as they slept in luxury hotels, had brought their own carnival to

Brazil. Yet given the financial largesse and alleged chicanery the World Cup was a tournament, a sporting festival, put on for their own personal enrichment rather than to benefit the struggling Brazilian nation. It had been further crippled in debt by a World Cup tournament estimated to have cost upwards of an astonishing $10bn. FIFA, in contrast, managed to make a whopping profit. Brazil kept building up debt for the privilege of staging the premier tournament of the sport its people loves.

As for the 2016 Olympics, the Brazilian government and Games organisers appeared to avoid further agitating their disgruntled hard-pressed citizens. Brazil's economy in 2015 remained in deep recession. At the beginning of 2016, economic forecasts warned that the country might suffer its worst recession in more than a century, deeper than even in the 1930s. Inevitably, it meant the 2016 Olympic were destined to be the austerity Games. Just ten months before the opening ceremony was due to take place the budget for the Games was slashed by 30 per cent. The Games were to be privately financed but with the public purse making up any shortfall if costs overran. For the Brazilian government it was something not to be countenanced. The cost of the opening ceremony itself would be ten per cent of the bill for the extravaganza put on at London 2012 to welcome the world to the British capital. Fernando Meirelles, the acclaimed Brazilian film director in charge of Rio's opening ceremony accepted the decision, observing, 'I guess I would be ashamed to waste what London spent in a country where we need sanitation, right, where education needs money.'

As a drastic measure to curb spending on the Olympics, plans for some permanent building structures were scrapped. Instead the organisers decided to erect tents. Rio 2016 communications director Mario Andrada explained, 'The days of lavish spending are over. We need to be creative in the way we find these savings.' He added, perhaps being mindful of the World Cup protests, 'People get upset about luxury and excess, we have to tighten our belts.' Despite insisting on the budget cuts Rio's mayor still sought to deliver a long lasting 'legacy' for his city's people, an attempt to justify vast spending on a 15-day sporting party. Eduardo Paes commented, 'When you get a thing like the World Cup or the Olympics, you need to use it for something else.'

As an example of how not to organise a sporting tournament, he cited the football stadiums dotted around Brazil without a football club to play in them. As the World Cup Final was being played in the rebuilt Maracana stadium in July 2014, Paes avoided making such comments in front of the leaders of world and Brazilian football. Now with another sporting extravaganza about to be held in his city threatening to gobble up public finance, the political imperative for Paes was to reassure his people, if not secure his position in office. As he is considered a possible future candidate for the Brazilian presidency, Paes had a vested political interest in delivering a successful Games. In doing so though he faced a string of criticisms from the quality of water at outdoor aquatic events, to police violence, and the forced relocation of residents to make way for the building of Olympic venues.

Paes harboured grandiose ambitions of boosting his country's image abroad; a familiar theme for Olympic organisers even since the Berlin Games of 1936. He believed organisational failures in the staging of the World Cup, despite its undoubted success as a pure sporting event, hardly helped his cause. In particular, he cited the holding of the World Cup opening ceremony in a stadium with the builders still to finish off their work. Paes lamented the world at large held a 'mistrust' in the Brazilian capacity to deliver infrastructure projects. In an interview with American journalists at the end of 2015 Paes bluntly told them: 'IT don't think the World Cup changed the way you gringos think about Brazil. It's like, these guys, they throw great parties. Stadiums starts at costs of 10, when they were ready they were at 20 or 30. Two or three times higher. There are some white elephants that aren't going to be used. There are lots of things that took a while to get ready. By the end of the day, it was much better than the international media expected.' It may in sporting terms have lived up to the pre-tournament hype of a carnival or festival to remember. Nevertheless there was tacit recognition of embarrassing failures, not least those multi-million dollar stadiums lying empty. In offering reassurances about the Olympics, Paes pointedly noted: 'The IOC is not FIFA.' The Rio Games, he insisted, unlike the World Cup would deliver a lasting legacy for the benefit of its citizens.

Brazil's World Cup of 2014 ended in disappointment on the pitch with the failure of the national team to even reach the final, let alone win the tournament. It ended in disgruntlement and even protest at the failure to deliver an easily discernible legacy for the Brazilian people. The country's politicians hoped infrastructure projects completed in time for the 2016 Olympics might satisfy those far from convinced by the wisdom of staging the two biggest sporting events on the planet at a time of deep economic recession. On the pitch Germany may have been the winners. Off the pitch, the Brazilian people turned out to be the losers thanks to the remarkable ability of a group of sports administrators, men deeply embroiled in allegations of widespread and systematic corruption, to manipulate the vanity and egos of politicians.

Select Bibliography

BOOKS:
A Game for Hooligans: The History of Rugby Union; Huw
    Richards (2006)
American Pastimes, The very best of Red Smith; Red Smith and
    Daniel Okrent (2013)
Basil D'Oliveira Cricket and Controversy; Peter Oborne (2005)
Basingstoke Boy; John Arlott (1990)
The Ball is Round, A Global History of Football; David Goldblatt
    (2006)
The Bloodied Field; Michael Foley (2014)
*Beyond Glory: Joe Louis vs. Max Schmeling, and a World on the
    Brink*; David Mergolick (2005)
Bodyline Autopsy; David Frith (2003)
The Cold War and the Olympics; Allen Guttman (1988)
Conversations with Myself; Nelson Mandela (2011)
Croke Park, A History; Tim Carey (2013)
De Valera, Long Fellow, Long Shadow; Tim Pat Coogan (1993)
D'Oliveira, An Autobiography; Basil D'Oliveira (1969)
Douglas Jardine: Spartan Cricketer; Christopher Douglas (2003)
The GAA v Douglas Hyde; Cormac Moore (2012)
The GAA, a people's history; Mike Cronin, Mark Duncan and
    Paul Rouse (2009)
The GAA & Revolution in Ireland 1913–1923; Gearoid
    O'Tuathaigh (2015)
*Game Over: How Politics has turned the Sports World Upside
    Down*; Dave Zirin (2013)

The Games Must Go On: Avery Brundage and the Olympic Movement; Allen Guttman (1983)

The Greatest Fight of Our Generation: Louis vs. Schmeling; Lewis Erenberg (2006)

Harold Larwood; Duncan Hamilton (2010)

The John Carlos Story; John Carlos and Dave Zirin (2013)

Joseph Goebbels; Peter Longerich (2010)

Judging Dev; Diarmaid Ferriter (2007)

Long Run to Freedom: Sport Cultures and Identities in South Africa; John Nauright

The 'Miracle on Ice' and the Cold War Lens; Chad Seifried, University of Louisiana (2010)

Mythos Olympia; Hilmar Hoffman (1993)

Nazi Games: The Olympics of 1936; David Clay Large (2007)

The Paul Robeson-Jackie Robinson Saga and a Political Collision; Ronald A. Smith, *Journal of Sport History, Vol. 6, No. 2* (1979)

One Day in September; Simon Reeve (2005)

Olympia 1. Teil – Fest der Völker; Leni Reifenstahl (1936)

Olympia 2. Teil – Fest der Schönheit; Leni Riefenstahl (1936)

Playing the Enemy; Nelson Mandela and the game that made a nation; John Carlin (2009)

Politics on Ice: The United States, the Soviet Union, and a Hockey Game in Lake Placid; Donald E. Abelson (2010)

Salute; Matt Norman (2012)

Scoring for Britain: International Football and International Politics; Peter Beck (2013)

The Soccer War; Ryszard Kapuscinski (1990)

Silent Gesture; Tommie Smith (2007)

Stanley Matthews; David Miller (1989)

Time to Declare; Basil D'Oliveira (1982)

Willie John: The Story of my Life; Willie John McBride (2004)

The Way it Was; Stanley Matthews (2000)

Wisden Cricketers' Almanack (1933)

ARCHIVES:

Anti-Apartheid Movement Archives (UK)

The American Presidency Project Archives, Santa Barbara, California

FIFA Records; www.fifa.com
IOC Records; www.olympic.org
Irish Military Archives, Dublin
Irish National Archives, Dublin
US Central Intelligence Agency; Declassified archives
US Congress Library archives, Washington DC
US Digital National Security Archives
UK National Archives, Kew, London
Major League Baseball Hall of Fame archives, Cooperstown,
    New York
Rugby Football Union Museum archive, Twickenham

SELECTED WEBSITES:
A Game that changed Germany and Hungary forever; www.
    thehardtackle.com (2012)
Max Schmeling: Joe Louis' friend and foe; The International
    Raoul Wallenberg Foundation; www.raoulwallenberg.net
    (2005)
The official site of Joe Louis; www.cmgww.com/sports/louis/
    bio
'The Soccer War,' at Soccer Politics Pages, http://sites.duke.
    edu/wcwp
World Anti-Doping Agency Independent Commission:
https://www.wada-ama.org/en/resources/world-anti-doping-
    program/independent-commission-report-1 (2015)
https://www.wada-ama.org/en/resources/world-anti-doping-
    program/independent-commission-report-2 (2016)
US Justice Department: http://www.justice.gov/justice-news
Basil D'Oliveira official website; basildoliveira.com
The Cold War and British debates over the boycott of the
    1980 Moscow Olympics, Cold War History 13, 1 (2013);
    historyandpolicy.org
New Zealand History Website; www.nzhistory.net.nz/culture

NEWS SOURCES
ABC News, United States
ARD, Germany
Associated Press (AP)

BBC News
BBC Newsnight
BBC Sport
Boxing News, London
Catholic Herald, London
CNN News
Daily Mail, London
Daily Mirror, London
Daily Telegraph, London
Der Spiegel, Berlin
ESPN, cricinfo
ESPN FC
Financial Times
Harvard Crimson, Cambridge, Massachusetts
Huffington Post
The Independent, London
The Irish Independent
Irish Times
Los Angeles Times
New York Daily News
New Yorker Magazine
New York Times
New Zealand Herald
Reuters
RTE News
Smithsonian Magazine
Sports Illustrated
Sunday Times, London
Sydney Morning Herald
The Times, London
Time
Washington Post
Washington Times